A GUIDE TO HISTORICAL METHOD

A GUIDE TO HISTORICAL METHOD

Edited by

ROBERT JONES SHAFER

David Bennett
Nelson M. Blake
Robert Crane
Samuel Eddy
Robert G. Gregory
Joseph Levine
Roderick MacDonald

Peter T. Marsh
James M. Powell
James R. Sharp
William Stinchcombe
Walter Ullmann
Stephen Webb

*all of the Department of History
Syracuse University*

1980 Third Edition

Wadsworth Publishing Company
Belmont, California
A Division of Wadsworth, Inc.

ISBN 0-534-10825-3 (previously ISBN 0-256-02313-1)
Library of Congress Catalog Card No. 79–55220

Printed in the United States of America

7 8 9 10 — 95 94 93 92 91 90 89

For Estelita

PREFACE

The gratifying reception of the first two editions of this guide encouraged us to retain most of the original organization, style, and point of view. Some major changes were made, however: (*a*) Chapter I was re-arranged to strengthen the definition of historical conceptions, method, and literature; (*b*) a new Chapter II was added to make clearer the first problems encountered by the beginning researcher; (*c*) a section was added on quantitative method; and (*d*) the material on writing was considerably expanded. We somewhat condensed the materials on the traditional auxiliary disciplines, the collection and recording of evidence, and on external criticism. Lesser changes were made in other parts of the guide. Some of the illustrative examples were replaced with more recent or otherwise apter ones. Appendixes were added on proofreading and on common abbreviations. The bibliography was updated.

The matter contained in this guide was developed over a period of several decades, primarily for beginning researchers in history. The experience of the authors, however, in university teaching, cross-disciplinary research, government service, and private business strongly suggested the value of such training in research method for many other fields of activity as well. Our society demands huge numbers of professional researchers, data analysts, and report writers capable of reducing the record of assertion, belief, practice, and decision to understandable order.

There is no natural or ideal order for the components of historical method. There is a general progression from collection through analysis to synthesis and communication of results; but analysis and synthesis occur throughout research, and the inquirer has constantly (not just at one stage) to beware of bias and try to keep to the rule of relevance. It is no service to beginning researchers to pretend that the components of method do not overlap, when they obviously do. Those of us who were reared on German and French guides of an earlier age were unnecessarily intimidated by hothouse strictures that reeked of logic rather than of practice. Nor is it a service to pretend that working historians consciously drag out "elements of method" very often to use in their work; having been learned, the method guides work habitually, until crises occur in investigations.

Where to begin is an agonizing problem for new researchers. Chapter II instructs them to use immediately some bibliographic aids in order to locate a few good treatments of the research topic. Read quickly through one or more of those, taking sketch or orientation notes, and setting down questions, tentative hypotheses, and outlines, to help guide the research effort. Spend only a few days on this, to get some orientation, some notion of the character and dimensions of the topic. Do not be afraid to read first the best studies of the subject; professional scholars do. You will later use contemporary materials or evidence.

We are rather prescriptive about some of the procedures discussed in the guide, not because there no alternatives, but because the beginner needs to get into research; he can puzzle later in his career over details of punctuation and grammar, footnote styles, bibliographic alternatives, and the like. Much is gained and little is lost by prescription in these realms, so long as it is remembered that it is designed to facilitate the development of orderly investigation and record keeping; and that that is done in order to permit concentration on the essential business of encouraging analysis and the development of a critical attitude. There is no magic in guides to style and craftsmanship. Footnote method, rules of quotation, clarity in composition, a sound research note system, bibliographic techniques, and the like, are the necessary building blocks of good research method, but the heart of the enterprise is in critical analysis and interpretation.

February 1980   Robert Jones Shafer

CONTENTS

LIST OF FIGURES

I

THE NATURE OF HISTORY

Man views his past with boundless fascination, savoring its drama and victories, weeping at its failures and follies, probing it for clues to the meaning of human endeavor. We feel a tug of sympathy, a link of shared human experience, with Socrates drinking the hemlock for encouraging rebellious youth, or with Joan of Arc, repelling the invader, only to fall victim to man's endless willingness to proclaim the unimpeachable path of destiny. The pageantry and majesty of China's remote past take on new colors as we eye the wrenching changes of her recent history. The historical approach appeals to our feeling for the relationship of events in time, both for the continuity of human experience and its immense variety. It encompasses the recurrences of heroism and bigotry, the apathy and misery of vast peasantries, and the growth and vicissitudes of the ideas of justice and brotherhood. It celebrates the glittering careers of Napoleon and Caesar, Kublai Khan and Pericles; and the achievements of St. Francis of Assisi and Muhammad, of Mahatma Gandhi and Albert Einstein. In short, human interest in historical literature probably will never die.

A. Meanings and uses of history

The word "history" has several senses in English. First, it refers to the events of the past, to the actual happenings. Examples might be as recent as the removal of American troops from Vietnam or as remote as the Persian invasion of Greece in the fifth Century B.C. Secondly, history means a record or account of events. Someone attempts to relate the events of Vietnam or to write a history of the Persian wars. Indeed, Herodotus, often called the father of history (that is, of history *writing*), set down his view of the causes and events of the war between the Persians and the Greeks. Finally, history means a discipline, a field of study that has developed a set of methods and concepts by which historians collect evidence of past events, evaluate that evidence, and present a meaningful discussion of the subject.

Historical literature has its greatest function as an addition to individual experience, giving to the single human being an understanding that men and women many times in the history of the race have confronted similar problems. The reader does not find in history that the problems are identical in detail, but that they are similar in their demands upon individuals and groups. The reaction is not simply intellectual; it is also emotional. The reader sees how recurrent are such problems as the necessity but the perils of resistance to tyranny, as the founding fathers of the United States had observed from the history of their own and earlier times that no man or group was to be trusted with absolute power. The reader observes also in history the frequent problem of greed in the development of property, argument over the values and dangers of freedom of expression, abuse of labor, the rivalry of culture groups, the competition of individuals for eminence and power, the lurking menace of demagoguery in free societies. This broadening of experience promotes sophistication and judgment in the contemplation of public decisions, and tends both to the reduction of parochialism or insularity, and to steadiness in consideration of grand decisions by elimination of the supposition that all current problems are uniquely terrible in the history of man.

A New York City newspaper printed the following editorial:

A Wise Woman, Clio!

"Large populations, made susceptible by literacy to new ideas, but unable to discriminate among them, constitute perhaps the greatest single menace to modern culture," the leading review in a recent issue of *The* (London) *Times Literary Supplement* proposes. "Never, it may be suspected, has pretentious novelty had a better chance of being accepted at its face value," the review goes on to say.

If this needs to be said to Britons, how much more so to Americans, so many of whom date the beginning of time and human experience from 1900, or a decade or so later, it may be. A contemporary school of pedagogy tends to confirm their belief that history is wholly irrelevant to or merely an escape from the problems of the moment. Certainly it can be both or either for pedants or antiquarians; a brute accumulation of mere fact or a shameless lust for antiquity as such. But most history readers today are staring into the past, not wistfully, nor with pride of knowledge, but with a purposeful scrutiny. As a modern historian recently said: "The prime . . . use of history is that it enables you to understand better than any other discipline the public events, affairs and trends of your own time."

History at least can save from severe disillusion those to whom every "new" idea or polity appears in the guise of a beautiful virgin. Clio, the muse of history, has known these meretricious hussies since the days of Herodotus. She has been around a lot and a long time. She knows that most of them are no better than they should be. In fact, she knew them when.[1]

---

[1] *New York Herald Tribune*, October 10, 1946.

Perspective was the term applied to this aspect of historical study by the Behavioral and Social Sciences Survey in 1971. It remarked that perspective "is no small matter," to help guard against the temptation of each generation to see its problems as unique, a temptation (said the survey) to which social engineers especially are prone.[2] A president of the American Historical Association put it in terms of a current exaggerated cry for "relevance," which expresses an "inarticulate existentialism, a headlong immediatization of the 'here' and 'now'"; a vulgar ignorance of the fact that even in "an age of disjuncture" it is the case that "many continuities . . . persist."[3] Reflective men in many fields of endeavor have pointed out that to ignore the past is to forfeit an opportunity to learn from experience. Even existentialists might want their constantly terminating presents to retain reality as pasts for more than a moment.

But historical literature by broadening the experience of the individual, putting him into touch with the life of the race, does more than prepare him for change and disappointment, and the shock of those things. It also provides him with approximate models of some of the possibilities of human action and organization. It is precisely this sort of extension of experience through historical memory that dictatorial governments in our own and other times have recognized as a threat to their continuation. Conceivably, those models could be provided the citizen on call by a computer. "If troubled by a fear that state power is becoming oppressive, punch program TX786N for models of past tyrannies." One fears that the urge to punch would come too late. One hopes that the models would be cast in historical form and not in either equations or social

---

[2] See Social Science Research Council, *Items*, March 1971. The survey was sponsored by the SSRC and the National Academy of Sciences.

[3] C. Vann Woodward, "The Future of the Past," *American Historical Review*, February 1970, pp. 711–26.

science generalizations; that is, that the need for human dimensions and art in such material would be realized. And finally one hopes that if in equations or in correct but juice-less verbalizations the models would have sufficient impact. How much better to have historical literature, full of the juices of richly varied emotional and physical life, a part of the heritage of the threatened citizen, ever present on a shelf for reading.

The terrible problem involved here is seen in the fact that the protagonist of George Orwell's *1984*, that terrifying novel of technological tyranny, is a rectifier of history. He is a slave of that all-embracing, all-seeing government of Big Brother, spending his miserable days managing the record of the past. Especially he sees to it that the thin record contains nothing on mistakes of the past, or criticism of Big Brother's horror world, or even the memory of persons who disappointed him (they become "unpersons" as the record of their lives is erased), a fictional activity all too reminiscent of the removal of the names of unlucky Soviet officials from the official encyclopedia. The record always favors the omnipresent and omnipotent and omniscient state. There is no history out of which to condemn and convict the regime for usurpation, to compare it unfavorably with others (lost are the virtues of Athens and Paris and Boston), to serve as a guide to protest, to lift up the spirit with the thought of past revolt and heroism (unpersons are Churchill, Gandhi, Washington, Spartacus), to show the transience of regimes, to indicate the unchangeability of change itself. This is the logic of the policy of uniformity, starting with fear of heterodoxy, becoming regimentation of opinion, hardening into a poisonous orthodoxy, and ending in a pathological terror of contradiction not only by the recently buried but by the most antique dead.

Historical study and literature have other important functions or virtues. One is concentration on the unique human sense of time. There are two sides to this. One is that for purposes of communication, studies must have some sort of organization, and the chronological often is useful. The other aspect of the matter is that humanity's acute sense of the passage of time is not merely culturally induced, is not eradicable, but results from the fact of mortality; to be sure, some cultures are more oppressed by it than others. The sensivity to time lends an appeal to literature that emphasizes chronology.

Another feature of much historical literature is that it tries "to see things whole," to show the multiplicity or variety of the human condition and experience. To be sure, other disciplines do this, but the results are far different—unless they write history. Religion, philosophy, and social science obviously have important things to say, but in their own fashions. If some people are satisfied with their efforts, others are not. This dimension of wholeness (less, of course, than completeness) and multiplicity in historical literature fills a need and demand. Related to it is the fact that history deals in part, and an important part, with nonmeasurable things, as pride, courage, commiseration, cruelty, leadership (only in part measurable). Again, philosophers and priests deal with these things, but if they do it like historians that is what they become. Even if no final judgment can be rendered on many nonmeasurable aspects of history, those aspects should be contemplated.

History is one of the most powerful studies for engendering empathy, an understanding of the motives, beliefs, frustrations, culture patterns, and hopes of other people. It is suited to this task by various of its qualities discussed above, and also by the fact that the best historians so immerse themselves in the times they study that they arrive at an understanding obtainable in no other way. Anthropologists and others can do this for the present and recent past; only historians can do it for the more distant past.

History sometimes serves the function of giving to groups that feel alienated and scorned a sense of worthwhile origins and of belonging or comradeship. That was the source of the vast popularity of the novel and television series titled

Roots, about the history of blacks in Africa and the United States. The function has been served by nationalist literature, which now sometimes is criticized; it has defenders, however, both for emotional reasons and on the grounds that nationalist unity is far from an unimportant force in the world today. We may guess that if superior beings come from space, a "human history" will be written to defend *homo sapiens* from too wasting a sense of inferiority.

Many statesmen have testified that the study of history prepared them for what to expect, in a general way, from human greed, cruelty, and folly, and from nobility and courage and wisdom. It is clear that men who are ignorant of history are apt to make superficial judgments—witness the views of the Germans Kaiser Wilhelm and Hitler regarding the martial qualities of English and Americans. To be sure, history does not repeat itself exactly; it does not give detailed guidance for action today. The past does not show us how to oppose Hitler tactically, on a given day, but reveals the danger of bowing the neck to tyrants and argues for opposition to tyranny even in the face of great odds, often suggesting some means that might prove valuable in gaining victory or pitfalls to be avoided.

History is much used in public life, nowhere more so than in the United States. Much of the belief, the action, and many of the leaders of our early history seem sufficiently contemporaneous to justify policy today. Our judicial system abounds in uses of history. Legislation is discussed and written in the light of precedent, recent and remote. Great political controversies swirl around passions roused by appeals to the sacred shades. When Daniel Webster and Robert Y. Hayne debated in the Senate the nature of the union in 1830, they appealed to the intent of the founding fathers. A century later, when Franklin Roosevelt was accused of trying to pack the Supreme Court, an almost unprecedented uproar arose over this asserted threat to the traditions of judicial independence and the separation of powers.

A powerful use of history was in a speech by Senator

Flanders of Vermont in 1954,[4] scoring the activities of the demagogic Senator Joseph McCarthy as "contrary to senatorial traditions," tending "to bring the Senate into disrepute," and calling for condemnation of his conduct. Flanders feared that the United States had entered into the "time of troubles" postulated by the historian Arnold Toynbee as indicative of a nation's decline. He compared McCarthy's exploitation of the communist issue with Hitler's and gave a picture of the senator as fuehrer. He pointed out that the Republican Party, of which Flanders and McCarthy were members, was a century old that year, and instead of the ideals of its first president (Lincoln) holding the spotlight, "We see the bright lights of television on the junior Senator from Wisconsin sitting at the table with his assistant whose lips are glued to his ear whispering, whispering, whispering." Flanders judged his party at a parting of the ways, to follow Lincoln or McCarthy. At least, Flanders said, the latter had given "us the opportunity to appraise our national political morality in this year of Our Lord 1954. For this opportunity we must ever be grateful." McCarthy was duly chastised for his irresponsible conduct, and Senate and country turned away from the witch hunt.

Historical studies long have served as weapons in controversy. The Protestant Reformation of the 16th century gave rise to a prolonged and often vitriolic dispute that extended almost to our own time. The character of Martin Luther was the object of intensive writing by Catholic historians, who often aimed at proving that he was an unworthy priest, guilty of vices that led to his break with the Church. Protestant writers seized on the weaknesses and immoralities of various Renaissance popes to attack the leadership of the Church and to validate the Protestant rupture with it. Another historical dispute developed with the growth of nationalism in the 19th century. Many scholars employed their talents to prove that their peoples had

---

[4] *New York Times,* July 19.

an historic right to political independence. Especially in eastern and southern Europe, nationalistic history often favored the position of one minority over those of others. The creation of a number of independent nations in that region following World War I did not settle the controversies between Czechs and Slovaks, Croats and Yugoslavs, or take historical argument out of political debate.

More recently, the controversy over United States entry into World War II gave rise to a polemic literature. There was much allusion to the experience of World War I as argument for or against involvement in World War II. Then, after World War II, an acute American awareness of the power of the Soviet Union, combined with a long-felt fear of communism, stimulated numerous theories of conspiracy concerning settlements among the great powers made at Yalta and Potsdam. Very often hindsight provided a perspective for evaluating defects in those agreements that in the minds of some were the result of sinister communist machinations, and the "historical" debate on the peace continues to enliven literature and politics.

As a final example, historical argument has been much used in the United States in recent years in connection with civil rights issues and the treatment of minorities. Historians, and their supporters in national and community affairs, often are divided into two schools of interpretation. One group asserts that in general American history shows a consensus on institutions and decisions, a pervading satisfaction and spirit of compromise. The other group declares that American history rather displays repression and violent protest as methods of action and reaction, and that violence is an indispensable and legitimate answer to bigotry and tyranny. Of course, it is not merely history showing one or the other of these pictures to be the more veracious, but the individual historians and others viewing that history.

Historians also provide data for public uses other than political polemics. They—together with social scientists, philosophers, and others—make various sorts of efforts to promote understanding of human society, and hopefully to suggest guidance for the future. Historical data are used to try to identify cultural conditions favorable to stated attitudes or institutions, in the hope that such knowledge can be used in decision-making in the future. Sometimes such data are prepared by historians directly for such projects, sometimes they are extracted from historical works by social scientists. In some cases, data can only be gathered and interpreted effectively by historians with the erudition to understand the time and place under consideration. In such instances, social scientists pluck raw data from the record of the past at their peril. Other disciplines also use historical studies: for illustrations, raw material for statistical or other generalization, or for instruction.

Coins, stamps, monuments, newspapers, films, and television employ historical themes and motifs. The events often are distorted or oversimplified. Sometimes that is justifiable. Sometimes the data are turned to the service of propaganda. But such uses only serve to illustrate the need for good historical writing. Finally, to repeat, many millions have found historical literature a pleasure to read. It provides something akin to the movement and variety of travel. It gives a sense of participation in the affairs of the race.

History also is a discipline, a field of study, with ideas and techniques attuned to the accurate and forceful presentation of the past. The method and aims of historical inquiry have been much refined and codified in the last two centuries. They now are eminently teachable; as a result, historical inquiry has been professionalized, and the level of performance has improved. At the same time, abundant disagreement remains in those areas of judgment, morality, ethics, and religious and social belief that cannot be codified and "taught" in an agreed manner.

The many achievements in the field in modern times include a revolution in our knowledge of ancient Egypt; great advances in technological and economic history; a new ability to grapple with the history of social groups; better history of public health, medicine, and science; and strides forward in the development of historical demography. Michael Ventris combined his knowledge of ancient Greek with the cryptography he learned during World War II to discover in the 1950s that the language of the ancient Minoan Linear B script was not Minoan but Achaean Greek, which he then deciphered with reference to a known language. That drove the history of written Greek back to about 1450 B.C., some seven centuries earlier than formerly believed, and indicated that Greek-speaking people had civilization many centuries before the classical age.[5]

B. Varieties of historical literature

Humanity's fascination with its past is illustrated by the great variety of historical literature. The most useful distinction is between narrative and analysis, although the two frequently are combined. Narrative is story, often with description as a simple sort of near-analysis, but sometimes with a great deal of profound analysis. Analysis is examination of topics, groups of events or ideas, with only incidental attention to individual occurrences. Fernand Braudel in his monumental and fascinating *The Mediterranean and the Mediterranean World in the Age of Philip II* stated that he is "little tempted by the event." That is evident as one goes through the hundreds of pages of this masterpiece of the *Annales* school of historiography. Individual "events" are important only as they suggest topics for more collection of evidence to permit analysis. The heart of the enterprise is in the sections supported by enough data to permit analysis of the role of gruels in the European diet, cases where wagons could compete with water transport, or the demand

---

[5] See I (D), below, for history and social science methodology.

for luxury goods shown as the prime cause of commercial and industrial development.[6]

Narrative at its extreme contains little analysis, and analysis at its limit has little narrative. Historical literature also can be categorized by the functions we listed for it in the preceding section: experience, instruction, depiction of identity, contribution to knowledge; or as the philosophy of history.[7]

Narrative history had its beginnings with Herodotus and other practitioners in the ancient Mediterranean world. This is a style that is literary and dramatic in character, though it is no longer thought proper to create dialogue in order to heighten the sense of crisis at key points in the narrative, as with the Melian dialogue of Thucydides, which so effectively illustrates Athenian pride in dealing with the small states of their empire. Narrative historians, with their attention to story, to great events and human interest, and to individual heroism and depravity, have only biographers as near competitors for public interest. Gibbon's *Decline and Fall of the Roman Empire* was a best seller in the 18th century, as was Macaulay's *History of England* in the 19th and Tuchman's *Guns of August* in the 20th.

Narrative history is important as a communication link between scholar and public. But there are fewer men capable of writing brilliant narrative history than of turning out scholarly monographs. Thus it is that the public acclaims Bruce Catton's *A Stillness at Appomatox*, or the rolling periods, drama, and gusto of Winston Churchill's historical works. Nor are these authors devoid of scholarship, although their purpose is the creation for a wide public of a feeling for the great men and deeds of the past.

---

[6] First published in France in 1949; English ed., 2 vols., London, William Collins, 1972. Braudel and Marc Bloch and the other historians associated with the *Annales d'historie économique et sociale* have had great influence during the last half-century or so.

[7] See III (B).

Critics sometimes chide the profession for excessive attention to scholarly analysis and too little production of stimulating narrative history. It is probably the case, however, that the apparently unslakable public appetite for good narrative history tempts from the ranks of academic and nonacademic writers most of the talent that exists for that sort of composition.

Historical biography has great appeal because of its concentration on one or a few interesting individuals. And now in the form of the new psychohistory it has attracted readers by the effort to apply psychoanalytic concepts to historical characters. But all biography tends to suffer from two weaknesses: excessive sympathy with the subject, and the fact that concentration on the life of an individual distorts perspective. That was the case with Plutarch's *Lives* and Suetonius's biographies of the Caesars, and their reputation is considerably less than that of Tacitus's works, despite the bias of the latter. Modern criticism of medieval hagiography, the lives of saints, generally has been severe because of their uncritical acceptance of legend. But biographers can, and often do, follow the canons of critical research, and respond to the latest concepts and methods of investigation and interpretation. In any event, biographies of historical figures will continue to be popular.

Analysis rather than narrative is characteristic of the bulk of scholarly production. Sometimes it takes the form of large and complex studies, as the work of Braudel cited above. Usually, however, it is a more limited study, a "monograph," the characteristic product of the modern professional historian.[8] Building on the development of critical scholarship in the 15th to 18th centuries, the monograph was refined by the "scientific" historians of the 19th century into approximately its present form. The emphasis is on meticulous research into source materials or evidence. Often

---

[8] Most historians were "amateurs" until the 19th century. There are critics who lament the change.

it is an exhaustive treatment of a narrow subject. It is, therefore, a child of science rather than of humanism. Although
influenced by the humanist tradition, it holds to the dictum
that accuracy is more important than art. It is obvious that
monographic studies often fail to integrate results into the
broader framework of history; also, most are dull. Some
monographic history, nevertheless, is well written, even
lively, and some carefully integrates the analysis into history in general. In any event, these criticisms are irrelevant.
Monographs are specialized works, intended for limited
audiences. That includes all sorts of scholars and public
and private agencies that have a use for carefully done analysis of historical events. Finally, the best of narrative historians, who find large audiences, will base their work on
monographic literature.

In view of the foregoing, it is not surprising that the
growth of history as a discipline shows an increasing tendency toward specialization in subject matter. The professional historian may still write a history of the world or of
a civilization, but such work most often is prepared for use
as a textbook. Increasingly, the professional historian tends
to think of himself not merely as a student of medieval history, modern European history, or United States history,
but also as a social, economic, or intellectual historian. The
broad avenues of political history that once held almost ex-
clusive sway give way to the narrower specialties of the
history of political parties, of institutions, behavior, or international relations. Historians have also been much influenced by the deep stirrings in many parts of the world
hitherto little studied by European and American scholars.
Africa, Asia, and Latin America have attracted great interest
in the period since World War II. It is apparent that the
historian is responsive not only to influences from within
the profession but that his outlook is broadly shaped by
fundamental changes in outlook and perspective within the
society in which he lives.

Not all specialized historical fields can be mentioned here, and those listed are merely illustrative. Intellectual and legal history offer typical examples.[9] Quantitative history is an important and rapidly growing specialty; it also is a method, and can be applied to most historical fields.[10] Psychohistory has some popular appeal, although the American Psychiatric Association is not sure it wants its members to write about living subjects. Freud tried to analyze Leonardo da Vinci, but there could be no invasion of privacy in that case; nor any analysis, critics say. There is no reason why notions of the psyche or other psychological concepts should not be applied to historical figures, so long as speculative elements are so identified. There is Marxist history in its many varieties. There is comparative history, more often praised than practiced, although some interesting work was done in recent years on slavery in English, French, Spanish, and Portuguese America. There is cooperative history, which produces some excellent reference works. There are histories of education, diplomacy, science, religion, sexuality, childhood, women, servants, blacks, Hispanics in the United States, and many more. Some are served by specialized historical journals. Some of the new specialized history is technical, suitable only for specialists; but some is lively and widely read, witness the popularity of histories of the black and female experiences in America.

C. Major problems in historical thinking

Intellectual problems in historical inquiry illuminate much of the nature of the discipline and some of its fundamental concerns. An examination of some of them specifically is useful in introducing the student to historical anal-

---

[9] John P. Diggins, "Getting Hegel Out of History: Max Eastman's Quarrel with Marxism," *American Historical Review*, February 1974, 38–70; Harry N. Scheiber, "At the Borderline of Law and Economic History: The Contributions of Willard Hurst," *American Historical Review*, February 1970, 744–56.

[10] See Chapter III (C) on quantitative history.

ysis, the demand for evidence of probabilities, and the problem of interpretation.

1. THE VALUES OF HISTORIANS

Historians carry their personal philosophies and values to their work and they affect the search for evidence and the interpretation of that evidence. That fact is a staple of modern training in historical method. It follows that historians should devote attention to their fundamental assumptions; to fail to do so, it has been well said, is to remain prey to unformed ideas rather than to escape the influence of philosophical problems.

Although historians do pursue the theory of history, for most it is an occasional activity; they are not theory oriented. That is mostly because the discipline does not lend itself easily to theorizing, as philosophers have found.[11] It is not clear how much yield may come from continuing examination of such matters as causation and contingency in their larger aspects. Special cases of causation and contingency apparently are more promising fields for logical probing.

Historians contend more about specific cases of causation and interpretation. In those cases, conflicting intellectual and metaphysical views produce a variety of attitudes toward miracles, stock exchanges, state censorship, race riots, and other matters of importance. That certainly is one reason that some American historians find the history of their country mainly one of consensus while others find it chiefly a story of violence, conflict, and repression. But the fact of disagreement in historical literature is no reason for not reading history. We do not abandon politics because statesmen fall out, or resort to witch doctors because physicians dispute, or repudiate science as its new findings

---

[11] See III (A) on the technical philosophy of history.

cancel some of the old. So history is rewritten. Fine. To have values is to be human.[12]

Some historians try to ignore the metaphysical and epistemological implications of their work on the ground that the discipline has little to offer in those realms. Others declare their views with whatever argument they can offer to support them. Yet others try to judge events solely in terms of the social environment in which they are embedded. Some people consider odious such a neutral attitude toward values, believing it must lead to either cynicism or despair. Others find it a gain to sophistication and a prop to tolerance.

It is at least understandable that some historians are wary of metaphysical inquiry when they consider the oscillations of fashion in that regard. Various ideas that at one time troubled the historical profession no longer are much regarded. An example is determinism, or historical inevitability, and the question of free choice. Most people—including most historians—now largely ignore the question. Those for whom determinism is a matter of transcendent importance naturally believe that only the naive can ignore it in practice. Modern historians are at least interested to the extent that most are aware that human choice is more limited—by heredity or by social and physical environments—than once was supposed.

Another once much-discussed idea that diminished in attractiveness is the "relativism" developed in the late 19th and 20th centuries. New knowledge from natural science, psychology, comparative religion, and other fields, resulted in a decline of interest in metaphysics and to doubts about the capacity of the human mind to deal with such problems. It led to the view that historians did not discover an historical reality that had an existence apart from men, but that men themselves *created* (observed, thought about, in-

---

[12] See VIII (C) on bias and subjectivity.

terpreted, composed) history. The English philosopher R. G. Collingwood argued that the historian's criterion of truth was an innate *idea* of history, which "every man possesses as part of the furniture of his mind." He contended that the historian uses this criterion in the light of his own experience, to judge the value of authorities coming down from the past, and in using his "constructive imagination" in supplying gaps in the record.[13] Such contentions led the American historians Carl Becker and Charles Beard to declare respectively that each man was "his own historian," and that history was "an act of faith."

To most historians, such contentions boiled down to two commonly accepted propositions. (1) The historian's cultural experience or environment affects his interpretation of evidence on human affairs, and that as a result interpretations of history necessarily vary with the social environments of historians. (2) Inference (i.e., supplying data not explicitly provided by the contemporary writers or artifacts) must be indulged in with great care. Thus, if the past must be interpreted in a variety of ways, the historian should be cautious about declaring the universal validity of his work. As Collingwood pointed out, a modern historian's experience might lead him to reject ancient Greek accounts of killing infants by exposure, but the fact of such exposure, if it is a fact, existed independently of what any one may think. Assumptions regarding human standards—e.g., of cruelty or justice—must be used only tentatively. A beginning researcher today cannot, for example, be sure what infanticide might be acceptable in a future world made virtually unbearable by overpopulation. As for inference as imaginative connection between authorities or evidence, it also must rest on assumptions; hence, on the cultural environment of the historian.

Relativism never seriously troubled most historians on the working level. On the theoretical level, relativism in the

---

[13] R. G. Collingwood, *The Idea of History* (Oxford: The Clarendon Press, 1946).

middle years of the 20th century was rather modified by arguments by epistemologists and others that human activity shows some "probabalistic" regularities, permitting assumptions and explanations in which we may repose considerable confidence. There also has been a new emphasis on the knowability of certain things that are not metaphysical in nature; for example, election figures, or the capacities of ox carts. To be sure, they can be linked with metaphysical questions, but that does not make them metaphysical in themselves.[14]

2. CONTINUITY AND CHANGE

The idea of the continuity of history is the foundation of the discipline. Social scientists often concentrate on change rather than continuity because they see human agents working change. But continuity is not something that merely "happens"; it also is induced, even pounded into the citizens of command societies to compel continuity of ideas of a certain sort. It is socially desirable to remember this, and it is one answer to the existentialist youth who has no historical memory or interest in one and thinks of everything as change.[15] The widely-read Oxford historian Hugh Trevor-Roper, speaking to a "history-is-irrelevant" crowd in 1969, said

> To those who say, with Marx, that it is more important to change than to understand the world, I would reply that even so, without understanding we cannot rationally change it. To those who see the past as an incubus from which we must set ourselves free, I would reply, with Freud, that obsessions are purged only by understanding, not by repudiation. We cannot profitably look forward without also looking back.[16]

---

[14] On probability see III (A), and on "regularities" see III (C) on quantitative method.

[15] See I (A) above.

[16] *The New York Times Book Review*, April 24, 1977.

History often *seems*, of course, to deal only with change. We hear it said that history is being made at a rapid rate today. What is meant is that national governments are being felled by violence, the role of women is changing, attitudes toward energy and the ecology are altering.

All this is true, yet change is only a small part of the human picture. Suppose that instead of the greeting, "What's new?" we ask, "What's old?" Obviously much of human behavior is immensely old. People marry and divorce, laugh and weep, work and play, worship and sin in 20th-century America, and they carried on these same activities in first-century Rome. Also old are our basic social and political groupings (family, village, city, nation, empire), our instruments of written communication (letters, books, magazines, newspapers), our educational institutions.

The complaint of the disenchanted youth that he is born into a world he never made has an obvious basis. Yet it is fortunate that this is true. If each generation had really to make its world anew, creating from nothing its patterns of behavior, its means of livelihood, its political and social institutions, humanity could do little more than struggle to keep alive. One of the great advantages of being human is that we inherit all these aspects of our culture. Each generation leaves only a thin new accretion on the huge reef of humanity's experience.

Respect for what is old gives us perspective on what is new. We soon perceive that the completely new in human affairs is rare. The 1961 achievement of the Russians in first orbiting a man in space around the earth was a triumph, but both Russia and America had experimented earlier with unmanned space vehicles. Nor were the so-called artificial satellites themselves wholly novel. Their launching would have been impossible without earlier experimentation with long-range ballistic missiles and military rockets. Equally necessary for modern space triumphs was the accumulation of scientific knowledge during earlier generations, knowledge about the laws of motion, the composition of the atmosphere and space, the uses of mathematics, and the transmission of electronic commands. So viewed, the question of who *invented* space travel becomes pointless. Man's curiosity and inventiveness over many generations played a larger part than any single man's genius.

Impressed by this fact of the *continuity of history,* the historian sees problems in long perspective. He finds the roots of today's racial tensions in lines of development that go back not merely to the Civil War but long before. In trying to understand Russian domestic and foreign policy, he studies not only Marxist ideology but the conditioning experience of hundreds of years of Czarist history. But the idea of continuity will not be found—except for hints and isolated anticipations—in ancient and medieval historians.

It is a 19th century idea, this concept of continuing incremental change in human society, of history as a developing process, of linkage rather than periodization, of the existence of the past in the present. It should be noted that even when historians speak of "discontinuities" in human affairs (e.g., the revolutions in Russia in 1917, Mexico 1910–17, or China in recent years), they do not mean that all the past was eradicated, but that the rate of change was abruptly increased. Much that was old remains. Scholars need to examine the continuities (often heavily camouflaged) as well as the discontinuities or changes in such post-revolutionary societies. In short, an historical approach is a vital component in the study of current affairs, giving adequate attention to both continuity and change.

3. THE INDIVIDUAL AND SOCIETY

Once upon a time it was thought that the good prince made good times and the bad king corrupted society. The element of truth in this notion is now modified by the view that while devils and saints frequently twist human affairs, they do not all by themselves form or shatter the foundations of society. Ancient Hellenic and romantic Victorian historians who subscribed to the "Great Man Theory" of history tended to give insufficient weight to the role of society (institutions) and culture (values) in forming the ideas of leaders, in structuring the problems they faced, and in molding the solutions they might attempt and achieve.

All men are, of course, born into society, into what anthropologists call a culture. Each culture has many institutions and values—that is, customs, associations, relationships, complexes of values or norms that are enforced in various ways. A man acts, consciously and unconsciously, in the light of the institutions and values of his culture—affected, to be sure, by his own qualities. Great innovators, leaders, villains, can move other men only within limits imposed by the culture—religious, economic, scientific, technological, and political. Julius Caesar could not start automobile manufacture. Muhammed could not have foisted Zen Buddhism on the Arabs. Adolf Hitler born into Samoan society in 1600 might have been simply an indifferent fisherman.

What are sometimes called "social forces" are the outcome of persons acting for change in the context of existing customs and forcing others to do the same. It certainly is the case that much of the activity of man in society, actions involving organized groups and institutions, is dependent upon agreement on ideas. Without this agreement, effective action is difficult. An electoral process will not work well if there is no firm agreement to accept the results. There is no physical safety without agreement on rules of conduct. There can be no discussion if opponents can howl down debate. It is obvious that human institutions have varied tremendously in place and time; there are no unvarying social forces, except in the sense that institutions of some sort will deal with certain broad classes of human needs—for example, food, sexual gratification, and procreation. There have been many societies with numerous important institutions that involved groups of people dedicated in at least some of their activities to maintaining and extending the rights and obligations of the group. It may be a church, a military institution, a chamber of commerce. Such organized groups have been much studied in recent times. We are better equipped than formerly to examine organization and structure, membership, doctrine, leadership, and linkages with other institutions.

There are three overriding requirements in the study of individuals and institutions: (1) That they be conceived of as interacting, but with the power of the individual much inhibited by the organized and established strength of the ideas and interests of men grouped in institutions; (2) That it be clear that the historian cannot understand an historical figure except in the context of that figure's own culture. Slavery and permissive homosexuality were facts of ancient Hellenic society, to be understood in that context, not in that of Victorian England; (3) That it be clear that historians are products of their own times—that is, of the institutions of their specific cultures, even if their culture encourages them to study others. Even in a culture that encourages individualism, men are not entirely free, either physically or spiritually.

4. Generalizations and Laws

"History repeats itself" is a saying more popular with nonhistorians than with historians. Franklin D. Roosevelt won the presidential elections of 1932, 1936, 1940, and 1944, an example, presumably, of history repeating itself. Yet if we compare these elections, the dissimilarities may impress us more than the similarities. In each election the Republican candidate was different, the issues were different, the campaigning was different, the popular and electoral votes were different. The same may be said of the numerous instances in human history of warfare, political assassination, religious persecutions, and many other phenomena. So the historian often will regard them more as illustrations of the uniqueness of human events than as proof of the uniformities of history.

Certainly history differs strikingly from the physical sciences. Space travel is possible because the course of a projectile and of a body moving through space repeats itself in a far more dependable way than the course of historical events. By the application of mathematics and "laws," certain results can be reliably predicted from certain antecedent causes. But history deals with so many independent variables, impossible of measurement or control, that it lacks this element of predictability.

Actually, the search for laws of history usually reveals some naiveté. The metahistorians are most ambitious in this quest.[17] Even in the field of science the idea of "law" is misleading; the more sophisticated scientists of the 20th century prefer to think in terms of statistical probability. Most historians regard the search for "laws" of history as a futile endeavor.

Yet there is ample room for less ambitious historical generalization. Comparative studies of revolutions show some similar patterns of events. It has been observed that peasants historically have tended to be politically apathetic and difficult to organize for action. Comparative studies show that no national group that used black slaves in America can claim a significantly superior benignity. These are sizable and important generalizations.

Such generalizations often involve some fairly simple relationships of cause and effect in which the historian can have considerable confidence. Or they are statements of statistical regularity, noncausal explanations. In any event, they are generalizations in terms of probability, not unvarying "laws." They should be carefully formulated so as not to outrun the evidence. This fault—outrunning the evidence

---

[17] See III (B) below.

—may be due either to poor conceptualization or to careless exposition; e.g., extreme terms such as "never," "every," "all," must be used cautiously; "forever" will never be used.

5. CAUSATION

What caused an historical event? Every student will recognize this as a favorite examination question. It also is a favorite question for historians to ask themselves. *What* happened is supposedly an easy question; *why* it happened is more difficult. What were the causes of the fall of the Roman Empire? Of the American Civil War? Of American entry into World War I? Each of these has been a sharply controverted question resulting in a flood of books and articles.

Nor are historians the only persons concerned with the causes of past events. Practical statesmen make implicit judgments about the past whenever they adopt a policy. The belief that a major cause of war is weakness and division in the face of threatened aggression was a reason for the abandonment of American isolation, for the organization of NATO and other defensive alignments, and for American involvement in Korea and Vietnam.

Simple people give simple answers to questions of causation. Asked why World War II broke out in September 1939, they are satisfied to answer that the war resulted from Hitler's order sending German troops across the Polish frontier. This is not an adequate answer. During earlier months, Hitler had ordered German troops into Austria and Czechoslovakia, yet no war resulted. What was different on the later occasion was Polish resistance to German attack and the decision of France and Britain to go to Poland's assistance. But instead of putting an end to our curiosity, such answers only raise new questions: Why was Hitler so determined to move against Poland? Why had British and French leaders decided that German expansion must be halted?

In short, the historian is led beyond the "precipitating" or "immediate" cause of the war—the invasion of Poland, to look at the "underlying" causes that made England and France accept that invasion as a reason for action. He will explore the Polish question back through the Versailles treaty, and on back to the partitions of Poland in the 18th and 19th centuries, and even back to the migrations of Germans and Slavs during the Middle Ages. Similarly, he may trace German militarism back through Bismarck to Frederick the Great and beyond, and Adolf Hitler's twisted mentality back through the horrors of trench warfare in World War I, frustrations in youth, to the unnourishing social environment into which he was born. To understand the mood of Britain and France in September 1939, the scholar must understand the impact of the Munich crisis and its aftermath, the earlier hope for appeasement, the French alliance system, and a whole antecedent chain of events over many generations. Not only will the search for the causes of World War II ramify backward into time, it also will spread out in space as the historian ponders the influence of Russia's relations with Germany and with England and France, Franklin Roosevelt's struggles with Congress over American neutrality policy, world economic conditions, and the state of military preparation in various countries of the world.

All of these may seem likely causes, but often it is difficult to prove an agency *connecting* events. It will not do simply to *correlate* them. Many ridiculous correlations have been observed, such as between the incidence of bathing and great changes in national attitudes or institutions (e.g., in Rome and the United States), or between stock prices and baseball scores. Some correlations, however, have been so striking as to lead to a presumption of causal relationship, and to a search for the link, as in the cases of cigarette smoking and various disorders of the human body.

The historian, therefore, believes in *multiple causation*. He mistrusts the glib amateurs who are always ready to write a book proving that Pearl Harbor resulted from the machinations of Franklin D. Roosevelt, or that Secretary of War Stanton was responsible for the assassination of Abraham Lincoln. Similarly, he is hesitant to believe that the influence of the frontier was the sole cause of American democracy and individualism, or that the pocketbook interest of the founding fathers was the sole cause of the American Constitution. He finds instead a plurality of causes behind historical events. Moreover, he always finds a chain of causes; that is, each cause has antecedent causes, and the latter are preceded by still earlier. Theologians or philosophers may postulate a final cause, but few historians will.

If historical events have so many causes, how can historians discuss cause intelligibly? The answer is that they cannot hope to ferret out all of the causes of complex events. Nor can they always demonstrate that their explanations of the relationships between data is causal—it often will merely seem probable, or, even more weakly, plausible. It sometimes helps to accept a logician's definition of the cause of an event as "the sum of the necessary and sufficient conditions for the event's occurrence." If the circumstance is not necessary for the event—that is, the event could have taken place without it—it cannot be the cause; if the circumstance is not sufficient to bring about the event—that is, if the circumstance could have occurred without the event following—it cannot be the cause.

This definition often is difficult to use in historical inquiry. It will yield little as applied to the problem of Hitler's invasion of Poland as a cause of World War II. It may be used with somewhat more confidence in connection with another alleged cause of the war. In the early weeks of the war the German government published a collection of documents intended to prove that the Poles had been guilty of atrocities against the German minority living in Poland. According to the Germans, these atrocities cried out for German intervention, thus were the real cause of the war. There are two problems here. Did such atrocities actually occur, or was the evidence of the German documents fabricated? This is a problem of historical fact, dealt with elsewhere in this book. But the other problem is one of causation. Even if such incidents actually occurred, were these the necessary and sufficient condition for the German action? On this, the evidence from captured German documents seems clear. Hitler was determined to seize Polish territory in any case, and the alleged atrocities served as a pretext rather than a true cause for his action.

The issue of the alleged Polish atrocities involves also the fallacy which logicians call *post hoc, ergo propter hoc* (after this, therefore because of this). Even if it could be proved that the German attack came *after* Polish atrocities, it would not necessarily follow that the attack occurred *because* of the atrocities. A series of causes is not a mere succession of events in time. Some kind of logical dependence of one upon another must be demonstrated.

Medical experimenters, testing the efficacy of the new Salk polio vaccine, conducted controlled experiments and subjected the results to statistical analysis before asserting that the vaccine gave immunity from polio. The historian finds it almost impossible to duplicate this procedure. Dealing with past events that never exactly repeat themselves, he cannot conduct controlled experiments. Yet under certain circumstances he can apply statistical tools. Suppose, for example, his problem is whether the black vote was the principal cause of Johnson's victory over Goldwater in the state of Virginia in the 1964 presidential election. The researcher could probably design a study based upon comparison of voting districts with high black registration with districts of low black registration, working in a comparison between this election and earlier ones, as well. The result of his investigation might well be a convincing set of correlations between the percentage of black registrants in a district and the amount of Johnson's majority in that district. Statistical analysis would then tend to support the hypothesis of the decisiveness of the black vote. But several cautions must at once be offered. Even in the hands of experts, statistical analysis has many pitfalls, and for the amateur the perils are multiplied. Consider, for example, a possible rival hypothesis that low-income voters played the decisive role in the election. Then the fact that districts with a large black registration might also be low-income districts would be a confusing factor in the analysis. More careful study might resolve this difficulty, but other problems probably would be encountered. These remarks should not discourage the student from using statistical tools, but warn against superficial thinking. Mere correlation does not establish causation; a logical connection between the two series of events must be established.

Not only do historians have to distinguish between true and spurious causes; they also must attempt meaningful generalization about the causes they identify. In this way, they may group together the attack upon Poland and earlier episodes and find convincing evidence of the aggressive character of the entire Nazi movement. Or generalizing still further about German, Italian, Japanese, and Russian behavior, they may find a large cause of war in the rise of totalitarianism. In a similar way they may make some generalizing statement about the kinds of action taken by Britain, France, and the United States in response to this totalitarian threat. The failure of the democratic powers to take a strong united stand in earlier years may seem another major cause of World War II.

The problem of causation, the most vexatious facing the historian, is beyond complete "solution"—that is, to the permanent satisfaction of all manners of men. It bristles with philosophical and practical difficulties. Are human events "determined," or can individuals choose paths to follow? Apparently the best we can do is assert that we seem to come nearer to free choice on some questions than on others. Could events have developed differently than in fact they did? Yes, if the antecedent causes had been different— which gets us no place. Is there any *absolute* way of determining decisive causes? Probably not; it depends on value systems. Should we therefore abandon efforts to find causes? Some historians do, preferring to deal in what they claim are noncausal explanations. But to abandon the search for causes would be other than human (that is, it is not likely to happen), and it would leave us with formless and meaningless historical literature. Why should we not regard the search for cause, with appropiate vigor and modesty, as the greatest of the conceptual and technical challenges posed to the craft? At least historians now know more about the causes of many complex historical events (e.g., the Protestant Revolution, World War I, the disruption of the ancient Roman world) than did the participants themselves.

6. MOTIVATION

Since history so often deals with an individual's actions, sometimes it is relevant to probe his motives. For example, on January 1, 1863, President Abraham Lincoln issued the Emancipation Proclamation. Did he do so because of abhorrence of slavery and to end it? If so, why did he wait almost two years after his inaguration? Or, even more pertinent, why did he limit the proclamation to regions within the control of the Confederacy, excluding exactly those districts where his authority was respected? The historian probably will decide that Lincoln's dislike for slavery is not an adequate explanation, since that dislike was held in check by a sense of duty to act within the Constitution, and by a sense of political realism that deterred him from antagonizing the border states. He may find more convincing motivation in Lincoln's desire to recruit black troops, weaken the Confederacy, and strengthen the moral standing of the North in English eyes.

But most of the evidence for all this is indirect; we are working by inference; it is better than nothing, but the historian will be troubled. Even when the person under study leaves testimony as to his motives, we cannot be sure that he is trying to tell the complete truth; in any event, some of his motivation may have been obscure to himself, if only because men often are driven by irrational considerations, or because his motives were too mixed for him to disentangle accurately.

Attribution of motives is seen to be a hazardous business. Our confidence in the result is weak. Of course, the historian is not alone with this difficulty. People often find it difficult to understand their own mixed and confused motives; or they may be unwilling to face them, and so leave "false" testimony to confuse the historian. Nor do students of the human mind give us unambiguous guidance. A psychiatrist, after long observation, may find a patient's motives obscure. Psychology has not agreed on a single theory of human personality. It gives us insights, but not answers. Historians thus will be cautious about blanket assignment of human motivation to self-interest, the will to dominate, or altruism.

Motivation may be seen as a special case of causation. But often the researcher must ask himself: Do the motives of this individual much matter in the interpretation of the events under consideration? In many cases it will be decided that it does not much matter, unless simple biography is the objective. For example, if the objective is examination of the reception and practical consequences of the Emancipation Proclamation, Lincoln's motives in issuing the document are of little importance. Nor does it matter much—from most points of view—how much, if any, political motivation was involved in President Franklin Roosevelt's advocacy of Social Security.

7. CONTINGENCY

Although most events in history appear to have their logical explanation in the continuous chain of cause and effect, some may seem to have a chance or accidental character.

That does not mean that events—other than miracles—occasionally occur without being caused by anything. It merely means that two or more chains of causation cross in an unpredictable and apparently chance fashion. That is what happens when an oak tree, roots weakened by disease, is blown over by a storm (one chain of causation) and "accidentally" falls on a husband and wife returning from a party at that precise time, for all the reasons that brought them there at that hour (another chain of causation). The chains crossed and the couple died.

It was in this sense that "chance decreed" that the era of oceanic expansion and competition for overseas empire should commence while the Germans were divided and could not compete. There certainly were adequate causes of the discovery of America by Columbus and of European expansion overseas; and adequate causes of German division in 1492 as compared with Spain, Portugal, France, and England. German division, however, had nothing to do with the time of the discovery of America or the beginning of the competition for overseas empire, but the fact that those things occurred when Germany was weak put her at a disadvantage. It was no accident that several nations wanted a weak Germany for political, diplomatic, and economic reasons, but they had long wanted that without reference to overseas empire. It was, on the other hand, a fortunate chance for Spain that the discovery did not occur a half-century earlier, when Castile was weakened by factionalism and not yet united with Aragon. And it was a fortunate accident for Portuguese expansion that France and England were so often in the 16th century distracted by internal troubles that Portugal did nothing to cause.

The German Kaiser Wilhelm in a new German empire late in the 19th century complained of the unfair accident of history that gave great overseas possessions to countries weaker than Germany. He demanded Germany's fair "place in the sun." The Aztecs might have complained in 1519 of the accident that their ruler when the Europeans arrived was a weakling.

The assassination of President John Kennedy was an unpredictable contingency, except that we know that some persons want to kill presidents, and we know that presidents expose themselves in public for personal and political reasons. The chain of causes that led Kennedy to Dallas was different from the chain that led his assassin there, but they met and Kennedy was killed.

Yet contingency in history often is of limited long-range significance. The battle is not lost because of the lack of a horseshoe nail. The force of nationalism finally acted upon the Germanies and brought unity and power. The Aztecs were doomed not by the weakness of Moctezuma but by the superior technology of Europe. Kennedy's death did not interrupt major historical sequences. In Germany, China, Alabama, events continued to follow events in a way that probably was little different from what might have been expected if Kennedy never had visited Dallas. Still, some role is played in human history by unexpected and unpredictable "accidents." The life of man is full of crossings of independent chains of cause and effect. That is what we mean by contingency. Historians today do not assign them to fate, demons, or other supernatural agencies.

D. History and other disciplines

Whether history is science or humanity is an old debate. Enthusiasts for the scientific view in the 19th century included the English historian J. B. Bury, who both thought history a science and believed that a universal "law" had been discovered in the idea of progress.[18] The German Leopold von Ranke did much to develop the attitudes and

---

[18] See III (B) on the idea of progress.

methodology of the new historiography in that age of scientific advance, emphasizing the critical use of sources, hoping that historians would set down exactly what had happened in the past. Another enthusiast was the French historian Fustel de Coulanges, who asserted that "History is a science; it does not imagine, it only sees."

That view has not conquered the field of historical inquiry even in the 20th century of yet more vaulting scientific achievement, and of some doubts about science. The English historian G. M. Trevelyan stated in this century that

> men are too spiritual, too various, for scientific analysis, and the life history of millions cannot be inferred from the history of single men. History . . . deals with intellectual and spiritual forces which cannot be subjected to any analysis that can properly be called scientific.[19]

But Trevelyan made his methods as critical, objective, and systematic as possible. That is about where we stand today.

Insofar as historical study and literature are concerned with men, events, developments, and institutions for their own sakes as examples of human activity, they are humanistic; and in much of their scholarship historians share methods and attitudes with other fields, as the critical study of the Bible and comparative literature, fields that, with history, have had a long line of development from the 15th century. Insofar as historical studies seek regularities and generalizations, they sometimes share the ground with social scientists, using parts of a methodology that mostly has been developed during the last century. The life of Marc Bloch, the great French medieval historian killed by the Nazis in 1944 for his work in the French underground, exemplified this attitude of sharing for enrichment. He favored continuing efforts by historians to improve their methodology and achieve greater precision. He helped found the *Annales d'histoire économique et social* as a jour-

---

[19] See IV (A) on historical "facts."

nal to open better communications between history and the social sciences.

But while most historians consider the discipline a humanity with its own aims, although it uses or shares methods and concepts with other fields, a minority disagrees. That minority of historians is enough interested in other disciplines, especially in the social sciences, so that a merger or near merger occurs in terms of research activity. That is fine, in most cases. It is only irritating when a few of the merged, in the usual manner of converts, preach merging to all historians.

The irritation somewhat increases on those occasions when it appears that some of the interest in merger is based on the hope of participating in the discovery of general laws and in the solution of contemporary social problems. Historians note that proclaimed general laws disconcertingly often are proved later to be rather less general than originally claimed. An historian with a quantitative bent said, in rejecting the social science view, that

> The social scientist is searching with an instrumental purpose for general . . . laws about mankind. . . . He is . . . willing to raid it [the past] for materials to test theoretical models drawn in the present. In contrast, the aim of many historians is to understand the past in its own terms as well as ours. . . . The historian focuses on the uniqueness of past time and place and human behavior, the historical context. He seeks to understand what differentiates us and our problems from those of our predecessors.[20]

What the searchers for laws want is the ability to predict, so they then can prescribe, at the least, goals for conduct. But even prediction by physical scientists about their fields has been often wrong. And some excellent social scientists complain that the massive effort of our times to improve predictability in grappling with the life of man in society

---

[20] Charlotte Erickson, review article on quantitative history in *American Historical Review*, April 1975, pp. 351–65, at p. 364.

is accompanied by irritating jargon and much pretentious and empty theory, with little increase in predictability. An especially sharp comment was made by the historian Hugh Trevor-Roper, who was told as an undergraduate student that the proof of a good historical interpretation of the past was that it could prophesy the future. Roper said in later years that was good enough for undergraduates, but "Marxism never prophesied Fascism, and Fascism nearly conquered the world." And he found the Marxist efforts to say that "Fascism was a thing that didn't count," were "arrogant and absurd."[21] So it seems also to many historians of the underdeveloped world, where they see large numbers of protofascist military regimes seeming to hold the Marxist predictions at bay. As a final comment, economics is the most quantitative of the social sciences, often described as the "hardest" (i.e., most nearly scientific), with the greatest predictive capability, yet a Nobel winner in the field declared recently that "there is little warrant for the belief that we know the laws of history well enough to make predictions of any great reliability."[22]

Despite their failures with general, and most specific, prediction, the social and behavioral sciences have done much precise, systematic, and sophisticated work on the regularities of human activity. It is because the work is so promising that so much energy is poured into it, and that historians use so many of the results and methods. The huge amount of this material only can be hinted at here.[23] Methods of quantification and of the manipulation of evidence in matrices and by equations and by computers permit new approaches to the study of man in society.[24] Social science work on polling methods has something to offer the stu-

---

[21] *The New York Times Book Review*, April 24, 1977.

[22] Kenneth J. Arrow, *The New York Times*, March 26, 1973. See I (C), above, on laws and generalizations.

[23] See II (C), below, for some comments.

[24] See III (C) on quantitative method.

dent of past public opinion.[25] Modern psychology is helpful.[26] An historian studying Sir Henry Clinton, British
commander during the Revolution, noted a hesitancy in
Clinton's execution of well-developed strategy, and he col-
laborated with a psychotherapist to provide a mutually acceptable explanation that seemed to satisfy the criteria for
interpretation in both fields.

Historians have been influenced by social psychologists
and sociologists who developed the concept of social norms
and values as determinants of group action. Social norms
include tangibles like clothing, housing, diet, ways of earn-
ing a living, and intangibles such as habits of thought, traditions, and ideas. Each social group has its own norms, and
newcomers to the group must learn them. In addition, the
newcomer learns the judgments the group has made—that
is, the social values the group attaches to the norms. The
majority in any group conforms in general to the group's
norms and values, and it is this demonstrable fact that
gives validity to limited generalizations about the group's
behavior. Social norms and values in any living society
are fluid, so are altered as a result of challenges. One approach to history is to regard it as a study of the origins and
development of social norms and values, although that
schematizes things more than most historians will allow.[27]

Many fruitful results will continue to flow from other
fields to history, but of course there is no reason to suppose
that either social scientists or historians have a monopoly
of "knowledge based on the most careful examination of
all available evidence."[28] Historians provide materials for
social science activity, point out the shortcomings of some
social science speculation that is based on improper selec-

---

[25] See V (C) 2 on polling.

[26] See I (B) on psychohistory.

[27] See I (C) on individuals and society.

[28] Morris R. Cohen, *The Meaning of Human History* (La Salle, Ill.:
Open Court Publishing Co., 1947), p. 36.

tion of evidence or otherwise defective study of the past, and produce generalizations of their own. In sum, interrelations between the disciplines have tended to the enrichment of historical literature and pedagogy rather than otherwise.

The public, of course, does not care whether history is a humanity or a social science. Nor are the views of adults automatically set by the selection and treatment of subjects in school and university in open societies, or always, it appears, in command societies. Thus, narrative and biographical history will find readers as far as we can guess at the future. History as a humanity and a literary genre exists almost independently of its relations with the social studies.

II

BEGINNING RESEARCH

The stages of an historical investigation can not be delimited precisely into chronological blocks. Thus, while much of the collection of data is concentrated in the early stages of an investigation, some is likely to continue well into the stage of final composition. Also, collection merges into analysis when the first research note is taken that consists of more than simple copying. Furthermore, it would be ideal if the beginning researcher knew about all aspects of method before commencing work; and if he or she could achieve sophistication by fiat! Lacking a prescription for such miracles, we here provide sketches of what is elaborated in later chapters on historical method, and the early steps of the research process, together with a discussion of the selection of research topics.

A. Historical Method

The elements of historical method as set down in our table of contents may be divided into the well-agreed-upon and the more controversial. There are three well-agreed-upon elements of method investigators must learn if they are to function effectively. They can be done much better with method than without it, and with great savings of effort. They are not just simple mechanics requiring little brain.

First is learning what the *categories of evidence* are, the critical elements that differentiate them, and what these mean to investigators. Second is *collecting evidence*. Much, but not all, of this collection must occur early in the research effort. This involves bibliographic search, description, control, and analysis or annotation. Huge accumulations of aids and techniques make this field more manageable than in the past. This element of method also involves means of recording evidence, of deciding what to record, and how and how much to process the material at this point. On both the collection and the recording of evidence there are many useful suggestions that can be made without much fear of contradiction. One of these is that bibliographic method is not child's play, or mindless paper shuffling, and that even professionals vary widely in their domination of such skills. Another suggestion is that good research notes do not simply drip from the unthinking and inexperienced pen. Taking good research notes is something few doctoral candidates manage until near the end of their dissertations. Both bibliographic method and note-taking can be taught, using well-understood concepts and techniques; neither is likely to be handled well by the uninstructed without a long and wasteful period of trial and error, which is quite unnecessary today. Finally, since so much of a researcher's time inevitably is consumed by bibliographic work and note-taking, rationalization of even the smallest processes may pay handsome dividends.

Third, the *communication of evidence* also is a subject that can be taught, at least in its essence, which is lucidity—that is, unambiguous expression. Without these operations, only miraculous intercession will contrive the same result. The opportunities for ambiguous expression in historical studies are appallingly numerous; the need for training and method is correspondingly acute.

The less agreed-upon, more controversial elements of historical method are more difficult to perform, and to talk about or teach. We have chosen to put these elements under the titles of external criticism, internal criticism, and analysis and synthesis. Under these heads we discuss the problems that all guides must, although they disagree as to how they should be labeled and treated.

External criticism determines the authenticity of evidence. It gets evidence ready for use in the study of human affairs—that is, prepares it for the processes of internal criticism and synthesis. In the case of documents, external criticism essentially authenticates the evidence and establishes the text as accurately as possible. It may deal with problems of forgery or the garbling of texts in copying. External criticism especially means determination of authorship and date of evidence, and these things are important also in judging the credibility of evidence. Such mental operations as analysis, assumption, inference, and synthesis, which are difficult and often hazardous, are common to both external and internal criticism. Although the beginning researcher probably will not engage in external criticism, he can develop the habit of thinking in terms of the critical approach used in authenticating materials.

Internal criticism determines the meaning and value, or credibility, of evidence. Although the difference between the aims of external and internal criticism can be simply stated—authenticity of the evidence as against its credibility in the explanation of human affairs, the processes share some interests and many mental operations.

Synthesis here means the blending of evidence into an

account that accurately describes historical events or solves historical problems. The operations of internal criticism and synthesis call not only for erudition and technique, but for intelligence, powers of discrimination, imagination, and sophistication. They necessarily are riddled with subjectivism, with value judgments, some of them acknowledged by the historical scholar, and some of them unacknowledged but nonetheless operative. These operations cause problems for historians, and between historians. It is in these areas that some historians most bitterly contend that some one and only that one conception of operations is proper. It is of these areas of what may be called types of interpretation that sometimes it is said that most working historians have relatively little interest in methodological theory.

Such comments are misleading. It is more accurate to say that many historians are lukewarm toward metaphysical and epistemological problems, and especially to efforts to schematicize research and interpretation as a whole. On the other hand, many historians who are tepid toward the more ambitious efforts to explain or integrate method, have a lively interest in discussions of portions of methodology —for example, bias, selection and relevance, organization schemes (chronologic, topical, geographic) in their influence upon interpretation and assignment of possible causation, probability, contingency, the uses of working hypotheses. It is for this reason that in this guide we put much of our material on methodological theory in sections dealing with *aspects* of method.[1]

We contend that parts of even the more difficult areas of historical method can be discussed by most historians without debilitating differences of opinion; for example, bias, probability, the importance of knowing the time of composi-

---

[1] See David Hackett Fischer, *Historians' Fallacies. Toward a Logic of Historical Thought* (New York, 1970), for a sophisticated but sometimes rather "theoretical" effort to deal with aspects of historical methodology; Cohen, *Meaning of Human History*, for a lucid treatment of broader theoretical considerations by a philosopher.

tion of documents, the difference between literal and real meaning, and the usefulness of at least some corroboration, whatever the difficulties of determining what is true corroboration, or what constitutes enough. Some of these aspects of method have been much refined in modern times.

As for those parts of the method that may always be subject to bitter debate, the student can be carried little further than the characteristics of some of the positions taken, and the need to form his own views on the substantive questions and on their importance to his own activity. There simply are some things that guides to method cannot do.

B. Selecting and refining subjects

Although some instructors supply students with subjects in order to plunge them as rapidly as possible into research, others prefer that students find their own subjects. Beginning researchers, however, often have great difficulty locating and properly refining a subject, even at the M.A. or Ph.D. levels. This is one of those cases where the theory is simple, but the practice difficult. A proper subject is anything you and your audience find satisfactory—that is, there are no "natural" subjects.

For our purposes we shall assume an audience of educated persons wishing to be informed rather briefly on a subject of some interest and importance, or of professors reading research efforts by students. Thus, we rule out trivia and formless anecdotes or jokes. The subject must have a beginning, a development, and a conclusion. On the other hand, we rule out (1) graduate research seminars, which demand some sort of clear originality, even a "contribution to knowledge," and (2) big research tasks—as the Ph.D. dissertation, a major report by the Department of Agriculture, or a treatise by the United States Army Historical Office. The following additional injunctions will be helpful.

1. Be sure that sufficient evidence is available for study of the subject. This sometimes can be estimated roughly by

the nature of the subject (see 7 below). Clues also may be gleaned quickly from the library card catalog, and from examination of the text, footnotes, and bibliographies of a few good studies of the subject.

2. The common admonition to select a subject that is interesting and important merely means that it should seem so to the researcher and to a fair part of his audience. That certainly means that the subject should not be frivolous.

3. The subject for this training purpose should be narrow enough to permit examination in some depth. Nothing will be learned by producing so generalized a descriptive paper that it might have been copied from a single account. One of the consequences of this requirement is that the original subject often is narrowed—or refined—to cover or emphasize only a segment thereof. Do not feel that this means that you are neglecting part of the subject; consider, rather, that you have a "new" subject.[2]

4. Do not choose a subject that is beyond your skills—for example, in languages, mathematics, geographic techniques, economic concepts.

5. Although you are not looking for a subject that will permit you to make a contribution to knowledge, you do want one that will permit the development of research skills, a large enough task. If something original can be produced also, so much the better.

6. The subject should have *unity* in the sense that it is possible to discuss it to some extent in isolation from the other subjects that surround it. (No easily imaginable subject is so large that it is not surrounded by yet other subjects.) This means that each of the following would be a

---

[2] See II (C) on questioning and refining a subject; VIII (B) on the working hypothesis, which puts questions to the research that result in a delimitation of its major divisions, and in effect shows how subjects are subdivided into others, each of which is capable of separate investigation; VIII (D) on relevance and selection, shows a somewhat similar process with another subject; VIII (E) 7, breaks yet another subject into parts; IX (A), defines a subject by the use of an outline.

suitable subject: (1) the Civil War; (2) the artillery in the Civil War; (3) the Union artillery in the Civil War; (4) Union artillery ammunition in the Civil War; (5) manufacture of Union artillery ammunition in the Civil War; (6) labor problems and the manufacture of Union artillery ammunition in the Civil War; (7) shortages of skilled labor and the manufacture of Union artillery ammunition in the Civil War.

7. As a final caution, some types of subjects are inherently difficult to study; for example, those involving activities that the participants therein try to hide (e.g., illegal or immoral actions), or activities of so commonplace a character that they seldom occasion comment (e.g., the household activities of an illiterate peasantry in a society dominated by a small upper class), or subjects concentrated on the beliefs and attitudes of common folk (e.g., in Baltimore in 1850) who did not write books or answer questionnaires. On the other hand, certain types of subject are apt to offer considerable evidence to the researcher: for example, a subject arousing large public interest on the part of a modern representative governmental system, and the concern of organized interest groups, and the press. Thus, the Spanish-American War, or Medicare, offer floods of documentation to the researcher.

C. Other first steps in the research process

Having chosen or been assigned a research topic, quickly locate a few good treatments of it. This may be done by using the library card catalog and major bibliographies. Bibliographies may offer comments on the items listed, which will help in choosing what to read first. Or a few articles in major scholarly journals of history and the social sciences may be selected for this early reading. The fact of publication in such journals is at least a minimum guarantee of quality. Or, when a book title is located that looks promising, an effort can be made to find reviews of it in scholarly journals in the year or two following the book's publication. Finally, the researcher may simply look at a book with a promising title, and quickly estimate its quality, and its probable suitability for this early reading. This process of quick estimation, or screening, will be discussed further.

A few such items having been selected, commence reading. This may be thoughts of as *orientation reading*. The object is to get some notion of the character and dimensions of the subject, of some of the attitudes toward it adopted by investigators, and of problems of evidence and interpretation. Notes should be taken, but at this stage they will not be the type of research note discussed later in this chapter. Think of these early notes as orientation materials, understanding that they will not form a part of the body of evidence used in composition of the final paper. If careful research notes are wanted on the materials read quickly for this early orientation, it will be necessary at a later time to return to the materials.

If the orientation process is thought of as involving the quick scanning of several hundred pages in about a week, it is clear that note taking must be sketchy. Try to get some idea of the *major subdivisions* of the project—chronologic, geographic, topical. If the subject is "United States Intervention in Latin America since 1898," it quickly will become apparent that different types of intervention have occurred. So a note might suggest a preliminary classification into economic, military, cultural, and diplomatic intervention. Also, it will be seen that certain chronologic divisions are evident: (1) much direct intervention to about 1933, (2) cessation of such intervention from 1933 to 1954, (3) direct intervention since 1954.

Such simple patterns, set down in writing, should in effect be *questioned by the researcher*. Why did this periodization occur? Was it because of developments in the United States, in Latin America, or elsewhere, or a combination of these? Was it because of economic, military, political, cultural, or diplomatic developments? Were the causes different in one period than in another? This preliminary questioning process might result in construction of a simple outline indicating the causes of intervention in specific cases discussed by the authors read.

At the same time the researcher should be considering two other matters: (1) does there seem to be difference of opinion on the character and results of United States intervention in Latin America, and (2) is it apparent that there are some problems of evidence in connection with study of the subject? The researcher should be able to jot down a number of problems in connection with these questions if he has read even a hundred pages in a standard college textbook of United States–Latin American relations. For example:

(1) Has U.S. intervention in Latin America ever been successful?

(2) How can scholars define "success" in intervention? Will this be different from the definitions of journalists, Secretaries of State, corporation executives?

(3) Are there "schools of thought" among scholars on U.S. intervention in Latin America in general? In Haiti in 1915? In Guatemala in 1954?

(4) How much, and in what ways, have Latin Americans expressed resentment of U.S. intervention? How is this related to the problem of "success?"

(5) Do views on intervention vary in accordance with an individual's political party, occupation, income level, religious faith?

(6) What is the evidence for the view that private business induced Theodore Roosevelt to declare and act on his "corollary" to the Monroe Doctrine?

(7) Are there special problems of evidence in connection with the local communism that ostensibly was all-important in recent U.S. interventions in Guatemala, Cuba, and the

Dominican Republic? How great was local communist influence in each case? How much of a threat did it pose to the U.S. in each case?

Such questions come, then, from what the researcher reads—by historians, social scientists, journalists, and others; and from his own thought processes. They are developed to give shape and direction to research. They will be applied to the evidence as it is collected, helping to determine what to look for, and what to take down as being relevant. Some of the questions may be adopted as tentative hypotheses quite early in the research process. In any event, from the beginning of his work the researcher should try to make sense of it by inquiring what it means, how it came about. If this is not done, there will be no basis on which to select from among the mass of data available. The researcher should not be disturbed by the thought that some of the early questions will be abandoned or changed and new ones developed later. This is unavoidable.

Either during this initial brief period of orientation reading and questioning, or early in the following process of collecting materials, it often is helpful to construct a tentative outline of the subject. This not only will help in the development of more questions to ask of the evidence, but it may very early in the research effort suggest that the subject ought to be drastically modified, probably reduced in size. This should be the case with the subject discussed above on intervention in Latin America. Clearly it is too large for a research paper of moderate length.

Developing questions to put to the evidence, and to the publications of scholars who have used some part of it, is a challenge to the researcher's sense of the fitness of things, of priorities in human affairs, of the ways in which men judge their own actions and those of others. Do not be afraid to ask the most important questions, being careful not to frame them to fit personal prejudices. Was the United States justified in invading the Dominican Republic because of a communist menace there? Has business been too influential in the making of intervention policy? Such questions give meaning, life, and interest to research. Of course, they shape research by setting up standards of relevance. That is much better than having no standards, and pretending to follow the impossible policy of collecting "everything," an error that has afflicted not only individual historians but huge government research and intelligence agencies.

After this orientation reading, with its attendant development of questions and of tentative outlines of at least portions of the subject, *systematic bibliographic work* must be started. A small amount only will have been done in searching for materials for the orientation reading. A thorough search for materials requires a knowledge of bibliographic method and bibliographic aids, which are discussed later in this guide. Here it is necessary to point out that the bibliographic effort necessarily must proceed hand-in-hand with some research notetaking from materials located. Research notes are discussed in a later chapter.

One reason that research notes must be taken before the bibliographic work is completed is that improvement of knowledge of the substantive aspects of the subject is necessary to guide the search for materials. A deepening knowledge of the research subject may well change the emphasis of research or alter the interpretation of evidence, with effects upon the search for materials. The difficult problem for the beginning researcher—and often a considerable problem for the experienced investigator—is to decide when to suspend the search for materials in order to take research notes and analyze some of the data found. It probably will work reasonably well if the beginning researcher locates—and makes working bibliography cards for—the materials on his subject that appear to be of major importance in the library card catalog and the major bibliographic aids appropriate to his subject.

Very likely the number of items located during this effort will be fairly large. It must, of course, vary with the subject, with the bibliographic aids available to the student, and with the latter's diligence and skill. But it is not uncommon for a student to spend a week on orientation reading, then another week on bibliographic work resulting in from one hundred to two hundred working bibliography cards. During this bibliographic effort it is necessary to develop some ability to screen or rapidly scan and estimate the worth of material. Such procedures present dangers; but so does an effort to explore thoroughly all materials encountered. Some screening can be done from bibliographic data in the card catalog or in other bibliographic aids: titles may show what a book covers, or its intent (e.g., levity or popularization); the publisher may indicate quality (a university press probably will avoid the frivolous, a communist press probably will view reality in terms of the expected clichés); the length may be indicative (110 pages is short for a useful economic history of Europe); the date of publication may indicate authorship too early for the chief area of interest of the researcher; editing by a well-known scholar suggests quality.

Many items must, of course, be examined. This sometimes can be done quickly. Coverage often can be judged by a scanning of table of contents and index. Quality can be judged tentatively by sampling pages and observing the method of dealing with evidence. Prefaces, introductions, bibliographies, and footnotes may give quick indications of the desirability of taking research notes from an item. After such a preliminary examination of an item, a judgment of its quality should be entered on the working bibliography card. If no further use need be made of an item—whether a study or contemporary evidence—that should be so stated, to avoid a second examination due to failure of memory.

From this first set of working bibliography cards should be culled (without discarding the others) the most promising items in the light of knowledge to this point, and in consideration of the emphases developed in the initial week of orientation reading. Research notetaking should be begun in these items.[3] Usually it will be best to begin with the studies by other scholars which appear most promising, leaving the contemporary evidence to a bit later.

The beginning researcher must identify as many items of probable value for his subject as he can, *whether or not they are in the holdings of the libraries he will be able to use*. There are three major reasons for this bibliographic effort: (1) to identify a large part of the materials, so as to permit a selection from the apparently best materials, either those immediately available, or possibly available through travel or by interlibrary loan or in microcopy; (2) training in bibliographic method, which is to some extent independent of "use" of the materials identified; and (3) it probably will enlarge and improve understanding of the dimensions of the research project itself.

---

[3] See Chapter V (C) on notetaking.

III

PROOF AND PROBABILITY

No facts speak for themselves to lighten the historian's task, not even facts as objects—a chariot wheel or a baby's crib—to say nothing of facts as events or ideas. So, facts must be made to speak, in the light of historians' varying purposes, erudition, sense of the fitness of things, and abilities to deal with problems of proof and probability. And there is the rub: proof is rare and probability comes in many sizes, only to be judged with art and a sense of responsibility. At least the extremes are clear: clearly improbable or unproven, or apparently highly probable, or even certain, for historians have no patience with metaphysical arguments that we do not "know" that Henry VIII once ruled in England. At the other extreme, historians find speculative philosophies of history pleasant to contemplate but insubstantial, like moonshine. To the considerable aid of probability in some contexts now comes to the discipline a new quantitative method, but its adepts warn of its limitations.

A. Plausibility, probability, certainty

The United States Secretary of State and the USSR Foreign Minister are discussing an armaments control agreement. Their mental comments are in brackets.

USSR: We seem to be making progress, Mr. Secretary. And I believe that the armaments treaty will make trade negotiations easier.

USA: [If he is satisfied, we should be asking more. And why bring up trade? Are they interested in that?] Possibly an armaments agreement will make many things easier. Technical interchange, for example.

USSR: [I think they are interested in both trade and technical interchange, but an armaments agreement is a political necessity for Washington.] Yes, technical exchange is of interest to the Soviet Union.

USA: [Is he suggesting "linkages" of issues as the price of a good treaty on armaments? It seems plausible; they like that sort of thing. Is technical exchange more important to them than wheat?] Apparently our wheat crop will be low because of drought.

USSR: [Some switch of subject! Besides, we doubt that, with acreage up ten percent. They want to raise the price.] We consider that technical interchange should include all aspects of electronics.

USA: [I'll bet they do. They won't get it. Why did he change the subject?] As you know, the United States government does not entirely control wheat sales abroad.

USSR: [Almost, though. Let's see if they will budge on sub missiles.] Possibly we should return to the submarine missile matter, Mr. Secretary?

USA: [They're alarmed by our breakthrough there. They'll give something for that.] I regret, Mr. Minister, that my instructions require me to give first priority to the verification of land-based missile activity.

USSR: [Sure, they do, with ours superior. Are they ready to give a little?] Possibly a compromise can be arranged.

USA: [Really? Or another three-week charade of double-talk?]

Another example is a date arranged between college students encountering each other on the campus:

Jack: Hello, Carla. Been meaning to look you up.

Carla: [Yeah? You dropped me like a hot potato two months ago.] Well, you finally ran me to ground.

Jack: [Real snotty. Probably refuse if I ask her out.] Been all tied up with basketball.

Carla: [No doubt. The complete Jock.] I suppose so.

Jack: [Some chill. Any use continuing?] I'm running for president of the Student Association, you know.

Carla: [Wants my vote.] I know.

Jack: [Waste of time, but give it a try.] How about going out to the Tropicana tomorrow night?

Carla: [Talk about buying votes! But he's fun, and his roommate, Tim, is a doll.] Just us?

Jack: [Oh, she's still got her eye on Tim.] Tim and Linda will go. What say?

Carla: [Why not?] Yummy!

Jack: [Is that sarcasm, or what?] Pick you up at nine.

These homely examples show conversations with mixtures of truth and falsity, and the participants trying to sort it out. But unthinking people give more credence to what they read than to what they hear in conversation. This may be justified if a conscientious person made a special effort to be truthful and accurate when writing; but it may not be, because writers suffer the same frailties as conversationalists.

The common sense evaluation we make in everyday situations therefore has its counterpart in the internal criticism of documents. To begin with, a single statement can be accepted as no more than very *probable.* Even the most truthful person may conceal or distort the truth under certain circumstances; the most accurate observer will sometimes be mistaken in whole or part. The researcher must judge as well as he or she can each statement that is important. The judgment is of varying degrees of *probability,* of being near or far from truth. Since this cannot be measured, only care and judgment will serve.

Not much help will be had from the notion of *plausibility.* Some statements strike us as plausible, easy to believe. Often that is because they are consistent with other information that we have about the situation, the known ideas and behavior of the parties, or of human beings in similar situations, or of what has happened earlier and later in a series of events. Much of that merely means that we have corroboration. In any event, the clever liar tries to make his untruths as plausible as possible. Still, evidence that does not seem to fit into the context will reduce the judgment of probability, until it is remembered that a piece of evidence may seem implausible only because of a mistaken interpretation of previously known evidence. On the other hand, there is a sort of implausibility that is easier to use: statements that run counter to our best scientific knowledge. Such implausible statements will meet a high degree of skepticism. Even from lies, however, some useful information may be extracted, usually from incidental information that indicates the cultural background of the liar.

So the researcher builds on probabilities with corroboration.[1] More attention to that might pare down the insubstantial treatises devoted to "national character."[2] Good historians judge well when they have all that can be expected with reasonable effort to form an explanation that is somewhat, moderately, or highly probable. They realize that their own values affect their choices and interpretations, but think it more productive to press forward rather than wrestle with apparently drastically diminishing additions to probability. They judge this preferable to being the sort of scholar who collects for a lifetime, finding refuge in an impossible search for all the evidence and an unattainable certainty.

The use of probability is common in law and public affairs. Examples were the investigations of the assassinations of President John and Senator Robert Kennedy and of Dr. Martin Luther King. All dismissed the likelihood of conspiracy, as did later investigations. In February 1977, for example, the Justice Department reported that in an

---

[1] See VII (E).

[2] See VII (C) on national character.

eight-month review of the FBI's handling of the King case it again appeared that James Earl Ray, the convicted murdered, acted alone. Facts found by the Warren Commission on President Kennedy's murder permitted no neat pattern, nor was one established by the fact that the President's assassin was a professed believer in Marxism who at one time renounced his United States citizenship. He was as much a misfit in the Soviet Union as in America. The crime apparently was the senseless deed of a mentally twisted man.

Some resistance to verdicts against conspiracy is based on a desire to strike out at enemies, or to bolster the sense of individual importance. Some comes from the fact that the workings of the American juridical system, with much use of appeals and retrials, gives the public an impression that proper verdicts seldom are reached. Another source of resistance is the widespread belief in "concrete possibilities," an ambiguity if ever there was one. Thus a sound tape of the Dallas tragedy that experts said contained "acoustical anomalies" was widely taken to mean that more than one gun had been fired. The same misplaced faith in concreteness operated when guns were fired to show the difficulty of shooting from one gun, in the time available, the shells allegedly used.

It was claimed that a "Confederate" conspiracy "must have" arranged the assassination of Lincoln. It was charged that racial bigots must have contrived the death of Dr. King. In President Kennedy's case, one group noted that his political and social programs antagonized southern whites, Dallas was a center of such opposition, so—; another group said the Communists had plotted Kennedy's death because he opposed their ambitions in Germany, Cuba, and Asia.

Unimaginative people do not realize the difficulties of conspiracy, and in any event think of it in terms of cheating at the poker club on Thursday night. Maybe their friends Joe and Peter will be close-mouthed, but there are more motives for revelation among proud and prominent judges, lawyers, and politicians. To assume a conspiracy among the members of the Warren Commission requires much naiveté; to assume their continued silence requires even more. No suggestion made as to why they would want to distort the evidence was very substantial, very probable. And it was a most improbable assumption that all members were irresponsible and corrupt, and foolish enough to believe they could hide a conspiracy.

As for conspiracies involving the assassins, the idea is too grand for the puny suggestions made in support of it. Little more than wild guesses have been made of a "second gun." Two men may make a conspiracy at law, but scarcely in history, if the word is to retain meaning.

The practical problems of conspiracy on a considerable scale make most asserted cases seem improbable. It recently was claimed that the newly revealed oil riches of Mexico had been known to a conspiracy of prominent men there for 40 years, but they prevented exploitation to avoid more penetration of foreign capital. This would have required a larger miracle (or series of miracles) than a successful Warren Commission conspiracy. Consider the temptations to break the agreement in time of budgetary crisis, or the dangers of passing the secret on as the older members died. The idea may be regarded safely as farcical, quite improbable. We may observe, finally, that historians show little disposition to look into rumored conspiracies, especially where competent investigations were made at the time, or when the conditions for success of the conspiracy were not present.

There is a logical approach to probability and other problems of meaning, through epistemology, the theory of meaning. It is mainly philosophers who carry on what they call the analytical philosophy of historical knowledge, and possibly that is as well, since philosophers find that historians handle problems of logic poorly. On the other hand, many professional logicians do not take the notion of a logic of historical thought seriously.

The analytical philosophy of history deals with the logic

of language, the method of science, and the analysis of concepts. Philosophers also do some work of less interest to historians in the realms of metaphysics (the nature of reality) and moral values. The work of epistemologists is taken seriously by historians, but little used by them, because the results are too abstract for ready application to their work.[3] One of the problems is that the analytic philosophy of history usually confuses logical order and causal order. The sort of causal explanation that the historian wants is a statement of probability or probable causal relationship; he does not want (and in any event cannot have) a logical explanation, a syllogism.[4] It is possible to declare that logical explanation suits logicians better, but not that it would be better for historical reasoning. Nor can historical knowledge be forced into general laws, because it is enough in historical literature to have generalizations that apply to certain times and places and not others, even in loose statistical terms such as "most" and "often."[5] Despite these at least partial failures, historians must be interested in such efforts by philosophers and others to differentiate the comparative objectivity of historical "facts" from "interpretations" or thought about the facts.[6]

B. The speculative philosophy of history

Very different from the closely reasoned logic of the analytical philosophy of historical knowledge is the specula-

---

[3] Morton White, *Foundations of Historical Knowledge* (New York, 1965), pp. 1–2.

[4] David Hackett Fischer, *Historian's Fallacies: Toward a Logic of Historical Thought* (New York: Harper & Row, 1970), p. 181ff. Fischer's explanation is about what most historians "feel in their bones," but it is nice to have it well reasoned and expressed.

[5] Ibid., pp. 128–30, for a good statement of this in discussing the efforts of analytic philosophers to force historical knowledge into the Covering (or Hempelian) Law model.

[6] Cf. Hans Meyerhoff, ed., *The Philosophy of History in Our Time* (Garden City, N.Y.: Doubleday, 1959), p. 188ff., for discussion of this effort.

tive philosophy of history, which substitutes imagination for proof and probability. It consists of syntheses of all human experience, so unattached to empirical methods that they sometimes are called metahistory (metaphysical history). The metahistorians, also called monists or systematists, have little influence on historical craftsmen. It is understandable, however, that these grand speculations should appeal to people seeking an "explanation" of human life.

A number of grand patterns or systems have been concocted since ancient times. They tend to locate the essence of causation in a single force, be it God, the spirit of the age, or the means of production. Often the system posits a scheme of stages through which human society passes in time (i.e., history). The system of stages may be either linear (i.e., ending in heaven, or the proletarian communist ideal society, or other ultimate perfection), or cyclical or recurring (birth–growth to maturity–decline to death, or spring–summer–fall–winter are popular).

Philosophies of history are created by individual human beings in specific cultural contexts and, therefore, reflect the experience and central interests of those individuals and some aspects of the cultural biases and social problems of their societies. Thus Augustine (354–430 A.D.), a Christian bishop, in the *City of God* wrote of his search for a satisfying religion and a meaning for human life in a period when the ancient institutions of the Roman world visibly were crumbling under internal and external pressures. Augustine's concern was with the epic struggle between good and evil, seen in Hebrew-Christian terms. He saw man's earthly life as but a pilgrimage to God, with the end of human history the Last Judgment. Such a philosophy of history, if rigorously adhered to, makes many aspects of human activity seem too insignificant for serious attention. It gives little room for causation except in terms of God's will. Augustine's view of human history ruled the Occident for more than a thousand years.

On the other hand, Karl Marx (1818–83) was very much
a man of the 19th century, angered by the social ills of the
industrial age, attracted to the socialist approach to their
solution, and sure that the scientific spirit of his day could
be used to build a new world of plenty and justice. He asserted that man's history showed that his chief motive was
materialist, and that the conflict of classes for control of
the means of production was the key to human history. All
else—ideas, beliefs, customs, laws—was "superstructure,"
essentially determined by the struggle for control of the
means of production. This struggle, Marx said, ran through
predestined stages. The capitalist stage of his own day
would lead to increasing popular misery, economic crisis,
and war. It would be succeeded by a dictatorship of the
proletariat, followed by a withering away of the state and
achievement of a classless, cooperative society.

This was an optimistic, monistic (one cause), essentially
unprovable system. Its predictive value has been limited.
There has been economic depression, but also a great improvement of levels of living in precisely the best developed
countries Marx believed first would become proletarian
states. Communist regimes, ostensibly founded on Marxist
doctrine, have not formed classless societies. It is not clear
that the terrible wars of our time are due primarily to contradictions or tensions in the capitalist system. Personal
frustration and the brute urge to dominate cannot, in our
present view, easily be dismissed as superstructure determined by control of the means of economic production.
So 20th-century interest in psychology modifies economic
interests inherited from an earlier day.

Arnold Toynbee compared civilizations and tried to discover the causes of their rise and fall.[7] Unfortunately, he
did not define civilization well, and often made points in
terms of that lesser breed, the nation, so that his scheme
was flawed at its base. He found that civilizations rose in

---

[7] *A Study of History* (10 vols., Oxford University Press, 1934–54).

response to challenges from the physical environment, and he conceived the challenges so loosely that he found only that the challenge could not be too little or too severe. Growth then was postulated to result from a spiritual challenge, to which the proper response was a higher religion and universal church. Some civilizations got started, but enjoyed little growth—were "arrested" or "aborted." But all civilizations (including the Western) finally stopped growing because of a failure of creativity on the part of leaders and a consequent loss of social unity as the proletariat withdrew support. The failure of creativity was due to the fact that the success of the response to an earlier challenge unfitted the creative minority to meet the next. So the "creative" minority turned to force and became a "dominant" minority. The civilization now was in the phase of breakdown, which was followed by disintegration.

The bulk of Toynbee's attention went to disintegration, which he found occupied the greater part of the histories of his civilizations. Western Civilization had been, he said, in the disintegration phase for several centuries. Although originally there was no way in the Toynbee system for a civilization to revive when disintegration began, in his later work he suggested that Western Civilization might survive by faith in God and creation of a brotherhood of man.[8]

The grand patterns are based on highly selective use of evidence. They also necessarily are based on imperfect knowledge of most civilizations. What individual really can know Rome, China, the Maya, ancient Egypt, modern Europe, and antique Babylonia? But the systematists are convinced they know how to select the "essence" of each civilization, suppressing detail. Also, they make comparisons or even identifications of developments in different civilizations, which most historians consider untrue if meant liter-

---

[8] This gives no idea of Toynbee's great erudition and often felicitous language, but it hints at the problems of supplying proofs for his system. Historians consider Toynbee's work philosophy or religion.

ally, and often misleading if meant as analogies. The very notion that civilizations are "born," or that they know "winters" is poetry, not analysis. A civilization is a condition of culture developed by successive generations of men. The men in the civilization die, but the civilization continues. There is no logical reason (available to us) why the civilization could not continue indefinitely. When a civilization weakens and disappears, it is because the men within it cease to deal successfully with their problems or are overcome by external forces too strong to withstand.

The grand systems or philosophies of history do have value. They stimulate interest in the broadest range of human history and offer some antidote to narrowly specialized scholarship. They certainly stimulate interest in causation. They sharpen the critical faculties of conventional historians who object to such systems. Insofar as the grand systems stimulate popular attention to social development and the fate of man, they may be accounted useful, even by those most dubious of their "accuracy." In any event, such systems must be scanned for dogmatism and over-simplification, however noble the motives of their creators.

Rather a different type of philosophy or law of history in the 19th century asserted humanity's majestic progress toward a perfect society—where poverty and crime would be unknown, wars would cease, government would be based upon the free consent of all, social justice would be achieved, and human intelligence would solve every problem. This idea was unknown to earlier ages. Greek and Roman thinkers imagined golden ages in the past rather than in the future, or else they inclined toward cyclical theories of history in which periods of happiness were followed by times of trouble. During the Middle Ages churchmen-scholars took history's meaning from St. Augustine.

It was not until the Renaissance that writers began to find in history a record of man's progress from barbarism and ignorance toward civilization and knowledge. Confidence in man's potentialities grew stronger during the 18th-century Enlightenment. It reached its apex during the 19th century, when scientific and technologic innovations transformed life, humanitarians achieved the abolition of slavery and other reforms, governments granted constitutions and widened the franchise. Progress appeared to be a law of life, a corollary to Darwin's theory of evolution.

And in the 20th century the medical art was transformed, which most people called progress. The ideal of care for the weak, poor, and indigent gained some ground, witness social security systems in many lands. Humanity's ability to produce goods—including food, clothing, and shelter—increased. The ideal of universal literacy grew, with at least a theoretical potential for some types of fulfillment.

But intellectuals today are skeptical. World Wars I and II offered little reason for optimism. Were Nazi gas ovens and Soviet purges evidence of increasing humanitarianism? Were guided missiles and nuclear warheads evidence of the beneficence of science? Would we be able to control population growth before it far outran our productive capabilities? Pessimists see us tobogganing toward disaster. Still, the idea of progress retains strong partisans.

This very large idea, a veritable philosophy of history, can neither be proved nor disproved. For one thing, "progress" cannot be defined satisfactorily, partly because it includes moral factors. Probably it can be agreed that it was premature to announce the doctrine on the basis of 19th century history; and its demise can not be proved from the events of the 20th. To some extent, the 20th century should be seen in terms of the destructiveness and irrationality that are recurring constants in human affairs. Peace and war, prosperity and poverty, learning and ignorance, have alternated many times in human history. Possibly "progress" must be limited to fields such as surgery or literacy; at least in them progress can be measured. In those areas progress ought to become more rather than less possible because of the continuity of history; that is, each generation has at its disposal a large cultural inheritance. If emotional or moral failings interfere with that development, the retrogression can be assigned to those realms, and how to describe them is not for the historian alone.

C. Quantitative method

One way of dealing with probability is by quantification. Quantitative method in historical study consists of explicit measurement, maximum rigor in conceptualization and execution, and sometimes the use of relatively sophisticated devices for counting and calculation. The fact of quantification is not new to historians; the other elements, however, have been adopted in recent years from social science by the cliometricians or econometric historians.

Historians always have been explicit, in fact, about some quantitative data; but they have made more implicitly quantitative statements, involving such terms as "significant," "widespread," "growing," "intensive." That often is more or less accurate, and good enough for the context. It will not do, however, to state that the expulsion of the Muslims from Spain in the 16th and 17th centuries "significantly" or "devastatingly" cut agricultural production, without providing quantification. Lacking that quantification, what the expulsion meant is not clear today, despite the confident declarations of generations of historians.

How often have we had tossed at us a phrase about "the especially rich soil of" Iowa, the Bajío of Mexico, or the celery swamps of the Amish near Canton, Ohio? And how often are we *not* given data on the contribution of the *soil*, as compared with other soils, and a discussion of the relative importance to the area of other factors—for example, rainfall, temperature, labor force (the Amish are formidable workers)? The reverse of this has been unguarded generalization about the "waste-lands" of underdeveloped countries—as the great "deserts" of Sonora, Mexico—where ultimately the soil proved highly productive.

The point is that problems of quantification exist. We

can leave them implicit or face them, deal with them sloppily or use the best methods available. If neither the aim of the study, nor the time or resources, are available for elaboration of quantitative questions, it is easy to say so.

Even relatively simple methods of counting and calculation sometimes yield useful results. That is partly because of (1) a better definition of problems, which (2) aids the proper identification of questions to ask and of data to seek. This has (3) led to quantification—in whole or part—of questions before thought not measurable. Finally, (4) the improved result sometimes is due in part to better methods of filing the data, often so it can be manipulated by machine in large-scale counting or in grouping into categories. These things suffice for many problems, where all that is needed is descriptive statistics aimed at showing the characteristics of groups when there is data on all the individuals. It is not difficult to calculate some totals and percentages and make some correlations to find relationships between characteristics.

Charles Tilly displayed the new methods and attitudes in a study of the counter-revolution of the Vendée that began in western France in 1793. He analyzed the economic and social structure of the insurgent areas, finding the characteristic social units and determining their distinguishing characteristics. Tilly described his logical procedure as including "nothing occult": use of generalizations already established, careful identification of the units of analysis, concern for identification of reliable differences, and stress on systematic comparison. These efforts brought important new questions: (1) What were the real differences between the areas in which the counter-revolution sprang up in 1793 and those that remained calm, (a) under the Old Regime, (b) during the early Revolution? (2) What was distinctive about both the organization and the composition of the *groups* that actively supported the Revolution, and those that actively resisted it, over the period 1789–93? (3) What significant change in the social situation occurred during the same period? (4) Is there any general knowledge available that helps to assemble coherently the answers to these questions and the fact of counter-revolution?

In addition, Tilly was imaginative and thorough in identifying, collecting, and using evidence, and in trying to avoid "the common propensity to conceive of historical process and historical explanation psychologically." "That," he declares, "encourages selection and use of those data which can be taken most directly as evidence of the intentions of participants in the actual events." And that, he says, causes "the probability that the major issues over which historians will disagree will be questions of motivation and responsibility." He proceeds to demonstrate that historians of the Vendée have, in fact, neglected important sources. As an example, they have argued the role and motives of the "peasantry" without examining the character of that group. Tilly finds the "non-noble, non-clerical mass of the rebels . . . quite heterogeneous, and far from strictly peasant in composition." Thus, "It is not evident *a priori* that one can attach a uniform set of motives to such a group, even if they did all join the rebels." And so it goes with reasoning, identification, enumeration, and calculation of simple percentages.[9]

Quantification has been useful in the study of voting behavior. McCormick brought into question the old generalization that democratic enthusiasm for Andrew Jackson caused a great upsurge in voting. McCormick made a large collection of voting statistics, voter eligibility requirements, and census and registration data, state by state. Inspecting this mass of material, he found it showed higher percentages of voter turnout in presidential elections before and after the Jackson elections of 1824–32, and in state elections. This led him to present what became widely ac-

---

[9] "The Analysis of a Counter-revolution," reprinted in D. H. Rowney and J. Q. Graham (eds.), *Quantitative History* (Homewood, Ill.: The Dorsey Press, 1969), pp. 181–208, from *History and Theory*, III (1963), No. 1.

cepted explanations. One was that candidates had such decisive leads in some states that many voters saw no point in turning out.[10]

Another example of large-scale data collection was a study of the effect of the British Navigation Acts, one of the measures used to regulate the commerce of the American colonies, just before the Revolution. The study involved some knowledgeable reasoning about economic factors, but usually not complex statistical procedures, although some intricate calculation was required. Historians long had disagreed as to whether the Acts helped or hurt America. The new study used sophisticated methods to examine all aspects of the Navigation Acts and their effects, including the relationship of the acts to other British economic measures that affected America (for example, bounties to encourage colonial production), plus the value to America of British military protection, including that against pirates. Values in all cases were stated in pounds sterling. The results were more convincing that those in earlier studies of the subject.[11]

Relatively simple statistical methods, combined with rigorous reasoning, and often laborious data collection, have in recent years yielded many other useful results. A better idea of the diet of black slaves in the United States (more nutritious than in the traditional view). A clearer picture of the iniquitous slave-breeding operations of pre–Civil War America. Better descriptions of degrees of attachment to causes or ideas also have been contrived.

The new quantification in history, on the other hand, sometimes demands tools that can be acquired only with considerable study. History faculties increasingly provide

---

[10] Richard P. McCormick, "New Perspectives on Jacksonian Politics," *American Historical Review*, LXV (January 1960), pp. 288–301.

[11] Robert Paul Thomas, "A Quantitative Approach to the Study of the Effects of British Imperial Policy Upon Colonial Welfare: Some Preliminary Findings," *Journal of Economic History*, XXV (December 1965), pp. 615–38.

opportunities or requirements for that study. The results of application of such methodology, furthermore, often are acceptable to the most nonnumerical historians, even though their understanding of the methodology is murky. There is, however, widespread dubiety about certain methods, and most prominently about efforts to answer counterfactual questions by the use of hypothetico-deductive models. These are methods of "indirectly" measuring by the use of equations. A much-discussed example is Fogel's study of railroads and American economic growth.[12] To establish the net benefit of railroads in 1890 he had to compute the actual level of national income and the level that would have obtained in the absence of railroads—that is, a counterfactual proposition.

To do the last, Fogel needed a hypothetico-deductive model on the basis of which he could infer, from those conditions that actually existed, a set of conditions that never occurred. So he tried to establish the difference between the actual cost of shipping goods (only agricultural) in 1890 and the alternate cost if there were no railroads. He recognized, and his critics pointed out, that in the absence of railroads society probably would have altered water and wagon shipment methods and distribution patterns. His computation required estimate of direct payments that would have been made for boat and wagon transport, and estimates of such indirect costs as cargo losses in transit, and expense resulting from time lost when using a slow medium, and the expense of winter interruptions of water traffic.[13] Much of this required mathematical operations that left untrained historians behind; it also increased their objections to "iffy" propositions. They harbor "suspicion of the synthetic figures extrapolated, guessed, and sometimes

---

[12] R. W. Fogel, *Railroads and American Economic Growth* (Baltimore: Johns Hopkins Press, 1964).

[13] For a good short discussion of the Fogel railroad study see his "The New Economic History, Its Findings and Methods," *Economic History Review*, XIX (December 1966), pp. 642–56.

borrowed from another period of time or another place to fulfill the requirements of the model."[14]

The quantifiers insist, however, that such propositions always have been a part of historical literature, although "implicit, covert, and subliminal." Fogel argues that when U.B. Phillips stated in 1905 that slaves were an unprofitable investment in the United States he used an implicit equation that was not good enough to give him an accurate answer.[15] Others have pointed out that in various guises synthetic figures have been used by historians for a long time. Counterfactual propositions were hidden in arguments affirming or denying that tariffs accelerated the growth of manufacturing in the United States.

Much of the new quantification therefore can be accepted without more than the normal examination of methods; the rest can be left to the vigilance of quantitative historians, who will not lightly approve dubious work. In addition, the following reflections are reassuring.

(1) Quantification has not made historians obsolescent. While many questions cry out for quantification (for example, economic and demographic history),[16] others have little or no quantifiable content. Quantifiers point out that although their methodology has wider application than once thought, it remains and will remain, rather limited in scope. Thus, historical literature necessarily must continue with "mixed methods." In addition, some quantifiers profess a belief that, except for some questions, mixed methods are best for historical inquiry and explanation.

(2) Moral questions are not obliterated by quantification, but sometimes made clearer by measurement of the

---

[14] Erickson, *loc. cit.*, 361.

[15] R. W. Fogel, "The Limits of Quantitative Methods in History," *American Historical Review*, April 1975, pp. 329–50.

[16] And great data banks have been and are being assembled by historians for many areas, such as voting requirements and behavior. This is no more than anthropologists and economists have been doing for a longer time.

surrounding circumstances. The recent great debates over
the profitability of slavery, for example, originally had a
high emotional content founded on the idea that the moral
problem of slavery was being ignored or even denied. Quite
the contrary. If slavery before the Civil War was, indeed,
profitable, as now seems the likely answer, the studies make
it seem more rather than less iniquitous. That is partly because it weakens the argument that southerners clung to
an unprofitable institution partly because they needed it
for psychological or social reasons. It is, in addition,
partly because the new explanations increase the profitability of slave-breeding, surely not a thing to reduce repug-
nance for slavery.

(3) Some criticism of quantification at bottom has been
objection to categorization that seems to the critics more
"sociological" than historical. That embraces a fear of
"laws" or pseudo-laws of society that seem to cancel out
the role of the individual or the importance of the unique
event. There is no reason for the critics to permit that in
their own work. Historians may remain as humanistic as
they please.

IV

HISTORICAL EVIDENCE

Historical facts are of various sorts, often slippery. It helps some to inspect their variety. It also helps to categorize the evidence used by historians, because that pushes the beginning researcher into the process of analysis. Categorization requires examination of the character and quality of evidence. Nothing is more important in research. We are here concerned with the different *forms* of evidence, and with the social and individual psychological factors that determine the *quality* and *credibility* of evidence.

A. Facts as values, ideas, objects, events

Just give us the facts, some people (even some historians) say. The difficulty in doing so begins with the problem that there can be no all-embracing and all-acceptable definition of historical fact. There are no measurable and unvarying units as in communication theory or chemistry. Each fact, on examination, turns out to be made up of a variety of facts. The Battle of Waterloo was a fact as event, but made up of many smaller facts as events (drum rolls, charges and retreats, heads mashed by cannon balls, orders shouted by officers); and it also was made up of facts as objects (field guns, boots, food depots, bandages, hills, streams, cadavers); finally, it consisted of ideas and values, which shaped the actions of men on the field—even the officers' shouted orders. And each of these facts as object, event, or idea can be further subdivided. So the Battle of Waterloo is only a single "fact" in certain contexts decided upon by the historian; e.g., the Battle of Waterloo demonstrated the genius of Wellington.

One of the problems of historical inquiry is that ideas in the life of men and women are facts as surely as are atomic bombs and chocolate soufflés. Ideas (and values and motives, as types of ideas) may be subjective facts, but they are real in their effects upon history. Remember, however, that even in the case of objects we often have only the mental images of them recorded by witnesses; that is, the evidence available to historians usually is not "fact" but *testimony* on the facts. In the case of ideas, we have impressions of states of mind. In the case of motives, we often make do with sheer guesses based on actions, incidental and tangential statements, or suppositions regarding character and intent; that is, we move from demonstrable proof to inference. And all this we put into language, itself a system of symbols. Such considerations led two scholars to state that "historians are occupied solely with images," although many of them did not realize it.[1] Similar problems also afflict social science. Students of humanity can not often set up experiments with controlled variables. We certainly cannot re-create the past to test hypotheses about behavior.

The activity of individuals, and the institutions, quarrels,

---

[1] Charles Langlois and Charles Seignobos, *Introduction to the Study of History* (tr. by G. Berry, New York: Holt, 1912), p. 219.

decisions of man in society are determined not only by the physical conditions of existence—the weather, mineral resources, soil types, virus disease, sun flares—but by the ideas men hold of their relations with each other, of their hopes of life, of the nature of property, of the sources of territorial jurisdiction of political units, of the nature of governance. How much of the triumph and disaster of human history has been molded by ideas of the divine right of kings, equality, freedom, nationalism.

Sometimes it is asserted that the life of man—especially, but not exclusively, civilized man—is almost entirely a history of ideas, that these are the engines that chiefly determine the direction of human movement. This means political ideas, regarding representative government, woman suffrage, nepotism; social ideas, as slavery, class distinction, incest; or spiritual or metaphysical conceptions, as damnation, or nirvana. But concentration on ideas is as conducive to error as interpreting history too heavily in terms of physical factors.

Also, we may say that (as if all the above did not offer difficulty enough) ideas are slippery things to grasp, often too slippery for the imprecision of language. In addition, ideas are difficult to identify, detect, weigh in individuals, because they involve often unexpressed, or poorly verbalized, beliefs, hopes, attitudes. Further, social changes over time bring new meanings both to words and to ideas. We must remember that words and ideas have histories.

We are interested in ideas because (1) they influenced past events; (2) they influence the historian's interpretation of past events; and (3) difficult problems of proof arise in connection with the effort to show the influence of ideas in human affairs.

We must distinguish between "single" (or bare) facts and linkages of objects and events with ideas. It is a fact that Sen. Barry Goldwater voted against the Civil Rights Act of 1964. It is a fact that some (probably many) blacks resented that vote. It is more difficult to be sure of the role of that Civil Rights Act vote in persuading blacks not to vote for Goldwater in the presidential election of the same year. Fortunately for the historian, it is possible to be confident of such things as the bare facts of the place and date of the birth of Napoleon, and about much of the physical scene at the Battle of Waterloo. It is much more difficult to discover the role of morale in the great battle or the later problem of frustration as a cause of the death of the ex-emperor. Also, we can treat certain facts almost without reference to values; e.g., the date of John Adams's death, or the weight of a nuclear weapon, or the time required for a given journey to the moon. Such matters can, however, by linkage with other events, objects, and ideas, enter into considerations involving value judgment; they may even be turned into aspects of a metaphysical question.

When historians say they deal with *unique* individuals and events, they wish to emphasize (1) that there are no unvarying units as historical "facts" and (2) their interest in particulars in addition to trends and generalizations. Historians do not use the word "unique" in its drastic literal meaning of completely different from everything else, but to mean "individuals" and somewhat different from other individuals or events. That is no looser or less respectable a professional rule of thumb than the social science view that human beings are "sufficiently similar" to be parts of quantitative generalizations.

Another aspect of "fact" is that historians must be prepared to use "tainted" materials and lies. Forgeries may be interesting in themselves as evidence of interest in a subject, and they may include veracious details. And who would not like to have tape recordings or shorthand notes of the lies told to historian questioners by Napoleon or Cleopatra? The admissibility of historical evidence is not restricted in the fashion of legal evidence, where the rules on direct, circumstantial, hearsay, and original evidence are designed not only to elicit the "truth" but to protect contestants and to secure for society decisions of approximate justice within tolerable periods of time. It is clear that historians are entitled—indeed, required—to indulge in conjecture (properly identified as to degree of probability) in a way that courts could not tolerate.

The evidence—documentary or other—available on the past often touches but fitfully the activities of man. We cannot know, of course, what or how much occurred of which we have no trace. In any event, no historian would want evidence on all of human actions, mental and physical, even if such a possibility were imaginable. But what we do have is unevenly distributed, and often in a merely accidental way. Much evidence that once existed has been destroyed, accidentally or purposefully. In many areas of human activity poor records or no records are kept, either because of the state of the culture (e.g., religious taboos against certain types of record), or because it was thought expedient to minimize records (e.g., in the world of espionage). The conversational activity of man leaves but intermittent traces (even in our age of "bugging"), and these often set down tardily and inaccurately. It is an old joke that it is easier to write the history of the ancient Mediterranean world because the record is relatively scanty. On the other hand, the historian of recent times often has the opposite problem in that the mass of evidence confronting him demands a selection process at once imaginative, soundly related to the purpose of the records, and operable within a lifetime.

B. The categorization of evidence

1. The most important distinction is between material (written or other) produced by a *witness or participant* in events, and material produced by others, meaning (a) persons living at the time the events occurred but who did not witness or participate in them, and (b) historians living after the event. To be sure, nonwitnesses contemporaneous with the events often leave us a record of their conversa-

tions with witnesses, or relevant evidence on encircling events or environment. Thus "contemporary evidence" is a useful category to bear in mind, encompassing witnesses, nonwitnesses, and a third class of nonpersonal documents (e.g., constitutions) and artifacts (e.g., bludgeons, coins, feather capes) produced at the time. It is suggested, therefore, that the most useful categorization with this purpose in view is into "contemporary materials" ("materials" is more neutral than "sources") and "studies." We suggest this, for example, for the bibliography. The value of this division is little frayed by the fact that occasionally a "study" is done by an historian who was a witness of or participant in the events he describes and analyzes. Finally, it must be remembered that various *mixtures* of evidential categories exist (e.g., an account of events left in writing by a witness may include both his statements based on observation and his recording of hearsay).[2]

2. There is some value in thinking of evidence as being either deliberately or unconsciously transmitted. Words produced with some thought of the future may include deliberate bias for that reason. Of course, material produced without thought of posterity may well have some sort of bias for other reasons. Furthermore, the division between conscious and unconscious transmission is not always clear.[3]

---

[2] The beginning researcher must understand—because he will encounter—the traditional, and often confusing, tags used for historical research. *Source* often means what we call evidence; but as combined in the term "secondary source" it means just the opposite (i.e., material not produced by a witness). The words contemporary, original, or primary often are combined with "source" to mean evidence. Note that what may be nonevidence ("secondary source") for one purpose, may be evidence ("primary source") for another: Mao Tse Tung's opinions of Karl Marx are not evidence for the life of Marx, who died before the Chinese communist was born, but Mao's views are evidence for studies of modern Marxism or of modern views of Marx the man.

[3] Sometimes it is hard to know whether a diary or memoir was written with posterity in mind. Annals, chronicles, and histories certainly have posterity in mind; but some "mere" records may not.

3. Evidence may be divided into *documents* and "other," in turn divided into sub-classes. This classification has practical use because most historical researchers (beginning and advanced) use little but documentary evidence. This has been so nearly true of most historians that in the 19th century Langlois and Seignobos in their well-known *Introduction to the Study of History* scarcely considered that the training of historians required attention to other forms of evidence, because "documents [are] the sole source of historical knowledge."

As will be seen below, documents should be considered to consist of materials in writing,[4] and especially there should be no question that the term includes materials set up in type. To use document as a synonym for manuscript was a practice—fortunately moribund—arising out of a desirable emphasis on better use of archival material, but also out of snobbery.

C. Documents

Most methodological problems and processes can be illustrated from documents. The following discussion is tied primarily to fairly recent documents, although much of what is said can be applied, with modification, to earlier times. Although one definition of document is any written language, it must be remembered that document sometimes is used for writing on paper-like materials, and the term inscriptions for the writing inscribed on hard materials.[5]

Writing was developed independently in several places: Sumeria in the Middle East about 5000 B.C.; somewhat later in Egypt; later yet in the Indus Valley, possibly in the mid-

---

Some artifacts were produced without meaning to transit information to the future, but others meant to do so, and being sure of intent often is difficult.

[4] And even for some purposes to include much "unwritten but verbal" material (e.g., tape recordings).

[5] See Chapter VI (B) for discussion of inscriptions.

third millenium B.C.; in China in the late third; in the Maya area of Central America about the time of the birth of Christ.[6] The Mycenaean Greeks imported writing possibly in the early second millenium B.C., the Minoans of Crete somewhat later. Alphabetic writing, in which symbols (letters) represent single sounds (rather than ideas or syllables), greatly increasing the effectiveness of communication by script, apparently was invented by Semites in the Palestine-Syria area about 1100 B.C.[7] From this old Semitic alphabet descended Greek, Etruscan, modern European, Arabic, and other alphabets.

It is obvious that the beginning of true writing in a culture makes a dividing line between the types of evidence available to the historian. With the production of documents, the nature of the record changes; it becomes more detailed, and more additive or accumulative. The culture develops an expanded memory. Without this transmission of masses of written data and ideas, civilization is difficult. The languages and the scripts used in writing all have separate histories (though sometimes affecting each other), that is, they change in time.[8]

Both design and accident affect the preservation of documents. The factors involved are: (1) quantity, possibly; (2) the physical materials used for writing; (3) the storage system; and (4) social conditions. It is plain that baked clay documents in dry climates may last a long time, and that writing on linen in a damp climate may soon molder away. Also, stone stelae are difficult to move, and may for that reason endure. This last factor is, however, affected by social conditions; e.g., by the presence of people who put old stone structures and artifacts to new uses.

---

[6] Some of these dates are conjectural, as are the possible influences of one script on another.

[7] Cf. David Deringer, *Writing* (New York: Praeger, 1962), for discussion of scripts having phonetic elements without being truly alphabetic.

[8] See Chapter VI (B) on paleography, linguistics, diplomatics.

As for storage, the ancients seldom were concerned with providing an historical record except as that was involved in magical, religious, or familial considerations, or some limited governmental purposes, and some business transactions. Storage often was secretion. Hoards of secreted documents keep turning up in modern times. Conditions may be especially favorable for documents hidden in a dry location. Documents of metal sealed in jars in Palestine proved resistant to the rots of time. Skin and paperlike materials also come down the ages well if secreted in dry airtight containers.

Social conditions affect the preservation of documents in many ways. Religious partisans (e.g., those of the Inquisition) or political groups (Nazi or Communist parties) may destroy documents, or prevent their creation. Preservation may be aided by a fad for collection, as in the Renaissance. In the United States today, single illuminated pages of medieval hymnals may be bought in cellophane wrappers at Macy's department store.

The amount of documentation may play a role in preservation. This relates to the number of literates, the requirements they have for documents (individually and as operators in institutions), the technology of documentary production, and prices. Requirements for documents may be affected by the nature of the economic and social system, or by such social phenomena as censorship or representative government. Requirements may also bear some relationship to storage and retrieval methods. There would seem to be no point in producing more documentation than can be handled effectively.

It is precisely this situation that threatens us today. Data handling techniques barely keep up with the production of documents. The population, information, educational, bureaucratic, and scientific explosions have vastly increased the pace of document production, the copies required or desired, and transmission from place to place. This includes material in letterpress, offset printing, mimeograph and other machine duplication processes, typescript, etc. It includes materials that are published and sold, that are scattered almost broadcast to the general public by pressure groups and advertisers and political parties, that are directed to large but specialized "publics," that are circulated only within business or government offices, and materials that are given security classifications by government officials and that scarcely circulate at all. The storage files of governments (national and local) and international organizations (United Nations, Organization of American States, NATO), of General Motors and Fiat, of chambers of commerce, of fraternal organizations and social clubs, are crammed with the wordage of the bureaucratized culture.

Great expenditures of money and technical talent are made to control this Niagara of verbiage. Mechanical, magnetic, photographic, and electronic methods of storage and retrieval permit the rapid and accurate manipulation of documentation. Unfortunately, the indexing and cataloging of the kinds of documents and the forms of evidence used by most historians have not kept pace with the new hardware. Historians of the future may do much of their collecting of evidence by electronic means, thus eliminating much drudgery. The historical craft now contributes to the process of putting material into proper form for electronic manipulation, and plans ways of doing so for more types of material.[9]

In this time of transition, however, the historian—especially of recent times—must hone a sharp edge to his skills in the use of the mass of available documentation. Classification of documents assists in locating, selecting, and judging their general quality. There is, however, no magic in the "categories" of documents suggested here; they are merely a convenience for getting into the subject, and of

---

[9] Actually, all major data producing agencies may be required to put their material in common machine language; some day the data may be at least partially indexed by electronic means.

use as an entry into the processes of verification and analysis discussed in later chapters.

There is a difference between published and unpublished documents. The latter have enormously multiplied in recent times. The distinction depends on whether there was public issuance; it has nothing to do with whether the documents are in manuscript or are printed or typed. Huge numbers of documents are produced by the great bureaucracies, public and private, of the modern world, sometimes using printing presses, but reserved for private circulation (that is, never published for public use).

Another distinction is between printed and manuscript material. Were words marked down in type by a machine, or inscribed by hand with a pen or pencil or crayon? Manuscript materials, as noted, no longer are thought the most important documents for historical research.[10] There may be little difference between a memorandum handwritten by Secretary of State John Quincy Adams and one dictated by Cordell Hull to a stenographer and transcribed by a typist. There is, however, a certain charm about the use of handwritten documents, although there are difficulties in their use; e.g., in deciphering badly spelled, poorly written and much abbreviated 16th-century Spanish from paper warped by subtropic heat and humidity, and faded and smudged by time and handling, and pages riddled by worms.

Documents sometimes are categorized in terms of (1) time of composition in relation to time of observation of the matter reported, or (2) the audience for which the document is intended, or (3) the intent of the composer. Such classifications are only marginally helpful. Time of composition in relation to observation is important in using documentary evidence, but it does not aid much in classify-

---

[10] Manuscript materials may still be of especial interest if they indicate: (1) relative privacy of testimony; or (2) documents not yet edited and printed for general use.

ing documents. The same is true of the confidentiality of documents. A bit more can be done with classification by intent.

Estimating the intent of the composer of a document is an important part of the process of judging its credibility or plausibility. Many documents are composed not just with the intent of telling as much of the truth as possible, but of editing or distorting the facts, either to improve communications (often laudable and proper), or to make a point or create an impression (ranging from minor fudging to towering lies). There are, however, documents composed either in a spirit of neutrality with regard to the facts, or with a sincere effort at truth. These include many (not all) simple records, commands or instructions, and more or less neutral "business" reports. The terms are imprecise, but efforts to tighten the categorization lead to subclassifications that create more confusion.

"Simple" record here means only a record; that is, a record that may be erroneous, but not because of intent on the part of the recorder. Tape records obviously have no intent; they reproduce sounds. It is presumed that machines get what is said in their range. Of course, their sensitivity is not infinite (whispers will be missed, noise may confuse), they are subject to malfunction, and the tapes can be doctored or edited to tell lies. Shorthand records taken and transcribed also are presumed not to deceive. Not many stenographers are spies, jealous of the boss, or insane. Finally, cameras and film have no intent, but their users may introduce such an element.

It is presumed that commands are issued to accomplish action, so that the issuer does not lie to his subordinate. Of course, some commanders do lie, and many issue ambiguous orders; and some orders are given for symbolic, hortatory, propaganda, or ceremonial reasons. Still, the general rule remains. Most corporation executives try to frame their orders in relation to fact in order to assist in obtaining what they want. So important is this objective that cadets in military colleges are rigorously schooled in the composition of succinct and unambiguous orders. They also are told of many instances in the history of military activity when poorly framed orders either caused confusion because they could not be interpreted correctly, or had no effect because their ambiguity invited disobedience.

"More or less neutral business report" stands as a common type of document resulting from the activity of men in institutions (government agencies, business firms, military establishments, churches, and the like), in situations in which the impulse to torture the record occurs relatively seldom. Examples are: the counting of barrels of flour by an employee of a large milling company, the report of a professional accounting firm on the financial condition of a corporation that hired it to make such a report, a report by an ambassador to his home government on the preparations he has made for a visit by his president to a foreign country. Most business receipts also are meant to be neutral and unambiguous.

We have moved from neutrality (but not certain absence of error) in the cases of simple records, to some (conceivably much) possibility of intent to deceive in instructions or commands, to a greater likelihood of intent to deceive in more or less neutral business reports. In the last case we no doubt passed the line of usefulness in categorizing documents in terms of neutrality or probable absence of motive for deceit. Probability usually is the most we can hope for historical research.

Government documents constitute a class that needs comment. They may pertain to national, provincial, municipal units of government, or to special districts (water, sanitation, education), or to international organizations. The documents are composed by men, not by disembodied entities. Government documents can and often do contain distortion and error due to selection and bias and mistaken facts and mechanical errors. They can contain lies, God knows. The *Congressional Record* reports as having been spoken on the floor of Congress words merely supplied the printer in typescript by an absent congressman's administrative assistant. We must not assume that the published report of congressional committee hearings contains all the record of its activities. In short, do not assume that government documents are especially entitled to uncritical acceptance.

Newspapers and magazines are a special class of document, containing various sorts of data. There is more or less straight reporting—reprints in full in the *New York Times* of speeches or legislation, or accounts by reporters of events they witnessed or men they talked to. There are cartoons, with or without captions. There are signed columns of interpretation, ranging from the profound to scurrilous superficiality. There are editorials, which are unsigned (usually) columns by owners or editors. There are fiction, fashion, song, poetry, and photographs.

The press sometimes is examined by beginning researchers with the hope of gaining intimations of public opinion. That is too much to expect. Samples of editorial opinion give leads to what newspapers and magazines of well-known orientation consider it desirable to print. The inference may be made that usually they will not depart too widely from the views of the majority of their readers lest they lose their allegiance. But any specific case may be one in which the editors have departed widely—purposefully or involuntarily—from the views of much of their usual audience. In the best of cases, this sort of sampling merely gives insights into the views of publishers and editors of known political affiliation or orientation, or with a specific religious interest, or an economic or occupational bias. How much they reflect or influence public opinion cannot be known.

Private business documents are important sources of data in many countries. Access to this kind of record is, on the whole, difficult to arrange. Often, a corporation's files are almost as closely guarded as the strategic plans of military general staffs.

Enough has been said about documents as a type of evidence to suggest the many difficulties involved in their use. And it is *use* that is required for the development of skill and judgment in research. No manual of method can do more than assist the student in developing his skills through practice.

D. Other evidence

1. PHYSICAL REMAINS

What is meant here is physical remains that offer no language:[11] man's own bones, his artifacts, the remnants of cultured plants, natural objects man has collected or moved, or traces of astral, geologic, or climatic conditions or events that may have influenced human existence. This sometimes is called *mute* evidence. Use of the term "physical remains" in this sense is merely a convenience, since in its plain meaning the phrase might be taken to include documents, inscriptions, and tape recordings. Items of evidence in the category of physical remains sometimes are called nonlinguistic sources, relics, or artifacts. The first of these (nonlinguistic) will cover all that we include in the first sentence of this paragraph; the other two will not.

Physical remains in our sense generally are collected and judged by specialists—e.g., anthropologists, archeologists, "prehistorians," epigraphers, paleographers, paleontologists. Obviously, such specialists also often use evidence containing words. A numismatist will uncover coins with and without inscriptions; his study of either type probably will require the use of documents.

Most physical remains are unpremeditated or unintentional sources—i.e., they were not created with the thought

---

[11] Except that language itself may be said to be a physical remain that gives mute testimony (i.e., some leads to human activity in time may be found in the elements of languages and in change in them over time).

of leaving a record. This is the case with all physical remains other than artifacts, and even with most of the latter. Among artifacts created at least in part for the edification of posterity, some public edifices are prominent. Still, we may assume that most artifacts are "unbiased" in the sense of deliberate effort to mislead. They are, on the other hand, highly biased in the sense of reflecting the culture patterns of the society in which they were constructed; they are "culture bound."

Our modern exploitation of physical remains has but a feeble parallel in the past. Research now is more systematic, on a larger scale, with better records, and many new scientific techniques. Photography revolutionized this type of research. Improved organization of research includes better circulation of results, permitting improved comparison of data; it also facilitates the corroboration of physical by documentary evidence and vice versa.

The use of physical remains other than artifacts was virtually unknown until recently. Historians do little of this work; they use the results. Anthropologists sift anthropoid bones, dating man's forebears by the carbon decay of ashes, by geologic strata, and by the known chronology of biologic species. Botanists trace the origins of maize from a wild plant, offering illumination of the growth of American Indian culture. Data are found in the traces of volcanic eruptions, tree growth rings, and sunken coral reefs.

It is from artifacts, however, that the historian derives most of the evidence from physical remains. Things made by men (artisans) include weapons, buildings, vehicles, clothing, religious objects, toiletries, medical equipment, jewelry, coins, fishing gear, and toys. Some artifacts are especially impressive, either by their great size, large numbers, or unusual quality. The great pyramids of Egypt and of the pre-Columbian Indians of Middle America testify to the complex social organization of their builders. From many types of remains we derive data on a culture's level of technological skills (by the quality of an iron sword, a wheeled cart, a woven cape, an arched stone bridge), its esthetic standards (are artifacts formed and decorated in an effort to please, and, if so, with what purpose—artistic, religious, political?), its social ideas, religious attitudes, economic organization.

Mute artifacts may require corroboration or explanation from documentary or other materials, or they may provide corroboration for documentary evidence. Swords of Saracen craftsmanship found in the ruins of a Frankish castle may be thought, with some confidence, to argue relations between Franks and Muslims. It may be more difficult to learn whether they were friends or foes, or both at different times. Were the swords gifts, acquired through trade, or booty of war; or all of those things at different times? Much supporting evidence, including documents, might be needed to solve the problem. On the other hand, mountains of fragments of pottery types made by one society, but found in the trash of another, may be thought more persuasive evidence of trade between states than an inscription on a monument stating that distant commerce flourished under King Thom the Great. And we have many examples in investigations of ancient and medieval European history of data derived from study of the remains of ships, carts, and roads, that provide impressive corroboration of the often merely incidental comments on economic life by chroniclers and official historiographers, whose orientation was political, civic, or religious.

2. ORALLY TRANSMITTED FACT, ERROR, MYTH

Orally preserved data are used primarily for studies of preliterate cultures (ancient and contemporary), and of today's literate society. Historians and anthropologists are prominent in the former type of work; they join in the latter political scientiests, sociologists, psychologists, and commercial pollsters.

For preliterate societies orally transmitted data are our

only verbal material. It gives us a record of some past events; and in myth, epic, ballad, fairy tale it also shows the transmission of values. Thus, the variations of the *Nibelungen* sagas indicate changing values from generation to generation among the numerous Germanic tribes that claimed the epic as part of their heritage. The usefulness of such oral record as an account of past events is often very limited, and scanty in proportion to the time between the account and the asserted event. Each generation of story tellers or troubadours embellished the inherited account and obscured the original core of truth. Thus the orally transmitted data of preliterate societies are generally a combination of fact and fiction. But the core of truth in the orally transmitted Homeric epics did permit Heinrich Schliemann to dig at Troy with some success.

More controversial are attempts to use the orally transmitted data of preliterate societies to establish models of the human mind. Jung the psychoanalyst tried to establish a collective folk soul on the basis of German fairy tales, and the anthropologist Claude Lévi-Strauss tried to use South American folk myths to establish the logical workings of the human mind. The less theoretical orientation of the historian is seen in Traian Stoijadonovich's *A Study in Balkan Civilization*, which uses myths in sketching a cross-generational portrait of Balkan civilizations.[12]

In analyzing our contemporary, literate society, orally transmitted evidence offers advantages. First, it is useful to interview the leading participants in great affairs, not only the five-star generals and presidents, but staff officers and advisers. Second, it permits a new approach to understanding popular opinion, as a step toward estimating its effect on affairs. This is of obvious importance in countries where there is overt broad participation in public affairs; it is also of some consequence in such modern "command" societies as the USSR, which has a varied and highly educated

---

[12] New York: Knopf, 1967.

population. Third, the rivers of material produced by typewriter, mimeograph machine, tape recorder, and printing press, drive us to any device that reduces labor. Fourth, oral communication has partially replaced some types of written materials, with the use of the telephone and air travel.

Oral evidence, especially when taken on tape, may allow a prominent individual to record his observations informally with little effort shortly after an event occurs. Such recordings are memoirs, but with the advantage of often shortening the time span between event and memoir creation, and of supplying, through the timbre of the recorded voice (and facial expression if there is video tape or film) emotional nuances not always evident in written memoirs. It is even better if the historian has a personal interview with an eye witness to the events he is studying.

The interviewer must establish a balance between the danger of antagonizing the witness with aggressive questions and the peril of permitting a monologue for the instruction of an ignorant visitor. Thus, it is helpful to test the respondent's memory and truthfulness by beginning with questions about uncontroversial matters the interviewer has verified from other sources. This establishes that the interviewer is familiar with the subject and, in addition, induces the respondent to transfer himself mentally into the target scene. After this, the interviewer passes to more controversial matters that require more emotional and nonverifiable responses. Such interviews usually are most effective when conducted by an individual pursuing a single subject; at times, however, a more institutionalized format is useful. A number of universities have oral history projects, recording answers of prominent men to questions posed by historians.

Mass interviews and sampling techniques are a development of recent decades, most used by social scientists and by research institutes or public opinion enterprises using professional interviewers. The quota type sample establishes for the target group its percentage of pertinent characteristics (e.g., sex, age, education, race, income levels) by surveying a small part of it. This is a model asserted to represent the larger target group in all pertinent (to the inquiry) respects. The model often consists of a few thousand individuals out of a target group of millions. Only the members of the model are interviewed, and their responses are supposed to represent those of the entire target group, within tolerable margins of error. One great difficulty is determining accurately which qualities of a population are critically important in setting quotas and in what proportions they exist in the model.

Another type, so-called random sampling, relies chiefly on statistical probability. Researchers select a numerical percentage of the entire group, supposedly without reference to the characteristics of individuals (e.g., by picking every 100th name in census reports), and this sample is interviewed. The random sample has the advantage of being relatively cheap. But supposedly random samples sometimes are, in fact, selective. Plucking names from a United States telephone book means that a significant fraction of the population (nonphone owners) is excluded. Use a Mexican telephone book and nearly all the population is excluded.[13]

There are other difficulties with sampling. Samples actually taken before about 1945 tend to be relatively unreliable because techniques were raw. Even when samples are reliable, historians may later have decided that the questions asked were of peripheral concern. Also, most sampling interview efforts are fashioned to make the answers easily quantifiable—i.e., the respondent is allowed only a limited number of choices. That usually distorts nuances of view that may be important, especially in gauging developing shifts of opinion over a larger span of time.

---

[13] There are other sampling techniques; e.g., area sampling consists of preselecting dwelling units for interview, then selecting at random the areas for interviewing.

Again, there is difficulty detecting certain types of distortion in testimony, even if many detailed answers are allowed. Finally, it is known that shallow interviews and questionnaires seldom measure "intensity" of opinion. The respondents have no stake in their answers and may respond irresponsibly; thus, their answers are a poor guide to their probable actions. One answer to this problem is the interview "in depth." But subjects for this procedure are more difficult to find, and the time-consuming process reduces the size of the sample.[14]

The study of past public opinion by historians has been a subject of some interest in recent years. It has benefitted from use of the methods developed for contemporary sampling. Some of those are concerned with the identification of direction, quality, intensity, and duration of opinion. Another useful area is concerned with indirect methods of questioning for the detection of attitudes and motives, which can be built up from responses to a variety of seemingly unconnected questions. All this is most clearly useful when adequate data (e.g., modern census returns) exist. It is more difficult of application when data are sparse or of the wrong sort.[15]

---

[14] A well-known example of this was the use of tape recorders by anthropologist Oscar Lewis to penetrate the "subculture" of the poor in Mexico and the United States, searching for the values of a group out of the mainstream of events. This was supposed to suggest the reactions (or lack thereof) to be expected from such groups given certain political or economic developments. Critics considered, however, that the great mass of response was too unstructured for most purposes.

[15] Cf. Lee Benson, "An Approach to the Scientific Study of Past Public Opinion," in Rowney and Graham, *Quantitative History*, pp. 23–63; Robert A. Kann, "Public Opinion Research: A Contribution to Historical Method," ibid., pp. 64–80.

V

COLLECTING HISTORICAL EVIDENCE

The Preface and chapter II have pointed out that the stages of an historical inquiry overlap. In the case of the collection of evidence, much of the activity is concentrated in the early part of an investigation, but some will occur later. Furthermore, collection merges into analysis when the first research note is taken that consists of more than simple copying. Collecting evidence is not, then, a simple process that may be delegated with a few instructions to secretaries or research assistants. When teams of collectors are available —for example, in large United States military history projects—their work must be planned and supervised with great care. Many decisions made during the collection of evidence require a sound methodology and sophisticated reasoning, and will have profound effects upon the results of the investigation.

A. Recording bibliographic information

Here, we are talking about *working bibliography cards.* Their purposes are (1) description, (2) control, (3) analysis or annotation. Each purpose is important, and all are looked for by the instructor in inspecting the student's working bibliography cards. These cards are not only critical to the control of the bibliographic effort, and important tools for the assessment of the character of evidence, they also will be used to make up the bibliographic essay and the formal, annotated bibliography. The following injunctions do not cover all the techniques of recording bibliographic data; they do constitute a teachable core that will put the student on the road to effective activity. We do not expect each working bibliography card to display all the devices available; only that some of them be so complex. Remember, when first encountering a new and apparently promising item (in card catalog, a bibliography, a footnote, etc.), make out a bibliography card. It takes a bit of time, but it pays.

1. Description

Each item will have its own card, and it is recommended that the form of the card catalog be followed, with such deletions and other modifications as may be appropriate. A 3 × 5-inch card usually is adequate. It will work best to file cards by author (the author, last name first, will be at the top of the card). At the minimum, the card must carry author (or editor or compiler), title, place and date of publication, publisher, volumes (if more than one), edition (if other than first; and occasionally the first must be mentioned), series of which a part (if appropriate). If the item is taken from the card catalog it usually will pay to enter the call number in the upper left (this seems a burden to professional researchers, too). Sometimes the number of pages should be recorded; e.g., if an indication of length will be useful as an estimate of coverage; or, to distinguish between editions of a work. Some scholars prefer always to enter the number of pages. The following procedures will be valuable:

1. Conserve space in entering bibliographic data, to leave maximum room for later entry of descriptive and analytic data.

2. Abbreviate. It is necessary only that you be able to read the cards. You can interpret them for the instructor. An occasional loss through over-abbreviation must be risked in a large research job.

3. Do use both sides of the card, but put "over" at the bottom of the obverse. This is better than two cards tied with a clip although sometimes that cannot be avoided.

4. Neatness is valuable; it is not essential. If cards done in script, with blots and coffee stains, are legible, there is no point doing them over in typescript.

5. Do include a separate card for each of the most important bibliographic aids used. This will be necessary for control purposes. It also will have the pedagogical function of helping the instructor to discuss such aids with you.

6. All signed articles in scholarly journals should have individual author cards. On the other hand, only one card is required for a newspaper; and often only one card is required for a popular magazine when a survey has been made of its contents and points of view and the individual authors or articles are not important.

7. Sometimes it will be useful to show where an item was located; e.g., if an item seems possibly incorrect, or possibly little known, a note can be made that it was found in such-and-such a bibliography.

8. Working bibliography cards should be filed alphabetically by author in a box where they are easily accessible. It is desirable to divide the file into at least "bibliographic aids" and "other." The latter also may be subdivided topically, chronologically, geographically, by types of materials, etc. Among the types of materials that it is most often

convenient to keep in distinct alphabetic files are public opinion materials (newspapers, popular magazines), government documents, and manuscript materials. There seldom is any reason to separate scholarly journal articles from "books."

2. CONTROL

The control of bibliography, in a large research task, requires meticulous attention to detail. It shows what has been done, and permits quick reference thereto. In a large research task it is easy to forget whether an item has been used, and to what extent. A record of the latter is useful on single-volume works; it is indispensable for widely used newspapers and popular magazines, multivolume histories or sets of documents, many types of manuscript collections. It is impossible to remember what has been done in such complex materials without a written record. Also, a card should be kept for each bibliographic aid (bibliography, government document guide, card catalog), showing when used, what categories looked under, and at least in general what principle was followed in taking cards from the bibliographic aid (e.g., "took all items on economic aspect," "prob got all will ever need on all aspects," "only took on 1789; see again later").

3. ANALYSIS OR ANNOTATION

Some working bibliography cards require annotation, if the items have been looked at. The annotation may amount to no more than "no use"; or it may point to need for further exploitation (e.g., "see ch. iv for excellent material on weegies"); or indicate a bias of the author; or note hiatuses in the coverage; or judge the quality of the work; or describe the arrangement of large sets of materials; and there are other types of annotation. Of course, some of the "control" material discussed in the preceding section also is annotation.

A critical attitude toward materials is indispensable. Certain types of analysis of the item itself (as apart from analysis of parts of the item) belong on the bibliography card. It is important to include views regarding the general character of the item that are generated in the course of research notetaking. Such general views should be transferred to the working bibliography card. Thus, it is best if the bibliography file is at hand while research is going on. Of course, this is not always possible, so a separate note to put the judgment on the bibliography card should be made. Does all this mean that judgments regarding the item will not be put on research notes? Certainly not. Only certain general judgments will go on the working bibliography card. Some of these later will appear in the bibliographic essay and in the formal, annotated bibliography appended to the final research paper. This process of bibliographic analysis and annotation requires labor, thought, and method.

B. Bibliographic aids[1]

Our modern bibliographic aids are a boon to the investigator. The labors of modern indexers, catalogers, compilers, editors, from which we benefit, constitute a great difference between historical research today and in earlier times. New techniques—such as pushbutton catalog searching, possibly of scores of associated libraries—promise further advances. The Bird Library at Syracuse University has consoles available to students by which they query the computerized cata-

---

[1] For additional bibliographic aids see American Historical Association, *Guide to Historical Literature;* and appropriate headings in library card catalogs (e.g., "United States" as subject, "History" as subcategory under it, and "Bibliography" as further subdivision under "History."

log and circulation systems to locate items in the collections.

It is important for the researcher to think in terms of *categories* of bibliographic aids. This necessarily involves consideration of the types of evidence likely to be useful for the given research task. These are by no means the same for all studies: newspapers, government documents, business records illuminate some subjects, but not others. Once the researcher grasps the principle of category in this context, he can apply it to any research task, looking for *items* within the identified *categories* of aids (e.g., Poore's *Descriptive Catalogue of the Public Documents of the United States* within the category of indexes or guides to public documents).

A few suggestions will be useful to the beginning bibliographer. (1) Diligence, system, intelligence, even imagination are needed in bibliographic work; without them, the

Figure 1.   Sample of author entry in card catalog

This is *not* the same as a "working bibliography card" in a researcher's own files, although they have some elements in common.

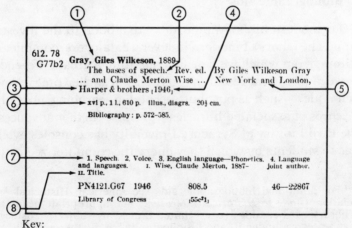

Key:
1. Author.   2. Title.   3. Publisher.   4. Date of publication.   5. Place of publication.   6. Pages and size.   7. Subjects under which listed in catalog.   8. Additional card in author-title catalog.

Figure 2.   Sample working bibliography cards

Some data are standard on most working bibliography cards; e.g., author, title, publisher, date and place of publication. The annotations vary with the nature of the item and the character of the research task; possible variations thus are so numerous that the few examples given here can be no more than suggestive. No diacritical marks are put on these example cards, on the grounds that scholars familiar with the languages will supply the marks when required in a manuscript. Students not firm in their knowledge of the rules for such marks should include the marks on the cards as they go along. The 5th, 9th, and 11th examples are bibliographic aids, which pose special record-keeping problems.

```
          Hennery, George
          A history of Spain.  NY: Macmillan, 1944.
               626pp


Seems good.  May want see for treatment of the May
riot, pp 66-90.  No notes yet.
```

aids will not be well used. (2) Be sure to use the prefaces and keys and other explanatory data in bibliographic aids; learn how the aid is organized, in how many volumes, what is covered and what excluded, and how the indexes work. (3) Do not try to determine library holdings by puttering about in the stacks; all the books on your subject will not be grouped in a few places, and some that the library owns will be missing during your visit. The library card catalog is the bibliographic aid designed to give you the library's holdings. (4) Keep records of what bibliographic aids you use, and how you use them (e.g., what subjects you scanned in the index, or what years you covered) or you will lose track of what you have done. It usually is most convenient to keep this record on a 3 × 5 card for each bibliographic aid, filed with the working bibliography (see the 5th, 9th, and 11th examples in Figure 2). (5) Librarians are a help, but seldom have the time or specialized knowledge to do much of your bibliographic work for you.

Figure 2 (continued)

```
924.1          Gonzalez, Carlos T. & Jeremy K. Smith eds.
SU has 2d      Coleccion de documentos ineditos para la
ed, with v.29 hist. de las constituciones de Mexico
missing        35 vols Mexico, 1942-49

XXXV:  iii-vi, essay on sources; viii-cvi, Bibliog (div
into: works on Mex consts., fed and state; texts of fed.
consts; text state consts).  A very few annotated.
I, iv-lvi:  Intro:  discn purpose, and genl discn hist Mex
state & fed consts.  Primary aim bring tog texts. Discn
hist emphasizes 'legalistic' aspects; remarks on fed
consts. standard, unexcptl; remarks on state consts. exclt,
full of new insights.
I-VI:  texts fed. consts., incl. not only those adoptd, but
those suggestd (ie by major gps or convetns); and constl
amends suggestd but not adoptd.  Texts in ea case taken fr
best available source, with fn discussn of source, its
status, accuracy, etc.
```

```
VII-XXXIV:  texts state consts.; again fr best possib source,
with discn source; here had much diffic locatg reliable
texts of many early state consts; and of total 116 state
consts since 1822, lack any text of 12.
     A very few fns to texts of consts; so few that wonder
why incl any.  Those few seem to be concentrated in the secs.
dealg with indiv liberties, and show some effort 'prove'
fine Mex record in this regard....And intro does same, by
stressg constl provns without adeqtly referrg to failures
to implement.
     3 state consts in 1940s incl; all others before 1940.
IX:  Michoacan and Jalisco.

 Jan. 65: took full notes everything on indiv liberties in
19th cent. in Michoacan.
 Mar.65: full notes on indiv libs. Jalisco in 19th cent.
Also detd that nothing else of value for those states except
XX, iii-vi, LX lxi-lxiii, some of I ((took full notes all
these cld use))
```

(reverse of preceding working bibliography card)

```
          Smith, Clark P., "Whaling in Argentina in the
          Nineteenth Century," Hisp. Am. Histcl Rev.,
          Summer 1955, pp 350-398.

 Definitive on number Arg vessels, amt catch, values, taxes,
etc.  Took full separate notes. Basd on Arg govt records.
```

Figure 2 (continued)

```
        Martinez, Lazaro
           Los cristeros.   Mexico: Editorial Graza,
           1943.   193 pp

   No value on substance of the movement and actions; but
   excellent example of a sympathizer's attitude.  Took a
   few notes on this; no more needed.
```

```
           Guide to documents in the archives of
        the Stark County Historical Society.
           Canton, Ohio:   Blucher Typographical, 1956.
                   201 pp

   Apparently done at least in part by employees or officials
   of the Society.
       Excellent organization, by topics within chronological
   divisions.   Index of names only.
   Jan. 66: used secs.  1 & 2 thoroly (took notes & cards)
   for econ history subjects on all townships exc Plain and
   Goward (tho material there).
   Mar 66: used secs 3-4 as in Jan. 66 above.
   Feb 67: used secs 1-4 for Plain & Goward twnships on
   econ subjects.
   Nothing anyplace on separate Amish activities.
```

```
           Feldman, Percy
           Exports thru London in the 19th century.
           London: Beverley, 1922.   567 pp

    Basd on wide variety contemporary materials, esp govt
   records. Judicious. But value of sections varies consid.
   due to unevenness of evidence available.
    Esp good on hardware (pp44-69), textiles (101-165), &
   processed foods (204-245); and have full notes on all
   these....Much less valuable on other commodities, and took
   no notes on them. Prob neednt look at again.
```

Figure 2 (continued)

```
         Johnson, Paul
            Military clubs in Tibet.  St. Paul, Minn.;
            Pine Tree Printery, 1934.    133 pp

no use
```

```
         Smith, Max
            Lumber booms of the northwest.
            NY: Putnams, 1924.    234 pp

   Baker, Hist Oregon, says not worth consultg; but S.
   Dobbs, The Bibber Company, says useful for IWW.
      ((prob shldnt bother to find?))

   Oct 66: Got copy. Baker right. Sec on labor of marginal
   use. Took few notes--all that worth.
```

Some of the many types of bibliographic aids are clumped into categories. The first seven of these are probably the most commonly used types of aids; the rest are less often used.[2]

---

[2] There are many other categories of bibliographic aids. Some of these have an obvious, specialized importance; e.g., guides to law and legal literature (Edward Schuster, *Guide to Law and Legal Literature of Central American Republics,* New York, 1937). There are guides to the appraisal of books (as the *Book Review Digest,* 1905–). Many other categories are either rather esoteric (*Numismatic Literature,* published by the American Numismatic Society, 1947–), or are of minor significance for bibliographic work (encyclopedias, biographic dictionaries). Library journals often contain listings or discussions of rare materials, but this is not a category of aid that ordinarily would be used in a simple investigation or in the first stages of a complex study.

Figure 2 (continued)

```
                  Readers Guide Per Lit

Jan. 65: took cards on all stuff in index under NICARAGUA
in 1917-29.
Sept 65: took cards on Literary Digest stuff only as in
index under NICARAGUA in 1930-33.
Dec 65: under LATIN AMERICA and INTER-AMERICAN AFFAIRS
 in index took everything for 1917-33 that might touch
 on Nicaragua-US affairs.
```

```
        Confederacion de Camaras de Comercio de los
               Estados Unidos Mexicanos
                 Boletin de la.....

1a. epoca, no. 1919-20, t.I, No. 1 (1 enero 1919) -
 t. II, No. 9 (Sept 1920). Took full notes my interests.
2a. epoca, quincenal, No. 1-12 (Jan.-June 1923). Used
 all.
3a. epoca, quincenal, No.1-52 (jun 1923-oct 1925). Much
 bigger format and more pp than 1st 2 series. Took
 full notes.

       Heraldo Comercial.  Successor to Boletin.
 Quincenal; every 2 wks fr 10 jan 1926 to 25 may
 1932, when ceased publcn.
       Took full notes all relevant subjects.
```

The items listed under these categories are merely illustrative. We cannot cover here even the more important
bibliographic aids. It is quite simple, however, to learn the
categories of aids, and to search for items within those categories.

Figure 2 (concluded)

Jones, Paul V.
Index of historical materials in
Argentine periodicals. 3 vols. Buenos
Aires, 1963.

Covers all that cld find in 12 libs in BAires and 3 in
Cordoba that "likely" to have such material. Does not cover
"some low-grade" periodicals. No nwpers (not even wklies).
Only minor efforts cover govt periodicals. Does incl univer-
sity periodicals. Almost 0 bef 1850, but he believes bec
little pubd. 90% material in post-1900.
  Index quite genl, and mostly basd on titles of articles
rather than analysis content articles.
Jan.65: took cards on all under MONEY, BANKING, TAXES,
 JOSE CARRANZA. Appar no other useful index categories for
 1886 money scandal ((tried several)).
Fb 66: lookd under VICTOR MARIATEGUI and made several
    cards.

Lockwright, George P
A history of Arg-US relns.
NY 1953.

Scholarly; well doctd; good bibliog; well org; marred on
close exam by bias vs US 'appeasement' of Arg in 1943.
  Author in Arg with Emby 1946-48...Suspect doesnt like
Args....Really assumes Peron wld have knuckled under to
stronger US line, but without giving reasoning.
  But exclt for resume and discusan (most things) Arg-
US since XVIII.
65-69: good analysis Arg natsm[took up notes]
75-79: on Arg milit; a miserable polemic; he hates Arg
milit, and can hardly describe their role because so busy
deplorg it[took no notes - not nec].

---

1. LIBRARY CATALOGS

Library catalogs are bibliographic aids in two senses:
(1) they assist *identification* of materials, and (2) they show
the *location* of items. The distinction for beginning researchers is important in that many assume that the holdings of a library necessarily represent a large part of the

extant items useful for a subject; in fact, of course, most libraries are too small and heterogeneous in their holdings for this to be possible.

Most library catalogs today arrange items on cards or on pages under one alphabetic arrangement from A to Z, with many subordinate A–Z arrangements. An older and usually less efficient type is the handwritten book or ledger catalog. This last, in its worst form, is a list of items set down as acquired, and it may be necessary to scan the entire catalog to learn the library's holdings.

The *card* and the *printed* catalog are the most common types in the United States today, and nearly all are arranged alphabetically. Some printed catalogs are merely reproductions of cards. The printed catalog is valuable in permitting a scanning of the holdings of libraries not directly accessible to the researcher. Some are catalogs of a library's entire collection; some are catalogs of special collections; e.g., University of California Library, *Spain and Spanish America in the Libraries of the University of California, a Catalogue of Books* (2 vols., Berkeley, 1928–30).

The printed catalogs of national libraries often are of especial value, both because they tend to be among the best libraries in a country, and because they usually have large holdings touching on national subjects, holdings often not found elsewhere. Sometimes publishers are required to deposit copies of all their issues in the national library. The Library of Congress is the "national" library of the United States. Its enormous collections may be scanned through its printed catalogs, the hundreds of volumes of which are widely held by libraries. The volumes have been issued in several series, beginning with *A Catalog of Books Represented by Library of Congress Printed Cards Issued* [from 1898] *to July 31, 1942* (167 vols.); a supplement to this for acquisitions from August 1, 1942, through 1947 (42 vols.); continued as *The Library of Congress Author Catalog* for 1948–52 (24 vols.); *Library of Congress Catalog . . . Books: Authors*, 1953–55; and *The National Union Catalog: A Cu-*

mulative Author List, 1956– . These printed author cards were supplemented, beginning in 1950, with the *Library of Congress Catalog: Books: Subjects* (73 vols. for 1950–66).

Following are some things to learn about card catalogs:

1. Beginning researchers tend to use the catalog poorly; they underestimate its complexity, do not understand how it is organized, and fail to realize that its proper use requires patience, care, imagination, and some (as much as possible) knowledge of the subject being investigated. Beginning researchers commonly miss many items in the card catalog through improper procedure.

2. Your library will have guides (often posted near the catalog) to the organization and use of the catalogs.

3. You should take down all or most of the data on the catalog card, and approximately in the order and positions found there. Usually, less work is involved in discarding data than in revisiting the catalog. Do omit data useless to your purpose (e.g., size of book, and usually the subject headings under which the card also is filed elsewhere in the catalog). Abbreviate as much as possible.

4. The catalog will contain several cards for each item: an author card, title card (beginning with the first word of the title that is not an article), and cards cross-filed under subject headings, and possibly cards under co-authors, editors, compilers, or a series title.

5. In searching the catalog under either author or subject it is important to note subdivisions. *United States* as author will have various agencies (e.g., Department of State) as subdivisions within the overall category, and each subdivision in turn will be arranged A–Z, and may have subdivisions itself. *United States* as subject will have many subdivisions, with these in turn subdivided. Not all subdivisions are marked by raised index tabs; they may merely be indicated by headings on the cards themselves, and must be searched for diligently. The complexity of the arrangement under such headings as United States or Great Britain makes evident the prudence of keeping records of how the

catalog was used (especially what categories and subcategories were searched, and whether cards were made on all relevant items found).

6. Most libraries post the rules for entries in the catalogs; e.g., articles (the, la, el, die, etc.) as the first word of a title are not counted (e.g., *La Historia de España* is filed under H); if a word is a person, place, and thing, cards are filed in that order.

2. BIBLIOGRAPHIES

Bibliographies may be published as books, parts of books, or articles. They are abundant and well done for some countries and subjects, scarcely exist for others. Most bibliographies are produced within the framework of the life and publication of a nation. The bibliography of each nation is a study in itself, with its own peculiarities. Bibliographies may be classified in many ways. The following bibliographies provide an introduction to the subject. Some bibliographies do not fit neatly into this scheme.[3]

(1) *Bibliographies of bibliographies:* These are lists of lists, and are an excellent place to begin bibliographic research. The coverage and other characteristics of each one must be checked carefully. An example: Cecil K. Jones, *A Bibliography of Latin American Bibliographies* (2d ed., Washington: Government Printing Office, 1942).[4] (2) *Bibliographies of countries or areas:* Many bibliographies cover a country or a culture area, or some division (e.g., chronological or geographic) thereof. The arrangement of such

---

[3] E.g., *International Bibliography of Historical Sciences*, Paris, annual, sponsored by International Committee on Historical Sciences; about 10,000 entries, from many countries.

[4] Other examples: Edith M. Coulter and Melanie Gerstenfeld, *Historical Bibliographies: A Systematic and Annotated Guide* (Berkeley: University of California, 1935); Robert L. Collison, *Bibliographies, Subject and National. A Guide to Their Contents, Arrangement and Use* (New York: Hafner, 1962); José I. Mantecón, *Ensayo de una bibliografía de bibliografías mexicanas* (Mexico, 1943).

aids varies: some are summaries of all work done to date, some are lists of new work published in a given period, some are combined bibliographies and discussions of trends and events in history. An example: *Handbook of Latin American Studies* (Harvard University Press, 1936–47; University of Florida Press, 1948–). An annual, covering many disciplines, including history; selection and annotation by many scholars; only the more important items are included; books, articles, some printed documents listed; includes materials published in many countries and languages.[5] (3) *Bibliographies of chronological periods:* Examples are Louis J. Paetow, *A Guide to the Study of Medieval History* (rev. ed., New York, 1931), a combination guide and bibliography, confined geographically or culturally largely to the Occident, although it contains some Islamic material; Lowell J. Ragatz, *A Bibliography for the Study of European History, 1815–1939* (2d ed., Washington, 1946). (4) *Bib-*

---

[5] Other examples: H. P. Beers, *Bibliographies in American History* (rev. ed., New York, 1942), with bibliographies by chonological period and by topic. Oscar Handlin *et al.*, *Harvard Guide to American History* (Cambridge; Harvard University, 1966), a combination of guide and bibliographies. E. C. Richardson, Grace C. Griffin *et al.*, *Writings on American History:* various publishers since 1904; irregular in later years; covers publications for 1902–03, 1906–40, 1948– ; there is an *Index to the Writings on American History, 1902–40* (Washington, 1956). Students of British history have bibliographies for each major period before 1789, beginning with Wilfrid Bonser, *A Romano-British Bibliography, 55 B.C.–449 A.D.* (1964), and *An Anglo-Saxon and Celtic Bibliography, 405–1087* (1957). For France: P. Caron and H. Stein, *Répertoire bibliographique de l'histoire de la France* deals with works published in 1920–31 on the entire history of France; somewhat similar guides exist for publication back to 1866; the important *Bibliographie annuelle de l'histoire de France du 5e siècle à 1939,* begun in 1955, appears currently with author and subject index; there sometimes are bibliographies in the volumes in the series *Clio: Introduction aux études historique,* published by the Presses Universitaires de France since 1937; also available is *Biblio: Catalogue des ouvrages paru en langue française dans le monde entier* (October 1933–). An example of an important bibliography in a scholarly journal is Robert Potash, "Historiography of Mexico Since 1821," *Hispanic American Historical Review,* August 1960, pp. 383–424.

liographies of local history: There is a large bibliographic literature on subdivisions of nation-states.[6] (5) *Bibliographies of other subjects:* There are many types of specialized bibliographies that do not fit under (1)–(5). Those on historical literature in general sometimes are excellent references for beginning research.[7] There are bibliographies on special topics.[8]

3. GOVERNMENT PUBLICATION GUIDES AND INDEXES

These come in many forms. Some nations are better served than others. The student must carefully read the prefatory material in such aids to try to learn what is included. Often much material has not been covered, and not infrequently the aid does not make this clear. There may be separate indexes or listings (even separate volumes) for legislative, executive, or judicial publications; or the publications may be divided in other ways. Some governments have state printing offices that print all government publications; other permit various agencies to handle their publications separately (even using private printers). There

---

[6] E.g.: James H. Easterby, *Guide to the Study and Reading of South Carolina History: A General Classified Bibliography* (two parts, Columbia: Historical Commission of South Carolina, 1949–50 [i.e., 1953]); Clarence S. Peterson, *Consolidated Bibliography of County Histories in Fifty States in 1961* (Baltimore, 1963); Charles Gross, *A Bibliography of British Municipal History* (New York, 1897); Joaquín Díaz Mercado, *Bibliografía general del estado de Veracruz, 1794–1910* (Mexico, 1937), on one Mexican state.

[7] E.g., American Historical Association, *Guide to Historical Literature* (New York, 1961), was done by many scholars, is highly selective and annotated, covers all culture areas and all times of recorded history, with sections on prehistory, auxiliary disciplines, and other subjects.

[8] E.g.: S. F. Bemis and G. G. Griffin, *Guide to the Diplomatic History of the United States, 1775–1921* (Washington, 1935); Karl W. Deutsch, *Interdisciplinary Bibliography on Nationalism* (Cambridge, Mass., 1956); H. M. Larson, *Guide to Business History* (Cambridge, Mass., 1948); Monroe N. Work, *A Bibliography of the Negro in Africa and America* (New York, 1928).

may have been several indexes in the history of a county and they probably vary in quality.[9] There also are guides (as opposed to indexes) to government publications.[10]

4. PRESS AND JOURNAL INDEXES

This category includes indexes to newspapers, popular magazines, and specialized (including scholarly historical) journals. Newspaper indexes are not numerous.[11] Indexes

---

[9] For the United States the indexes are: Benjamin Perley Poore, *A Descriptive Catalogue of the Government Publications of the United States, September 5, 1774–March 4, 1881* (Washington: GPO, 1885); John G. Ames, *Comprehensive Index to the Publications of the United States, 1881–93* (2 vols, Washington: GPO, 1905); United States Congress, *Catalog of the Public Documents* (Washington: GPO, 1896–). P. and G. Ford prepared a series of tools with which to approach the information in the British Parliamentary papers: *Guide to Parliamentary Papers* (1956); reprint of Hansard's *Catalogue and Breviate of Parliamentary Papers, 1696–1899* (1953); a *Select List of British Parliamentary Papers, 1833–1899* (1953); and *Breviates of Parliamentary Papers* for 1900–16 (1957), 1917–39 (1951), and 1940–54 (1961). The British government issues an annual catalog of its publications entitled *Official Indexes, Lists, Guides, Catalogues,* for which Her Majesty's Stationery Office (H.M.S.O.) has produced two introductory guides: *Government Information and the Research Worker* (1952) and *Published by H.M.S.O.* (1960).

[10] E.g.: Anne M. Boyd, *United States Government Publications* (3d ed., rev. by R. E. Rips, New York, 1949); Everett S. Brown, *Manual of Government Publications, United States and Foreign* (New York, 1950); Jean Meyriat, *A Study of Current Bibliographies of National Official Publications* (comp. by the International Committee for Social Sciences Documentation, and published by UNESCO, 1958); L. F. Schmeckebier, *Government Publications and Their Use* (rev. ed., Washington, 1961).

[11] E.g.: *New York Daily Tribune Index* (30 vols.; New York: Tribune Associates [1876–1907]; the *New York Times Index* (New York: New York Times Co., 1913–), published monthly, then cumulated (years before 1913 indexed later and now available on microfilm); Lester J. Cappon and Stella F. Duff, *Virginia Gazette Index, 1736–1780* (2 vols.; Williamsburg, Va.: Institute of Early American History and Culture, 1950); Herbert O. Brayer, "Preliminary Guide to Indexed Newspapers in the United States, 1850–1900," *The Mississippi Valley Historical Review,* XXXIII (September, 1946), pp. 237–58. The Brayer guide is being brought up to date by W. R. Griffin and J. L. Rasmussen.

of magazines and journals are of many types. Care must
be taken to understand the coverage of each index.[12]

5. INDEXES TO BOOKS PUBLISHED

This might also be called "national bibliographies." It encompasses aids that help one learn what has been published
in a given country. "Help" is used advisedly, since no national bibliographical system covers all items published.
They vary widely from country to country, and over time
in a single nation. In many cases, this is one of the more
difficult bibliographic tasks. Only professional bibliogra-
phers are likely to have a firm grasp of the intricacies of
national bibliography in many countries. Both public and

---

[12] E.g.: *Poole's Index to Periodical Literature, 1802–1881* (rev. ed.,
2 vols., Boston, 1891; later supplements cover 1882–1906) covers
United States and English periodicals; *Reader's Guide to Periodical
Literature* (New York, 1907– ; monthly, with annual cumulations),
chiefly indexing popular magazines of general circulation, and probably of value mainly for public opinion estimates; Columbus Me-
morial Library of the Pan American Union and the New York Public
Library, *Indice general de publicaciones periódicas latinomericanas*
(1961–), a quarterly cooperative index of Latin American periodicals; Franklin D. Scott and Elaine Teigler, *Guide to the American
Historical Review, 1895–1945: A Subject-Classified Explanatory Bibliography of the Articles, Notes and Suggestions, and Documents*
(Washington: GPO, 1945); *Social Sciences and Humanities Index*
(New York: H. W. Wilson, 1916–), originally (covering years 1907–
1919) *Reader's Guide to Periodical Literature Supplement*, then *International Index to Periodicals* (covering 1920–65), and continuing under the present title to cover more scholarly journals than the
Reader's Guide; Public Affairs Index (Bulletin of the Public Affairs
Information Service; New York, 1915–), issued as weekly bulletins,
with cumulations five times a year, the fifth forming the annual
volume. The best guide to scholarly articles concerning United States
history appearing before 1958 is the *Writings on American History*.
After that date, consult the indexes in *American Historical Review,
Journal of American History* (formerly *Mississipi Valley Historical
Review*), *Journal of Southern History*, and *William and Mary Quarterly. Ulrich's International Periodicals Directory* (16th ed., New
York and London: R. R. Bowker Co., 1975–76) not only lists periodicals by subject but states whether abstracted or indexed, and in
most cases gives collective indexes that exist.

private agencies may be involved in the preparation of lists that contribute to a national bibliography. The national bibliography usually will exclude some categories of publications (e.g., comic books, government publications).[13] National bibliography is apt to be a complex and frustrating matter for nations that have had printing since the 15th century; in modern underdeveloped countries it is difficult because of poor organization of society in general and of printing and library and scholarly work in particular. For the United States, national bibliography may be followed with a considerable degree of coverage and accuracy.[14] That also is true of Britain.[15]

---

[13] See LeRoy H. Liner, *The Rise of Current Complete National Bibliography* (New York, 1959).

[14] Charles Evans, *American Bibliography: A Chronological Dictionary of All Books, Pamphlets and Periodical Publications Printed in the United States of America from the Genesis of Printing in 1639 down to and Including the Year 1800: with Bibliographical and Biographical Notes* (14 vols.; Worcester, Mass.: American Antiquarian Society, 1903–59), arranged chronologically; Joseph Sabin, *A Dictionary of Books Relating to America, from Its Discovery to the Present Time* (29 vols.; New York: Bibliographical Society of America, 1868–1936), covering to the mid-18th century, overlapping Evans, but with additional items, and arranged by authors; Ralph R. Shaw and Richard H. Shoemaker, *American Bibliography: A Preliminary Check List for 1801–[1819]* (New York: Scarecrow Press, 1958–); Orville A. Roorbach, *Bibliotheca Americana; Catalogue of American Publications Including Reprints and Original Works from 1820 to 1860 Inclusive, Together with a List of Periodicals Published in the United States* (4 vols.; New York; Roorbach, 1852–61), organized by author; James Kelly, *The American Catalogue of Books, Original and Reprints, Published in the United States from January 1861 to January 1871* (2 vols.; New York: Wiley, 1866–67); this last was continued by annual issues of the *American Catalogue of Books* (9 vols. in 13; New York, 1877–1911), listing volumes in print in 1876–1910; *The United States Catalog* (New York, 1900–28); *The Cumulative Book Index* (New York, 1898–), listing United States publications, and since 1928 including books published in English in other parts of the world; *The Publishers Weekly: The American Book Trade Journal* (New York, 1872–).

[15] See *British Museum General Catalogue of Printed Books*, 263 vols. published in 1965–66, covering all the Museum's acquisitions to 1955. Catalogues of each year's additions are being published beginning with 1963. Massive and unselective though this catalog is, it does not exhaust the printed sources for British history, especially

6. MANUSCRIPT AND ARCHIVAL GUIDES

Of these numerous guides, some are modest, some large and complex. Professional scholars depend heavily on manuscript guides and indexes.[16]

7. INDEXES TO DOCTORAL DISSERTATIONS

Many doctoral dissertations never are published; some are not published until long after the degree is granted. But they must be consulted by researchers because some are excellent and complex studies that need not be repeated. It often is important to search for dissertations in more than one discipline (e.g., history, economics, political science). Unpublished dissertations may be borrowed or microfilm copies bought.[17]

---

those for the two centuries following the invention of printing. Early printed material may be checked in A. W. Pollard and G. W. Redgrave, *Short-title Catalogue of Books Printed in England, Scotland, and Ireland . . . 1475–1640* (1926) and in D. G. Wing's sequel for 1641–1700 (1945–51).

[16] Examples for the United States: *Guide to Records in the National Archives* (Washington; GPO, 1948; with later supplements); Philip M. Hamer, *A Guide to Archives and Manuscripts in the United States* (New Haven, 1961); *National Union Catalog of Manuscript Collections* (1962–); Historical Records Survey, *Guide to Depositories of Manuscript Collections in the United States: California* (Los Angeles, 1941); Grace C. Griffin, *A Guide to Manuscripts Relating to American History in British Repositories Reproduced for the Division of Manuscripts of the Library of Congress* (Washington, 1946). The inventories of French archives are dealt with in H. Courteault, *Etat des inventaires des archives nationales, départementales, communales, et hospitalières au 1 Janvier 1937;* and a *Supplément,* by R. Boutier, covering 1937–55. Two examples for Latin America: Lino Gómez Canedo, *Los archivo de la historia de América. Período colonial español* (2 vols., Mexico, 1961), including archives in Spain; *Guide to the Latin American Manuscripts in the University of Texas Library* (Cambridge, Mass., 1939).

[17] Dissertations in history in the United States and Canada in recent years may be found in: *List of Doctoral Dissertations in History Now in Progress at Universities in the United States* (Washington: Carnegie Corporation, 1902–38, annual volumes; American Historical Association, 1941– , usually triennial volumes); *Doctoral*

8. SCHOLARLY JOURNALS

Searching scholarly journals for book reviews is not ordinarily an efficient way of compiling bibliography. The exceptions are with materials of very recent publication that have not yet appeared in bibliographic compilations, or those underdeveloped countries that lack such compilations. Some scholarly journals, however, as we have noted, do publish bibliographic lists regularly, and less often print extensive bibliographic review articles. They also sometimes describe manuscript collections and discuss fields of historiography.

9. GUIDES TO REFERENCE BOOKS

Guides to reference books sometimes are helpful to the researcher. They assist in finding specialized materials dealing with aspects of subjects under study.[18]

10. BOOKSELLERS' LISTS

Sometimes booksellers' sales catalogs list items that pass quickly from one little-known (or even entirely private) collection to another; e.g., Maggs Brothers, *Spanish Amer-*

Dissertations Accepted by American Universities, 1933–55 (New York: H. W. Wilson, 1934–56, annual); *Dissertation Abstracts: A Guide to Dissertations and Monographs Available in Microfilm* (Ann Arbor, Mich., 1952–), an annual, continuing the preceding item, and representing an expansion of a microfilm abstract guide for 1938–51.

[18] Listings of reference books are in American Historical Association, *Guide to Historical Literature,* listed above; Eugene P. Sheehy and Constance M. Winchell, *Guide to Reference Books* (9th ed., Chicago: American Library Association, 1976); Louis Shores, *Basic Reference Sources* (Chicago, 1954); A. J. Walford et al., *Guide to Reference Materials . . . with Emphasis on Current Publications and on Material Published in Britain* (New York, 1959); Helen J. Poulton and Marguerite S. Howland, *The Historian's Handbook. A Descriptive Guide to Reference Works* (University of Oklahoma Press, 1972).

ica and the Guianas (London, 1935; listing 800 items in 118 pages).[19]

11. ITEM LOCATORS

These aids show the researcher where to find examples of materials he had identified previously. Ordinarily, they are not usefully consulted to identify items. Two types are (1) union lists,[20] and (2) microprint guides.[21]

C. Research notes

Making research notes involves relatively simple forms and complex analysis. It thus is both a set of procedures and an art.

1. THE MECHANICS

Memory alone will not serve in historical research; the evidence is too abundant, too diverse, and often too ambiguous. The mechanical side of note taking must be accepted in the sense that practice is accepted by musicians and the sanitary and materials-handling aspects of chemical research are accepted by its practitioners.

Three types of notes may appear in the files: (1) research notes proper, containing substantive data; (2) notes referring to other parts of the research note files; and (3)

---

[19] See Archer Taylor, *Book Catalogues: Their Varieties and Uses* (Chicago, 1957).

[20] E.g., *Union List of Serials in Libraries of the United States and Canada* (2d ed., 1943, with supplements in later years); Louis F. Steig, *A Union List of Printed Collections of Source Materials on European History in New York State Libraries* (New York, 1944); Winifred Gregory, *American Newspapers, 1821–1936: A Union List of Files Available in the United States and Canada* (New York, 1937).

[21] Library of Congress, *Newspapers on Microfilm* (6th ed., Washington, 1967).

notes directing the attention to the possibility of further research on a stated subject in a given source.

There is no size or material for research notes that is best suited to all tasks. Whatever suffices is appropriate, with the following provisos: (1) that all the sheets or cards be of the same size, for ease of filing and indexing; (2) the size be suitable to the materials of research (e.g., certain types of statistical research can employ quite small note cards); (3) that index cards and file drawers can be found for the note material selected; (4) that the weight and expense are bearable; (5) that the material will take a proper impression and will stand the expected amount of wear.

Although most researchers today prefer loose-leaf note materials, some perform acceptably with bound notebooks. Loose-leaf materials have the great advantage of permitting physical shuffling of notes.

The following suggestions will be helpful:

1. Adopt a standard method of recording things, including a set place on the note sheet for the elements involved (source, pages, heading, etc.). We prescribe a system here, for pedagogical reasons, but other procedures may be equally acceptable.

2. In the upper left corner put the source, abbreviated (full data will be on the working bibliography card).

3. Put a short heading or descriptive phrase in the upper right corner. This describes the content of the note, aids in filing and organization (not the same things), and reduces the need to read long notes over every time you contemplate using them.

4. Put pages and volumes of source. If this is put only in the source citation in upper left, it will apply to the entire note. If more than one page and/or volume of citation is involved, it should be put to the left of the part of the note to which it applies.

5. Abbreviate as much as possible, and be telegraphic (e.g., by elimination of articles).

6. Using the reverse of note sheets or cards causes prob-

lems; so does not using them. The reverse certainly should
not be used for material that requires a different heading
(indexer) from that in the upper right corner. Even when
the continuation on the reverse is on the same subject, it
makes the physical matching of notes more difficult, turning over the notes is a chore, it often increases illegibility,
and it interferes with quick riffles through the note pack
in search of specific material. On the other hand, the multiplication of continuation sheets, clipped or stapled together,
also causes problems. Some of the problem of using the reverse too frequently can be solved by changing to a larger
note sheet.

7. Material that you interpolate into quotations should
be in brackets.

8. Quotations that contain quotations should be so indicated by single quotation marks within double.

9. Legibility (to the researcher) is necessary, beauty is
not. Do not type over notes that have been taken in longhand simply to improve their appearance.

As nearly as possible use a note sheet for one subject only.
This generally accepted principle is easier to state than to
demonstrate. What is a subject? Think about it. The fact
is that it is impossible to follow this injunction with all
notes. Sometimes it simply would be too much labor. Sometimes the definition of subject changes in the course of research. But it is a help to follow this principle as nearly as
possible. It permits the physical grouping for analysis and
composition of a major part of the evidence on a part of the
subject. It also greatly simplifies the problem of cross-
indexing, a heavy chore in any sizable research project.

Notes must be filed by categories, divided by indexers, if
they are to be easily usable. Some classifications will be
suggested by the descriptive titles of research notes and
by the divisions of working outlines. The first file categories
set up almost certainly will be modified later to some extent,
and some notes shifted. Another problem is that often a
note may be put into more than one file category. As a prac-

tical matter, there is no complete answer to this (unless the researcher has a staff of helpers, or is pursuing one of the relatively rare subjects little affected by the problem). The following are procedures of some value: (1) duplicate (or multiple) notes may be made, but researchers will not want to accept the labor or expense involved in large-scale application of this "solution"; (2) cross reference notes may be made, and put in appropriate research note file categories, referring the researcher to a note in another category; (3) many schemes are used that involve coding with numbers, letters, or colors. Thus, a note found in file bin A–1 may bear (most usefully at the top of the note sheet) codes directing its use in other categories also. At the proper time, therefore, notes with a given code may be plucked out of all file bins and combined with those notes in the file category in question.

2. PRELIMINARY ANALYSIS[22]

All note taking that is not mere copying involves analysis, some of it simple, some sophisticated. Analysis is involved in the simplest process of selection. A student investigating the relations between church and state in a country having church and state to some degree united will, of course, read the church's records; and in making notes, he will have to decide which subjects dealt with in the records were of merely ecclesiastical interest and which were relevant to the state as well as the church. The processes of condensation and paraphrase also involve selection, comparison of data (from the memory), reformulation, even judgment. Sometimes all this is implicit rather than explicit in the note; but sometimes there is explicit com-

---

[22] We have found it useful to emphasize that the instructor will look at and discuss some of the student's research notes, and that all of the notes will be turned in with the completed paper. This helps to force analysis of materials from the beginning of the process of note taking.

mentary. Nearly all note taking should involve implicit analysis (i.e., simply copying merely postpones the process of analysis, and involves some duplication of effort); some will involve explicit analysis. Not all materials require the latter. The purpose of the research and the nature of the material dictate what is taken down. It is, however, a good general rule to perform as much analysis as possible when the original note is made (of course, much later analysis involves the use of many notes on the same subject or complex of subjects).

The following suggestions will be helpful:

1. Summarization and paraphrasing are highly necessary skills. Train yourself to avoid taking many materials down verbatim. Beginning researchers woefully overestimate the use they will have for direct quotations. It will be found that often a page, even a chapter, occasionally a book, may be summed up in a few lines for the researcher's purposes.

2. Inevitably, the criteria for selection of data change in the course of a research task. In the early stages of the task selection is bound to be especially difficult. Again using the example of investigation into the relations between church and state in a country with an established church, the student might begin by ignoring church worship on the assumption that this subject would concern the church alone. Later in his investigation, however, he might find that changes of ceremonial in worship aroused public feeling to such a pitch that state intervention was demanded; the student would then have to begin taking notes on church worship.

3. The "corroborative note" often is a special breed. Sometimes it will state that the data in one source virtually or strongly supports that in another, and is of about the same value (i.e., the data and/or argument may not have to be repeated in the corroborative note). Use of this device depends both on the correspondence between the sources involved, and on the value to the research in the given case of small variations in testimony or other evidence in cor-

roboration of evidence. For example, the diaries of men who attended a secret meeting could be used in this corroborative manner in an attempt to establish what took place.

4. Some "negative" notes are likely to be taken—for example, notes stating that no evidence on a given subject appeared in such-and-such a place, where it might have been expected that such evidence might appear. Interpretation of this absence of evidence depends on the particular circumstances in each case.

5. It is important to recognize that often it is not sufficient to take down summaries of statements found either in the accounts of witnesses or in studies. In many cases the note, at the time it is taken, should also include discussion of the cited sources of the study being used (or the fact that no sources were cited, if that is the case), or discussion of the argument used by the historian, or indication of what it is that the witness bases his statements on (visual observation, from what distance, under what circumstances; etc.).

An essential set of procedures—mechanical and mental —is here disposed of in few words out of our conviction that the skill required to take research notes competently can only be learned by practice. Figure 3 consists of examples of research notes, illustrating both the forms involved and examples of the process of preliminary analysis.

Figure 3.   Examples of research notes

The following examples of research notes are illustrative, and do not cover the variations to be found in a large research note file. Research notes all will be on sheets or cards of one size. The examples below, however, divided by lines, do not show the blank spaces that would occur on many note sheets. Brackets [ ], often used to indicate interpolated material, may be indicated in research notes by double parentheses (( )) when a typewriter lacks brackets; this cannot be done in finished manuscripts. Of course, many research notes will be handwritten, in which case brackets can be drawn. (No diacritical marks are included in these notes. For comment see introduction to Figure 2.)

```
P Notte, C Eur & Asia, II, 63              Graustark threat China aid

Says no doubt Graustk made the threat ((cites only Madrid Noticias Graficas
5 nov 82)); but consid doubt if had any notn really tryg get Chinese aid
((cites no evid, and does not give reasong)).

II, 78 cites letter (Archives Nat., Paris), Count Marko, Fgn Min Graustk to
Ch. Clouvier, Grstk Amb to Paris, suggestg possib threat such a connecn ((but
no more analysis than on p63; & no indictn effort find corrob or contradictg
evid elsewhere)).
```

```
NYT editl 4 nov                    Winkler's tariff speech 3 nov 82

Says Pres W good on econ issue, but "less than candid" on moral issue. On
whole creates strong suspicion W playg politics rather than searching for
best solutn fr pt v USA.

        ((NYT doesnt say why less than candid; & remember NYT havg feud with
        admin on other issues at this time))
```

```
NYT 5 nov 82  datelind Graustark 4 nov     Graustark govt reacn W's tariff
                                                  speech 3 nov 82

Graustark Fgn Mintr today in speech to Natl Assoc of Manuf dinner stated W's
speech "demagogic," lackg in desire find real solutn.  Main interest speech
was Fgn Min hint that Graustark might turn to China for assistance.

        ((corresp not at dinner; says no handouts text; got data fr "friendly
        guest" at dinner; corrsp pts out govt often uses this method express
        "unofficial" displeasure))
```

```
Vaughan, Intl Rels in XIX, II 78

I ((sic)) 142:  Says Marko in letter to son Jules, sept 82 ((no day given, and
no collecn or repository cited)) asserted that "he was convinced that the
activities of anarchists 'require me to recommend the use of a Chinese threat'".
```

Figure 3 (continued)

Cong. Rec,105th cong,2d sess,1892,CI,Part 5,9553-9674   Cong debate on W's
                                                           3 nov speech

These pp contain speech 18 senators on issue. 5 suppt speech without reservn;
5 suppt W, but not enthused over speech; 3 rail vs speech; 5 vs W, but not
hydrophobic in criticizing speech....The 10 fav are Dems; other 8 Repubs; so
reactns ff strictly party lines.
    The 3 rabid critics incl Clark of Ohio, as usual vs any tariff reducn,
flagwavg, etc; and Simme of Idaho, who simply seems to distrust W.
    On whole speeches concentrate on econ issues, tho all allude to moral
questns, and two make big fuss ca moral issue (altho they disagree with each
other on definitn). Everyone claims be vs appeasement, but define it diff.
    Very clear that most wld vote for some tariff reducn, but far apart on amt.
    16 mention Graustark threat to turn to China; 3 say it empty threat; several
others simply vaguely worried; a few pt out that no official threat; clear
majority think it possib serious; 3 couple with US need maintain milit str.
    Most remarkable thing ca debate as whole is restrained, responsible tone
as compd with debate in jan 82 over the Constantinople incident. ((Of course
the only thing that cld restrain Smythers wld be a muzzle.))

K Botsch, US & Graustark 2d ed   cong reactn to Graustark threat on China

69: says cong up in arms ca the threat ((cites cong record 105th cong 2d sess,
1892,CI, Pt 5, 9553-9674, but gives no analysis or reasoning)); does not pursue
the subject, except to say that this "no doubt" one of reasons for increase in
naval approps only two months later ((no evid adduced)).

Amb Carl V Platt, US Emby London, to Secy   Graustark feeler to China for
State,10 jan 85 (in Docs Fgn Aff, XX,86-88) aid in re crisis with US on tariff

Amb states that got hands on ((doesnt tell how)) fr reliable source copy of
apparent message Graustark Fgn Min to its Min to China, dtd 8 nov 82. US Amb
pts out message hints at Graustark milit aid in return China econ concessns
if internatl tensions dev as at present.
    Text Graus. message printd. Is, indeed, merely hint. And no direct
indicatn that US involved in internatl tensions mentnd.
    Editors of vol state ((88 n)) that it is however a fair presumptn, given
date of message, and reptd speech of Fgn Min a few days bef in wch threatnd
agreement with China in retaliatn US tariff changes, that Graustark made the
feeler with US in mind. Editors pt out however that since no word of the
message leaked out till Amb Platt got copy over 2 yrs later, Graustark
didnt push the threat very far.

U Gotlieb, Kans & Intl Politics   Kans business & Graustark tariff issue

29: says no quesn but that Kans business much arousd, esp over packagd products issue, and put massive pressure on public offcls ((citing J Dousel,
"Kans and the tariff," Am Hist Rev, Jan 1910 -- but without discussg the
char of Dousel's evid))
76: says Chambers of Commerce very active in puttg pressure on pub offcls
((citg N Rutt, "Tariff Issues in West," Ec Rev, Feb 1949, and statg that
Rutt's view is solidly fded on exam offcl records 18 Chambers of Commerce in
Kans))
101: says "public opinion in Kans was arousd by this threat to US sovgnty
by Graustark" ((citg Kans C Star 7 nov 82--pretty dubious way showing all
Kans arousd))

Figure 3 (continued)

```
Memoirs J Cloud                        reason for Winkler's 3 nov 82 speech

19:  says he present as W's Secy Interior 28 oct, 3 pm White House when
P House of Dem Natl Comm presented analysis reactn tariff policy and urged
nec speech.  Cloud claims argument that seemed to impress W most was dissatis-
fcn in orgzd labor.
49:  prints excerpt of letter fr P House to J Cloud, 7 jun 84, alludg to
meetg of 28 oct 82 at White House, mentiong that both present at that meetg,
and statg "President Winkler was moved to make the famous speech of nov 3
primarily by my rept on agricultural unrest on the West Coast."
49-51:  Cloud rambles on at gt length refuting House's statements, ptly on
grds Cloud has better memory, ptly on grds West Coast agric in good shape
at that time, and cites statistics to prove latter ((fr Dept Agric Statistical
Bull, 12 jan 83, pp 72-79, 111-115))
                ((check on this))
```

```
Martinez, Docs Mex, IV, 190-195        influence sheepherders on 98 tariff

     See note filed under AGRIC & 98 TARIFF
```

```
  Sandy, "Calif and 98 tariff"             mining interests and 98 tariff

     Material on this in article.  I only took notes on Calif agric
     and the tariff fr it.  See if expand study.
```

```
Rept F Pizarro to crown 5 nov 1537        amt gold div at Sacsahuaman
(in Doc Ineds, III, 234-246)

   Doc reprinted fr orig in Arch de Indias.
   Rept written nearly 2 yrs ff events.
   Says total 11,345 lbs (ie pesos) gold, wch he saw weighed, and certificate
to that effect signd by him, by Friar Montesinos, by Assessor Guzman, the
Treasurer Calderon.  He incl copy certificate, and notes it sent with his
orig rept of nearly 2 yrs bef, tho Crown now claims it cant find it.
   He incl affidavits by Montesinos and Guzman that 11,345 was amt, & that they
signd certif.
   Claims story was another 5,000 lbs. gold in another bldg he didnt have
weighed, but kept himself, a lie.  Says 1 of 2 men claimg this, Urquiza,
was not at Sacsahuaman at time weight taken, but near Arequipa, 200 miles
over mts.  Incl affid signd by 8 impt conquistadores to this effect....Says
another accuser, Pi y Margall, was present at weighg, but known trouble-
maker, and his (F Piz's) personal foe, due fact Piz had to discipline him
once for cruelty to Indians ((a laugh, coming fr F Piz))....Rest of rept is
self-praise of gt services of Piz to crown.

((about all can tell fr this is that Crown suspicious of Piz; and that Piz
can get people to testify for him...and that even this early a conquistador
notd for cruelty to Indians considerd it politic to indicate to crown that
he was careful of Indians--ie knew crown concernd))
```

```
Oviedo, Hist nat III                   relatns bet Pedrarias and Balboa

98, 182 et seq:  Number of incidents described by Oviedo, claiming he
witnessd them, in wch Pedrarias actd arbitrarily, & contrary to royal
orders, persecuting old settlers who were there bef his arrival.  Three of
these involvd Balboa.  One of them involved Oviedo.  Says (182)"Here the
orders of His Maj are interpreted by only one man, Pedrarias Davila"....The
language thruout indicates strong dislike of Pedr.  On other hand, Oviedo
is proud of his task as historiographer, seems to have consid affecn for objec-
tive reptg, so that I doubt he inventd all these incidents, or even Pedrarias'
genly arbitrary character....Further, Oviedo shows no animus vs Balboa, nor
any affecn for him, and finds little to criticize (or praise) in his actns.
          ((copy this note also filed under ADMIN JUSTICE COLONIAL ERA))
```

126

Figure 3 (concluded)

V. C. Smith, "Diary," Univ Wisc Archives   corroboration deal on 1882 tariff

   Under entry for 8 oct 1882 he gives an approx 2500 word summary of speech
Winkler at White House dinner Democ state chairmen, 7 oct 82, wch Smith
attended. ((His acct almost exactly agrees with that in Robinson Memoirs.
I had fotostat of latter & compared them. The differences are of no imptce.))

Walker, My Exper in Politics   no evid on Dem Natl Comm activ on 1882
                                                                     tariff

   Nothing herein of value on subject, altho several historians hint that
there is. Actly, they make unwarranted inferences. Is useful testimony
on several allied subjects ((and I have separate notes)). Fact is, Walker
in Europe for 3 wks bef the critical Dem Natl Comm meetg until a wk
thereafter ((see his ltr to daughter in Natl Arch, 9 sept 82, filed under
MISC my files)).

VI

USING EVIDENCE: EXTERNAL CRITICISM

Using evidence requires knowledge of (1) external criticism, which determines the authenticity of evidence; (2) internal criticism, which determines the credibility of evidence; (3) the grouping of evidence in relationships of various sorts; (4) the interpretation of evidence in the light of many factors and in the absence of others; and (5) exposition or the comunication of evidence to others. These subjects are treated in Chapters VI–X. Although external criticism, subject of the present chapter, is a process relatively little pursued by beginning researchers, it is useful for them to develop the habit of thinking in terms of the critical approach developed in this chapter. They should look at all evidence in this critical manner. And the specific problems and techniques of external criticism will be useful to an understanding of the pitfalls of internal criticism and synthesis. The techniques of external criticism are modern;

they have been developed in the Occident since the Renaissance.

A. External criticism

1. ITS AIM

The aim of external criticism is to get evidence ready for use in the examination of human affairs; that is, to prepare it for internal criticism. External criticism authenticates evidence and establishes texts as accurately as possible. It sometimes is said, rather misleadingly, that its function is negative, *merely* saving us from using false evidence; whereas internal criticism has the positive function of telling us how to use authenticated evidence. External criticism also sometimes is referred to as "lower" and internal as "higher" criticism. Another way of putting the matter is to say that external criticism deals with the document, and internal with the statement or meaning of the document. The types of problems attacked by external criticism include forgeries, garbled documents, partial texts, plagiarism, ghost writers, interpolations. External criticism deals with both intentional and accidental errors in texts.

External criticism especially means determination of the authorship and date of evidence, which may prove or disprove the authenticity of the evidence, and almost certainly will aid in its examination by the processes of internal criticism. As a concept, external criticism is not difficult; as a process, it can be frustratingly complex. The phrase—but not the process—sometimes is criticized, but it has the values of traditional use, brevity, and some semantic content. Let us remember then that there is nothing mysterious about the difference between external and internal criticism; at the heart of it is the difference between authenticity and credibility. Remember this, and there should be no confusion because we look *inside* a document in engaging in external criticism, and of course we use other (outside, external) materials when engaging in internal criticism.[1]

Beginning researchers seldom engage in external criticism, because: (1) they have enough other problems to occupy them; (2) they usually lack materials requiring external criticism, or do not realize that they require it; (3) they usually lack the skills to engage in such activity; and (4) millions of pages of documents have been authenticated and published.[2] Physical remains have been similarly proved, cataloged, indexed, stored, often put on display. Many unpublished manuscripts in archives also have been authenticated at least partially or tentatively.

Many professional historians seldom or never engage in external criticism. If the need arises (and it varies considerably from field to field), they either can apply to reference books and manuals for aid in doing their own authentication or restoration of texts, or refer the material to a specialist, who may devote all his time to external criticism, usually in a relatively narrow field. Some of these specialists are discussed in VI (B), where their work is entitled "auxiliary disciplines."

2. Determination of author and date

The author is wanted because: (1) there is a suspicion that the document is wholly or partially false; or (2) it is needed for internal criticism. The document may proclaim an individual as author, or a class of author (priest, lawyer,

---

[1] There are many "overlaps" between external and internal; e.g., although information on author and date are the essence of external criticism, they also are needed for internal criticism.

[2] In some elaborate and admirable sets of published documents, not only is material furnished on authentication but also analyses that result from internal criticism. A famous example is the *Monumenta Germaniae Historica*, in 125 volumes, begun in the early 19th century and finished in 1925. In some other sets however, the editors tell us little or nothing about the methods they used in authenticating documents and the textual purity of many items is open to doubt.

soldier) may be indicated, explicitly or implicity. If it turns out that the asserted author (individual or class) surely did not compose the document, the next step is to determine the sort of falsehood involved. For example, if the forgery is a 16th-century Spanish document claiming to be a letter by an English Admiral, we may at least learn what sort of lies Spaniards thought it worthwhile to tell about Englishmen at that time.

The date is wanted because it can (1) show whether the asserted or implied date of composition can be correct, (2) show whether the indicated author can indeed have been involved, and (3) orient the researcher for the processes of internal criticism. The date is that at which the document was composed or the object made, not the date of the material treated in words or the date at which artifacts of a given type ordinarily were constructed. Sometimes a year, or week, or even a day or hour is needed; for some purposes, a century will suffice reasonably well. There are cases in which the date can be closely determined without much material on authorship being available (e.g., a Latin list of household objects, reliably dated from papyrus type, ink, structure of language as Latin of the third century A.D., but conceivably prepared by various sorts of persons for any one of several purposes, and in one of a thousand places).

Determination of authorship and date involves one or all of the following: (1) content analysis, (2) comparison with the content of other evidence, (3) tests of the physical properties of evidence. Division might also be made between the social and the physical properties of the evidence. Content analysis is, then, examination of the social content of the evidence. Comparison with the content of other documents either means direct comparison by the researcher, or the consultation of reference works, which are, in the end, founded upon many comparisons and classifications of pieces of evidence. Such reference works now exist in profusion, and include many types of information: inscriptions, signatures, seals, letters, various types of governmental papers, church materials, the records of such institutions as universities and craft guilds, and many more. Often they have been prepared with great care by specialists, and may be of the greatest assistance in establishing the authorship and date of newly discovered or studied documents. The availability of this mass of carefully prepared materials, often with extensive commentaries, constitutes a major difference between the historical method of the last century and a half and earlier times.

The language of the document may in itself provide useful general indications of where and when it was composed. The Latin of Roman times changed considerably over the centuries, as has English since the Norman Conquest. Specialists can assign dates to certain constructions and vocabulary, and even in some cases pinpoint regional usages that provide a clue to place of authorship, or to the place of origin of the author. The content of the document may provide data to permit general classification of the author; e.g., a man with a good but unspecialized education, or an ecclesiastic, or a lawyer. Sometimes yet more data exist, permitting judgment that it was composed by a member of the United States Congress in the years just before the Civil War, with an indication that he was a good friend of Henry Clay. That would lead to research on Clay's acquaintances.

a. Content analysis.

1. Anachronisms may be useful in establishing (or invalidating) authorship and in fixing (or loosening) the date. This includes anachronisms of spelling, in the use of words in certain senses, in the structure of language, in types of scripts, in references to objects or events or persons who have been (or can be) reliably dated and fixed in place. Simple examples would be an asserted author of the first half of the 15th century using the word "America," or an asserted 17th-century letter writer using the expression "didn't get to first base."

2. Dating may be suggested by mention of dates that are or can be reliably fixed: religious beliefs, astral events, domesticated animals, floods, battles, construction projects, elections, all may be revealing.

3. Script may be compared with known samples of an individual's hand. There are reference books containing samples of the writing of important individuals.

4. Tests of consistency include consistency of sentiment with the known predispositions of a culture, consistency of an individual's statement with his presumed cultural, general, or occupational background. As to the internal consistency of the document, one should question whether it seems to be of a piece, or whether there are indications of multiple authorship, and if the latter of what sort, and how divided in time.

b. Comparison of pieces of evidence.

By comparison of pieces of evidence contemporary with that under consideration, we may learn what have been the usual styles of composition and forms of documents in given places, offices, times, for given purposes. In some cases, we may find other documents with identified authors, and so similar to that under study that the latter may be ascribed either to that author or to one of that class. In even happier cases, an authenticated document by a known author states that he wrote another document that clearly can be identified as the one under study.

c. Physical properties of evidence.

Most of the tests for the physical—as opposed to the semantic or cultural or social—properties of evidence are of modern origin; many of them were devised only in recent decades. Since the 17th century we have had systematic treatises on some of the physical properties and appearance of paper, parchment or vellum, inks, seals. These include such things as color, weight, gloss, grain, watermarks. More recently, this sort of material has been subjected to chemical and spectroscopic analysis. Measurement of the age of materials now is possible through analysis of the decay of radioactive carbon.[3] On a humbler level, parts of documents have been matched by the shapes of stains going through the pages, or the paths of wormholes.

3. FORGERIES

Forgeries include complete documents (or artifacts) or forged interpolations into documents. Plagiarism (unacknowledged use of another's words) is a special form of forgery. Documents garbled because of either forged interpolations, or accident (e.g., bad copying), or the merging of documents are treated later in this chapter under restoration of texts.

Monetary gain is one motive for forgery. Fraudulent wills are by no means rare. Many historical, literary, and government documents are forged for sale. Fabricators of this type of material are sensitive to the market. In our day, collectors yearn for love letters exchanged by the young Abraham Lincoln and Ann Rutledge, so forgers supply them. Visitors to Mexico lust for ancient artifacts, so the descendants of the Aztecs make replicas and "authenticate" them.

Other forgeries are committed for political profit or in support of causes. Many a modern electoral contest has been livened by the appearance of fake documents that cast a sickly light on a candidate. Governments sometimes manufacture documents to "prove" claims. The history of religion is thick with proven forgeries, and with documents and holy artifacts of dubious origin. Some forgeries are made in pursuit of fame (e.g., by a scholar, or an explorer); some are at least in part the result of esthetic pride, satisfaction in work well and cleverly done. There have been forgers who

---

[3] See B6, below, which describes modern scientific methods of dating.

enjoyed making mischief; yet others seem to have been driven by frenzy, but this sometimes is difficult to distinguish from devotion to a cause.

Determining authenticity thus means whether a letter offered by a bookseller on Fifth Avenue for $25,000 as from an ardent Napoleon to Josephine, is in fact the manufacture of a Parisian penman of today. Or whether the baseball-sized shrunken head offered a museum collector at Iquitos, on the headwaters of the Amazon, is a Jíbaro tribal masterpiece, or the uncle of a Chinese entrepreneur of Lima, who smokes such delicacies for the market. Is the cobbler's bench an 18th-century occupational artifact, or a Hoboken-made approximation for the split-level trade? Is a postage stamp genuine, a forgery, or a facsimile (an acknowledged forgery)?[4] "Historical evidence" has been and is being fabricated in appalling amounts.

4. RESTORATION OF TEXTS

Documents sometimes contain "corrupt" passages. Some may be produced by the conscious interpolation of forged sections, others may be the result of poor copying and transmission of the text. Diarists sometimes alter the entries in their own journals through insertions or changes long after the event. Sometimes this is done in the sincere (though possibly mistaken) belief that accuracy is improved. Sometimes changes are meant to make the diarist appear more clever, a better prophet, or less harsh-minded. For later publication as pamphlets, Cicero, we are told, so altered the texts of speeches he had delivered. Modern ghost writing presents us with problems of authorship. Sen. Barry Goldwater once said that he had employed many "ghosts," with the result that, unhappily for him, extant Goldwaterian

---

[4] There are even cases of fake facsimiles; e.g., the supply on order of an asserted facsimile of an authentic title page, which is in fact simply an invention of the seller.

documents do not always present the actual Goldwater point of view. Hence, ghosted sources must be used with caution.

Plagiarism poses the difficulty of finding the source from which something was lifted. A special type of half-stolen, half-invented material is found in the speeches inserted by Greek and Roman historians in their narratives. Thucydides included orations delivered by Pericles and the other protagonists of the Peloponesian War, but noted that he gave only some parts of them word-for-word, as a rule reporting no more than the general drift of a speaker's language. The content of the speeches also shows that we do not have verbatim accounts, since all orators speak in a unique "Thucydidean" Attic, even when they are Spartans and Corinthians of Doric speech.

Detection of interpolations and multiple authorship generally is done by finding anachronisms or inconsistencies of style. In the book of Genesis, God is sometimes called Yahweh and sometimes Elohim. Since proper names were vitally important to the Hebrews, not only for naming a thing or being, but also for defining its nature, such differences probably mean that at least two authors were at work. This becomes certainty when there are doublets in Genesis—that is, recounting the same event twice—doublets that are consistent in that one set always uses Yahweh, and the other always calls God Elohim. It must be that early traditions were put together in ancient times to make the version of Genesis that has come down to us.

In dealing with corrupt passages, most scholarly work is not concerned with forgeries, but with passages that make no sense. A great deal of such textual criticism has been done by Biblical scholars. They must work with manuscripts that are copies of copies; the originals are lost. In the case of the Old Testament, the books or parts of the books were written down between the eleventh and second centuries B.C. The oldest surviving manuscripts long were those made by the Jewish Masoretes in the ninth and tenth centuries A.D.; then some made in the first century B.C. were found among the Dead Sea Scrolls, discovered in 1947. These much older documents are less likely to have suffered from the mistakes of copyists than the later ones. Another version of the Old Testament is the Septuagint, a translation into Greek made in the third and second centuries B.C. It shows what the Hebrew text was like at that time. It is not always to be preferred to the Masoretic text, however, since not all the translators were equally proficient, and also since the translation was made from texts brought to Egypt from Judeah some centuries earlier. Fourth, there is the Samaritan Pentateuch, which was (and is) used in northern Palestine, whereas the Masoretic text was derived from the version used in the south around Jerusalem. The method of Biblical scholars is to collate these four versions; that is, to bring them together for line-by-line comparison, so that the original text of which these four versions are descendants may be reestablished as closely as possible.

Study of these texts of the Old Testament shows that most corrupt passages were caused by careless copying and that little or no effort was made to deceive. Most mistakes, moreover, are simple and understandable ones, mindlessly repeated by scribes. There is the copying of a line, phrase, or word twice. There is, in reverse, the omission of a word, phrase, or line. There are spelling mistakes. There is the mistaking of one word for another which looks like or sounds like the correct one. Biblical scholarship has convincingly shown, incidentally, that the transmission of the text of the Bible has been, on the whole, amazingly accurate.

The same method of collating manuscripts is used also in establishing the texts of classical authors. In some cases, ancient works have come down to us as a single manuscript or papyrus, so that there can be no collation. Textual criticism then becomes a complicated (and somewhat chancy) business and requires a good knowledge of the language of the document and sometimes of dialectical variants. It also requires a knowledge of the culture of the author and of the milieus in which generations of copyists lived. The spellings and meanings of many Greek and Latin words changed between the classical period, when the ancient literature was written down, and the middle ages during which it was copied. When there is a single manuscript, then, difficulties arise. Lines in poems sometimes can be restored by study of the meter. Words that do not fit in or are foreign to the poet's dialect can be excised, and similar-sounding words that fit the poet's meter, dialect, and style inserted. Such emendations are not always right. It is known that the texts of the plays of the great Athenian playwrights have been contaminated by interpolations inserted by actors who imagined that they had hit upon some particularly happy line.

Broken Greek (or Latin) inscriptions often can be restored with some accuracy; first, by determining, where possible, the original length of the line. From the fifth century B.C. on, Athenian inscriptions were almost always written in *Stoichedon* style; that is, with the letters engraved rigidly in both horizontal and vertical rows and without spaces between words and (usually) sentences. Public decrees almost always begin with the set formula, "Decreed by the Council and People, (the tribe) So-and-So was in Prytany, So-and-So was First Secretary of the Council, So-and-So was Archon, So-and-So was Chairman (of the Assemly), So-and-So moved (as follows). . . ." If a part of this opening is preserved, the rest often can be filled in, establishing the number of letters in each mutilated line below. The language of official Greek inscriptions tends to run in set phrases, vocabulary, and style, and the study of bureaucratic usage of any period is an important help in restoring damaged texts. Furthermore, the subject matter of public acts also restricts the possibilities for restoration. Decrees, for example, authorizing naval expeditions will have nothing to say about the sacrificial calendar of Athens. The same principles may be applied to the restoration of partially destroyed papyri or parchments.

Some words and phrases never can be recovered. Numbers are especially subject to error, because they are unique terms whose correctness is not controlled by the surrounding context. Plutarch says that around 445 B.C. the Athenians kept 60 triremes in commission every year in peacetime for training purposes. The number is impossibly high, because 60 ships would have cost Athens more than half her annual income, and we know that more than half her budget was spent on other things than the navy. Plutarch's text must be corrupt. All manuscripts, however, read "60," so we must use our wits. The easiest emendation, the one that would most probably correct a copyist's mistake, would be to change "60" to "16" since the numbers are as similar in Greek as in English. We get probable confirmation that this is right from Thucydides, who remarks that at a moment of extreme danger in 440 B.C. when the Athenians had to use all available warships at once, they sent out 16 ships in advance of their main body.

The tasks of detecting forgeries and interpolations, and of emending corrupt passages, demand of young textual critics that they be, above all, *erudite*. They cannot know too much about the period in which they are working, and most of all, about its language.

B. Auxiliary disciplines

"Auxiliary" here merely means that in an age of specialization, historians may need consultants in fields other than their own. Physicians and scientists have the same need. For historians, such specialties may be useful for external or internal criticism. The historian today has available a huge mass of accumulated, classified, interpreted data, and specialists to help with it.

Most of the auxiliary disciplines of interest to historians have been developed in Western Europe since the Renaissance. Much of the work in these fields has been done in the last two or three centuries. Some specialities are wholly the work of the 20th century.

Some modern historians minimize the change that has occurred in method, partly through the development of the auxiliary disciplines, partly through conceptual changes. They insist that no one has surpassed Thucydides in certain respects, and decline to discuss the areas in which his conceptions and methodological tools were not the equal of ours. Such partisans of the past also often exaggerate how much older historians anticipated later methodological developments merely because they had some inkling of what later would be worked out in detail.

Modern methodology, much of it developed by the auxiliary disciplines, at least has increased the area of historical knowledge about which there is relatively little controversy, thus freeing inquiry to some extent to concentrate on the more difficult aspects of investigation. The latter may still be handled largely by "common sense," as many historians aver, but even in connection with such problems as bias and causation the level of sophistication, and the understanding of the problems—even their insolubility—is improved.

The auxiliary disciplines were developed in Europe, and so have tended to be somewhat culture-bound. This was especially true in earlier generations, but some of the bias remains. This is merely to say that the specialists first focused their attention on European and related Near Eastern antiquity. Such specialization not only was a reflection of ethnocentrism; we now see it as a necessity. In most of these specialties it is not possible for an individual to function well in more than one or a few cultures. To take an example, it is enough to be an expert in the authentication, decipherment, and interpretation of Greek (conceivably Latin also) inscriptions. There is no such thing as a universal epigrapher, who flits from Greek to Egyptian to Mayan to Chinese.

The great pioneers in Europe in the epigraphy of Greek and Latin inscriptions, or the diplomatics of medieval European official documents, or the philology of ancient European languages were not only compiling materials in their relatively narrow range of interest, and constructing rules for authentication, dating, and the like. They also were laying the foundation for construction of similar systems of organized knowledge for all societies that had similar cultural phenomena. So, in later years, the term philology has fallen from use, replaced by the term linguistics, which all understand to be universal in its interest. So, too, it is clear now that Mayan inscriptions are as worthy of study as Cretan. And archeology, as a science or art devoted to the material remains of cultures, embraces all the human experience. But within the field of archeology scholars are Egyptologists, Assyriologists, Sinologists, and the like. The universal digger can only be an amateur.

1. SPECIALTIES DEALING WITH LANGUAGE AND WRITING

Linguistics. This is the study of language. It is a modern term for a discipline that is both humanistic and scientific, and is driving from use such older terms as philology, associated in the past especially with the study of the Greek and Latin languages and literatures. The rhetorical and analytical study of language was developed in ancient Greece and India. With Europe's introduction to Sanskrit in the 17th century, comparative linguistic study broadened its scope. But scientific linguistics did not begin until the 19th century with European recovery of the lost languages of Babylonia and Egypt. The decipherment of the old Greek script of the Mycenean period is a triumph of the 20th century. Maya writing resists full decipherment.

Paleography. This term for the study of "ancient" handwriting, by extension can be applied to the study of all handwriting and to the materials involved therein. As developed in Europe it meant ancient and medieval European writing, and the forms of the manuscript (i.e., bound handwritten book or scroll). The discipline deals with the decipherment or reading of handwriting, dating, and determination of location where prepared. Both external and internal evidence are used in the process. The discipline was built up by finding examples that clearly could be deciphered and identified, dated, located, in order to compare them with others not so easily interpreted. Thus, the subject is inescapably culture-bound. Research involves the forms in which letters were put down, the use of abbreviations and punctuation, the material on which written, the instrument used, the inklike substance used. It requires knowledge of the practices of authors, scribes, booksellers, and many other aspects of specific cultural practice. Huge amounts of Greek, Latin, and medieval European scripts have been printed for the guidance of scholars. Many modern European manuscripts cannot be read by scholars without some paleographic training.[5]

Epigraphy. This is the study of inscriptions, which are in some part studied as a specialty, and in some part inextricably a part of the work of scholars interested in other things as well. Actually, it is the paleography of inscriptions, which are documents incised on a hard (as opposed to a paperlike) substance. The specialty was developed in early modern times in Europe, beginning with Greek and Latin inscriptions, then extending to Egyptian and Near and Middle Eastern cultures, and finally to the Far Orient and America. There is no reason to regard inscriptions as special sorts of documents, although they present special problems. There is the physical difficulty of moving or copying many inscriptions. Sometimes the resistant nature of the material required extreme brevity and abbreviation, which has impeded decipherment. One of the achievements of the specialists has been the copying and publication in great series of volumes of all known classical inscriptions. Presumably the same will some day be done for other cultures. Inscriptions have been left on stone, metal, clay, wood, ivory. They exist in Mexico, China, India, and elsewhere.

---

[5] *Papyrology* is a branch of paleography that deals with writing on papyrus. Extant papyri are largely from Greco-Roman Egypt.

They were prepared for religious, political, and social reasons; to promote public or private business; to memorialize kings, fathers, wives, and sons.

Diplomatics. Diplomatics is the critical study of official or business (rather than literary) documents. It sometimes is considered a branch of paleography. Jean Mabillon in 1681 published the first important treatise on the subject, founded on his study of medieval European documents. The documents with which this specialty deals are both public and private. The former are issued by public authority and include legislative, administrative, judicial, and diplomatic documents. The private documents are issued either by individuals or by corporations (e.g., municipal or monastic organizations), and include many sorts of materials, including conveyances of real property. Mabillon systematized the examination of the different forms and parts of official documents by some of the public offices of medieval Europe. The same sort of examination later was made of such materials in other places and times.

Seals. These long have been used in Occident and Orient, in ancient Greece and in China. The most intense European effort has been devoted to medieval seals, and especially those put on public documents. The subject thus is part of diplomatics. In medieval Europe seals were used for the business of monarchs and by bishops, municipalities, monastic houses, and private individuals. The study is mostly of the impressions (usually in wax) made by the seals on documents. The specialist is concerned with the materials, the legend, and the way the seal was put on (or tied to in many cases) the document.

2. HERALDRY

Heraldry, a system of symbols on shields that identifies a person, family, or organization, arose among the medieval European nobility. It is complex, requiring specialists, and sometimes legal interpretation. Some arms or heraldic devices came to be signs of authority. Family, corporative, military, and ecclesiastical devices are used today. Specialists in medieval European heraldry help in the identification of artifacts that carry such devices as their only "signature," and in following the marriage alliances of the nobility that were so important in both public and private affairs, and were reflected in heraldry.

3. GENEALOGY

The study of human pedigrees is related to heraldry. A number of aristocratic societies in East and West from ancient times paid much attention to genealogy. The study draws on other specialties—e.g., paleography and chronology. Although preliterate peoples often kept oral records of genealogies, both of public leaders and of private families, as did ancient literate Greeks and Jews, genealogy was put on a scholarly basis only in recent times. Much professional—and possibly even more amateur—genealogical work is being done today.

4. NUMISMATICS

This is the study of coins and medals. Coins were invented by the Lydians of Asia Minor at the end of the eighth century B.C., about the same time by the Chinese, and independently in India four centuries later. They contain important information, and are durable, and often were hidden, so that many have been preserved. The most important are gold or silver, marked by public authority with an official sign that guaranteed (supposedly) their weight and purity. The locations of hoards of ancient coins give us data on the circulation of coins struck at different mints, thus an idea of the routes and volume of trade. The debasement of coinage—as common in China as in the West—is good evidence of financial or economic troubles. The artistic and technological levels of cultures may be judged from coins.

Sometimes data of aid to chronology is on coins. All sorts of cultural information is contained on coins—religious, political, economic.

5. CHRONOLOGY

Chronology, the measurement of time and the placing of events in time, has been known in a number of cultures.

We know that the fixation of events in time sequence arose long after urban life developed. Much of the earlier material that we have relates events in terms of regnal dates ("in the fourth year of the reign of King Phool, the city was rebuilt"), or lists of monarchs or other royal or ecclesiastical officials. This is the case with much of the early written record of China, Egypt, India. Thucydides had such materials, and noted the difficulties involved in relating them to each other; i.e., in achieving and being confident of the accuracy of an uninterrupted sequence of events from the past to the present. None of these people had a reliable original referent from which to reckon time. Romans ultimately adopted the notion of datings things A.U.C. (which meant from the year of the foundation of Rome in what we call 753 B.C.). Some Romans knew then, as we know now, that the events and dates asserted often were legendary.

A Christian monk in the sixth century invented the Christian era, positing that Christ was born in 754 A.U.C. Although this was nearly correct, it did nothing to overcome the legendary nature of the earlier dates asserted for the A.U.C. system. Furthermore, use of the Christian era was not general in Europe until the 11th century, and some areas of the continent did not accept it even then. In addition, there was disagreement as to when the Christian year should start, and for many centuries December 25, January 1, March 25, and Easter all were used for the purpose. This only hints at the difficulties presented by the systems of dating used in medieval European documents.

Another problem is how to correlate dates between the

systems of different cultures. Possibly the most difficulty is presented modern scholars by the Maya system. There were no cultural relationships between the Maya and the civilizations of the Old World. The Maya had a year of 365 days, and many Middle American people used a "calendar-round," which repeated itself each 52 years. The Maya also used a "long-count" that indicated time elapsed since a date in their chronological system that is thought to correspond to about 3000 B.C. This presumably was the date of some mythologic event, as were the Maya calculations that reached a hundred million years into the past. The specialists can read the Maya calendric symbols, and relate one Maya date to another; the problem is to relate the Maya system to Christian era dates, so that developments of the European past can be related in time with developments in Maya history. The oldest date in Amerindian glyphs yet found comes from the Olmec culture, and is thought to correspond to 31 B.C.

6. SOME NEW SCIENTIFIC TECHNIQUES

In addition to these traditional specialties, historians recently have been getting new help from science and technology. A computer was used to study Stonehenge in Britain. The old supposition that the pattern of stones had an astronomical significance was tested in a program that matched eclipses and other astronomical dates with the pattern of stones. The calculations demonstrated that the locations of all of the stones could be accounted for if the structure had been reared in 1500 B.C.[6]

Many of the new techniques are used to date artifacts or the remains of flora and fauna. Charcoal remains are examined to determine how much a certain radioactive isotope of the element carbon, with a known half-life, has disintegrated since the charcoal was created. This dates the

---

[6] Gerald S. Hawkins, *Stonehenge Decoded* (New York, 1965).

material burnt, which permits assumption regarding non-carbon artifacts found nearby. Radiocarbon dating showed that important early cultural developments in the Balkans north of Greece and in Western Europe antedated those of the Aegean and Crete, thus either were developed independently or were based on the older Middle East.[7]

Another technique dates clay artifacts from the thermoluminescence of their metallic crystals—the light they emit when heated. It requires that the object have been subjected to fire (e.g., in the making of a vase). What is measured is the radiation the artifact has received since being subjected to the fire. It is the only reliable technique for dating sites older than 50,000 years (beyond the range of radiocarbon dating) or younger than 500,000 years (too recent for potassium-argon dating). Thermoluminescent testing also is used for interpreting the technique of making artifacts, and for determination of faked objects.

Many other techniques are used. (1) Electron microscope pictures of obsidian found in Greece showed when it was formed by volcanic eruption, proving it the same age as the obsidian of Melos, and ruling out some other possible sources of supply. (2) Bones may be dated by the rate of amino-acid racemization; that is, the amount of change following death in the polarization of light in the amino acids. (3) Valuable work also is done in the spectro-chemical analysis of glass artifacts. It may be done by burning samples in a spectrograph, and projecting the vapors through a grating to identify the components by the different wave lengths of light from the elements. Or X-ray fluorescent equipment can be used to analyze an entire glass object, with counters to read the characteristic radiations of elements in the specimen. Or the artifact can be subjected to neutron bombard-

---

[7] Difficulties of various sorts exist with regard to the reliability of radiocarbon dating. Some of them are solved by checking radiocarbon dates against Bristlecone pine growth rings that go back more than 7,000 years.

ment in a nuclear reactor, which changes the structure of a fraction of the atoms of many elements in the sample. The new forms, radioisotopes, lose radioactivity on an individual timetable of decay, which can be measured. This permits calculation of the rare earth ingredients of glass. Many samples, analyzed in these ways, possibly combined with archeological evidence, then may be classified, so as to establish the supposition that certain types of glass are associated with certain places and times. This bears some general relationship to the ways in which some of the traditional auxiliary disciplines built up bodies of evidence to serve as norms. But the scientific techniques were not available until day-before-yesterday.

VII

USING EVIDENCE: INTERNAL CRITICISM

Authentic evidence may lie or mislead, intentionally or un-intentionally. The letters of Cortés to the King of Spain on the conquest of Mexico misled both out of the intention of Cortés to glorify his deeds and out of his inability to understand much of American Indian culture. The authentic outpourings of Adolf Hitler teem with misunderstanding, exaggeration, misconception, and lies. The historian is interested in lies as well as truth, but he must be able to distinguish between them. This is the task of internal criticism: to determine the credibility of evidence. It thus deals with statements about specific things or ideas or customs. The beginning researcher will spend much of his effort on internal criticism. He must be aware that this process, described in this chapter, will overlap with the processes of synthesis and exposition dealt with in later chapters. It is the details dealt with by internal criticism that later will be fitted into patterns or relationships. Of course, relationships and tentative hypotheses will be generated in the course of internal criticism.

The division of subject matter in this chapter has proved workable; it is, however, no more logical than some other schemes for internal criticism. At this point, the student should consult others chapters: IV (A), "Facts as values, ideas, objects, events"; III (A), "Probability, plausibility, certainty"; VIII (C), "Bias and subjectivity." Note that although many materials in those sections are directed to clarification of the mind of the *investigator*, they also are applied in internal criticism to the mind of the *witness* (i.e., the source of the evidence).

A. Literal meaning and real meaning[1]

Internal criticism must begin with understanding of the words of the document in their literal sense. Sometimes this is complicated by language foreign to the reader, or by obsolete or technical terms, odd spelling, a lack of punctuation, or the use of abbreviations. The author may have been using words in some oblique sense—for example, ironically or allegorically. Much time and care, and the use of reference books, may be involved in this process, to determine if the literal and real meaning are identical.

Place and time influence the meaning of words. The English spoken in London differs from that of New York. Even more important are the changes in language over the years. For example, the Fundamental Orders of Connecticut of 1639 states: "we the Inhabitants and Residents of Windsor, Harteford and Wethersfield are now cohabiting and dwelling in and uppon the River of Conectecotte and the Lands thereunto adioyneing. . . ." A modern dictionary defines "co-

---

[1] Langlois and Seignobos, *Introduction to the Study of History*, 148ff., called this determination "positive criticism," which is succeeded by the "negative" internal criticism of the good faith and accuracy of authors. This illustrates the apparently unavoidable ambiguity of many of the tags used in discussion of historical method.

habit": "to live together as husband and wife; the word usually implies sexual intercourse, and is applied especially to those not legally married." Is this the meaning of the statement in the document? Were Puritans experimenting with free love? Then we discover that "cohabit" has as its archaic meaning simply "to live together." Later in the document the right to vote is awarded to all "freemen." The first dictionary definition of "freeman" is "a person not in slavery or bondage." So, were all men and women not held in servitude allowed to vote? A familiarity with 17th century usages rules this out. Freeman must be defined in its second dictionary sense: "a citizen; person who has all civil and political rights in a city or state." Thus, the vote in Connecticut was restricted to those ranked as "freemen."

The investigator must follow "the rule of context"—that is, he interprets the meaning of a statement in view of what precedes and follows it. He must not isolate phrases and sentences from the rest of the document, as American isolationists have done with such parts of President George Washington's Farewell Address of 1796 as:

> Europe has a set of primary interests which to us have none or a very remote relation. . . . Hence . . . it must be unwise in us to implicate ourselves by artificial ties in the ordinary vicissitudes of her politics or the ordinary combinations and collisions of her friendships or enmities. . . . Why quit our own to stand on foreign ground? Why, by interweaving our destiny with that of any part of Europe, entangle our peace and prosperity in the toils of European ambition, rivalship, interest, humor, or caprice?

These statements are quoted as meaning that Washington opposed foreign commitments for the United States under any and all circumstances. But a reading of the whole message shows that he qualified his meaning:

> It is our true policy to steer clear of *permanent* alliances with any portion of the foreign world, so far, I mean *as we are now at liberty to do it;* for let me not be understood as capable of patronizing infidelity to *existing engagements.* . . .

Taking care always to keep ourselves by suitable establishments on a respectable defensive posture, we may safely
trust to *temporary alliances* for *extraordinary emergencies.*
[Italics added.]

Documents produced under such unusual circumstances
as wartime censorship or totalitarian control may contain
a different meaning than a literal reading would reveal. In
broadcasting radio reports to America from Nazi Germany
early in World War II, William L. Shirer tried to outwit
the censors. He describes his tactics thus:

> For the last few months I've been trying to get by on my
> wits . . . ; to indicate a truth or an official lie by the tone and
> inflexion of the voice, by a pause held longer than is natural,
> by the use of an Americanism which most Germans, who've
> learned their English in England, will not fully grasp, and
> by drawing from a word, a phrase, a sentence, a paragraph,
> or their juxtaposition, all the benefit I can.[2]

B. Other sources of error in internal criticism

1. A CATALOG

Among the most common sources of error in internal
criticism are: ignorance, in its many degrees and guises;
bias, an ever-welling fount of human error; falsification, of
wholes and of parts; failure of the senses, with men and
women too apt to suppose that they cannot see and hear
awry; cultural difference, within or between cultures; self-
delusion and mental unbalance; mutilation of evidence; and
the misuse of evidence by adherence to a dubious scheme
of interpretation. Two or more of these, or other, sources
of error may be present at the same time. Most of these
sources of error may affect either the author of the evidence or the researcher using the evidence. Put another

---

[2] William L. Shirer, *Berlin Diary: The Journal of a Foreign Cor-
respondent, 1934–1941* (New York, 1941), p. 511.

way, error may exist in the evidence, or it may arise from the use made of it by the historian. Bear in mind, also, that error may be either willful or inadvertent, and that it may be either total or partial—that is, the piece of evidence may be a mixture of the true and the false.

The motives for deliberate falsification run the gamut of human drives and social thrusts: lust, greed, political ambition, jealousy, timidity, levity, and the like. Error is intruded into the record unintentionally in more ways than can be listed here: ignorance (e.g., inability to understand what was witnessed), failure of the senses, or mistakes in spelling or transcription or translation. It is difficult to know whether bias and mental unbalance led to deliberate or unintentional error; possibly the question in many cases has no meaning. Courts and historians sigh when confronted with the testimony of children, the enraged, the mad, or the culpable weaving fancies to hide their guilt. We know that the limits of human credulity are wide, indeed, corresponding to such needs as ego-bolstering and fear-reduction.

2. OBSERVATION OF THE DETAIL

Much of historical research is concerned with determination of the accuracy and value of observations of details made by witnesses of events. The analysis of stubborn problems and the construction of grand generalizations comes only after details have been gathered, often corroborative testimony on the same small subject. These little building blocks of knowledge are best cast into the form of the loose-leaf notes recommended in Chapter V, each as nearly as possible confined to one subject or detail. This is where knowledge of history begins, much of it dependent upon the testimony of witnesses. The ability of the witness to observe thus becomes a matter of prime importance. There are physical and social aspects to this ability.

a. Physical ability to observe

This includes the condition of the witness, and external conditions that affect his observational powers. The sight and hearing of the witness may be either naturally good or defective, and affected by illness, drugs, age, or by noise, or by intervening objects. Also, sight and hearing may be affected by the distance of the reporting witness from the event or object: Was he at the top of a big stadium, or at the lower edge of the arena? Beside the thing observed, or across a broad and crowded square? Next to the jury box, or in the back of the courtroom? Also, witnesses may be weary or bored; attention may be sharp during part of an observation, lax during another part. When no information is available as to the physical ability of the witness to observe, the investigator can only hope for the best, fear the worst, search for corroboration, and use the data with caution.

b. Social ability to observe

Social ability to observe concerns the familiarity of the witness with the subject matter, and his willingness to observe to the best of his ability. He should understand the language spoken, and not have to guess at many of the meanings. Imperfect knowledge of languages is productive of much dubious testimony. A report of a battle by a man unfamiliar with military affairs may be worse than useless —positively misleading. An account of a court trial by an observer with little knowledge of the substantive or procedural law in use may be sadly deficient. A man of one culture reporting on another may be ludicrously wide of the mark. The accounts of Amerind actions and culture by Spanish conquerors often were badly in error. Also, willingness to observe may be inhibited by social conditions. A witness under the eye of secret policemen may be unwilling to peer too intently at events. A member of a chamber of commerce or of a social club may find himself under severe pressure to conform. Finally, we must be aware that observation often is affected by prejudice, so that the eye apparently beholds and the ear apprehends what the mind wishes them to report.

3. REPORTING THE DETAIL

This concerns the fashion and frame of mind in which the document was composed, so it may be classified in terms of (1) the ability of the composer to report, (2) time of composition in relation to the observation of the events or objects reported on, and (3) the intent with which the account was set down.

a. *Ability to report*

This is much like the ability to observe. Bias (personal and cultural), pride, ambition, and other mental states play a similar role in both processes. Additional factors here are facility with language, access to recording materials, and the conditions under which the record was set down or recited. The presence of secret policemen, censors, enemies, or others might inhibit reporting. Ability to report may also be affected by literary, religious, legal, or other cultural conventions.

Controlling or recognizing bias means control of the researcher's biases and recognition of those of the witness, for everyone has the bias of his interest and culture, skills, temperament. The historian must remember that he is looking at the evidence through the prism of his own culture and time. That is why history so often is reinterpreted: different things and patterns are seen, partly because new generations of historians are looking for new things, partly because they are not interested in seeing others. In the end, possibly three rules should be followed: (1) the problem should be actively recognized, (2) efforts should be made to identify one's own biases, (3) it should be realized that biases often are unacknowledged or unrecognized, and influence us willy-nilly.

In terms of the witness, it must be remembered that much of historical research deals with biased people under stress. There are many ways of looking for biases in witnesses. Crude methods may suffice, or it may require subtlety. Bias may be covert or overt. Bias may be indicated by an institutional connection. Finally, we must ask if an author is aware of his "point of view."

b. Time of composition

With the lapse of time even highly accurate observations by a witness may become lost or confused. This is the factor that distinguishes journals or diaries, kept more or less as events occur, from memoirs composed long after events. Of course, the former may be used for the composition of the latter.[3]

c. Intent of composition

Many documents can be described usefully in terms of the purpose of their composition. The question is: did the composer wish to report as nearly truly as he could, both in terms of accuracy and of coverage? So we observe classes of documents in terms of degrees of probability that the composer would not purposefully distort what he had observed. Quite often intended and accidental distortions go hand-in-hand. For example, Bismarck's memoirs, *Thoughts and Reminiscences*, written after he left office in 1890, are an unreliable account of the German statesman's involvement in the Revolution of 1848. In part, this is a result of Bismarck's desire to hide his earlier lack of interest in

---

[3] An unrelated matter, often confused with the time witnesses set down their observations, relates to the time nonwitnesses record their views. It is clear that if the composer was not a witness, and consulted no witnesses, it usually matters little whether he wrote 50 or 500 years after the event.

German unification; in addition, the account suffers from simple lapses of memory. Bismarck could not remember the details of his actions some 40 years earlier, and he was too vain to check the records.

d. Types of distortion in reporting

This includes lies of commission and of omission, partial truths, twistings, favorable interpretations—the vocabulary is rich in phrases in this area. The motives for deliberate distortion in reporting are as varied as human hope, fear, and hate. Special attention must be directed to distortions introduced by the nature of the audience for which the document is intended. It is presumed that the views a man confides to paper for his own eyes only may be more accurate than those he prepares for other eyes, but this is a probability only. The account may be so sketchy as to invite misinterpretation; it may appear to be private, but in fact have been meant to be read, immediately or later; and some men are so constituted that they must lie even to themselves. When a document is composed for an audience, some conscious or unconscious editing occurs. It might be thought that the greater the size and/or the heterogeneity of the audience, the more editing would occur in order to communicate clearly the heart of the matter to people with various capacities and knowledge. This rule must be used carefully; it is rather clearly applicable at its extreme limits (e.g., the family group and the total national population), but more difficult to apply as a rule to groups of moderate size.

In any event, we might expect a chemist to report an experiment one way to a lovely but not scientifically-trained young lady, another way to a college faculty, another to a chamber of commerce, and yet another to a television audience. The author's expectation about his audience will have affected differently a letter from Benjamin Franklin to a French lady, a White Paper issued by the government of the United Arab Republic while at war with Israel, and a public report by a tobacco company celebrating the non-toxic quality of its cigarettes. It matters whether the audience is friendly (one's own foreign ministry) or unfriendly (an enemy nation's government), educated or uneducated, rich or poor, young or old, interested or not, and how interested (e.g., as legislators listening to a report on a pending bill, or physicians hearing a speech on foreign policy).

e. Additional possible clues to intended veracity

A good reputation and no apparent motive for distorion incline us to consider an author a good risk in terms of reporting. Downright indifference to the subject on the part of the reporting witness often seems especially encouraging. Indifference can, of course, be feigned. Researchers are happy to find witnesses making statements damaging to themselves, supposing that this will not be done unless an unavoidable truth must be displayed. But men may so testify inadvertently, or in fright or hysteria, or to distract attention from other matters. It may seem encouraging to credibility to find detail in an account on matters unconnected with the main line of testimony, on the supposition that there could not be a motive for distorting testimony on such incidental matter. But here again we have only a probability.

Some of the difficulty of judging veracity may be seen in Joseph Goebbels's two accounts of Nazi Party life in Berlin in the 1920s. *Kampf um Berlin* (1930) and *Vom Kaiserhof zur Reichskanzlei* (1934), although written by a master propagandist and political liar, are, on the whole, remarkably honest and objective. The reason is not that Goebbels suddenly developed a passion for truth, but that the truth served his political purpose at the time of writing. Since the Nazi Party had outgrown its miserable beginnings, he could afford to be honest about—indeed, glory in—the time of political inconsequence and financial difficulties, as well as the repeated setbacks suffered in its struggle for power.

C. Some illustrations of error and distortion

1. A FICTIONAL SCENARIO

Strikers at the Star Textile Company's Worcester, Mass., factory, were being addressed in 1922 at the plant gates by a member of the leftist Industrial Workers of the World. The "Wobbly" told them in the Italian language to leave their union and join the IWW and fight for a classless society. About 30 uniformed company guards, pistols in hand, moved through the crowd toward the speaker. Men in the crowd shoved and kicked the guards, and a few brandished knives, clubs, and lengths of pipe. A guard shot a striker. Strikers then knocked down some guards. The guards fired into the crowd, which retreated. On the ground lay some figures, some still, some writhing. Eleven guards had been injured, six seriously, and one died of his injuries. Three strikers had been killed outright by gun shots, and twelve others wounded, two of whom eventually died of their wounds.

Public opinion in the United States was aroused by the newspaper accounts. Headlines shouted "Worcester Massacre," "Anarchist Riot at Worcester," "IWW Battles Police," "Working Men Slain in the Streets." This sampling indicates editorial polarization. Much of the reporting was equally slanted. At that time newspaper operations were heavily influenced by their publishers, mostly conservative. Early accounts in procompany papers featured an announcement by a Star Textile Company vice president, based on his observation of the affair from the second story of a building near the gate where it occurred:

> I saw it all. A radical agitator had infiltrated the union pickets, and urged them to attack our plant. He was screaming and gesturing like a crazy Bolshevik. At any moment the mob would have stormed our gates. When our guards, under orders, tried to remove the anarchist from our property (We own the access road to the gate.) the mob attacked them with knives and clubs. The guards fired to save their lives.

Investigation revealed that the company official was not reporting the Wobbly speaker's remarks as of his own hearing; he was too far away to distinguish words, and in any event the official did not know Italian. In one of the trials resulting from the affair, the official admitted that he had the words of the Wobbly speaker indirectly from Italian speaking strikers. What the official did observe were the gestures and facial expression of the IWW speaker, and he probably could hear what he described as his "emotional" voice. It also turned out that the official's fear of labor violence had been heightened by the fact that his uncle, a banker, had been killed in the Wall Street bombing of September 1920. The company official was opposed to labor unionism and was convinced it was linked with communism and anarchism. Obviously, both his physical and his social ability to observe and to report objectively were questionable. All this could be brought out in the 1920s in the United States through investigative reporting and court proceedings. The same sort of difficulties exist, of course, with older testimony that never was subjected to query by reporters and attorneys.

The labor press and its sympathizers among the commercial papers at first featured the testimony of a supposedly unbiased casual passerby:

> I saw the whole thing. I was walking about a block away from the factory gate when I saw company guards march up to the pickets, who were standing there peaceful like. The guards walked right up to the pickets and began to fire without anyone having offered them any hurt.

It turned out that the observer, although not an employee of the Star Textile Company (hence, supposedly objective), had two brothers who were. Also, the observer was five feet three inches tall, and could not see or hear the Wobbly addressing the workers, because he could not see over the crowd, because he was too far away, and because it turned out that a line of heavy horse-drawn construction carts was rumbling down the unevenly paved street where he was walking. But before this had been brought out, he had told the newspapers:

> That speaker was just telling the pickets that all labor groups ought to cooperate, that that was the only way they could beat the millionaires and trusts, and that they should be careful not to use violence, because that was what the crooked newspapers and courts wanted.

During one of the trials that followed the Worcester Massacre, the following exchange occurred:

Labor Lawyer to *Company Official on witness stand:* Why does your company employ so many Italian immigrants.

Company Lawyer: Objection.

Judge: Sustained.

Labor Lawyer: You have a training program. I assume it is conducted in Italian.

Company Official: Yes.

Labor Lawyer: Do any company officials speak Italian?

Company Lawyer: Objection. This line of questioning is irrelevant and immaterial to the issues in this murder trial.

Labor Lawyer: Your honor, we contend it is highly germane to show the labor policies of the Star Textile Company.

Judge: Objection sustained.

Labor Lawyer to *Company Official:* You have asserted that you consider that most of your employees are loyal, though occasionally led astray by radical agitators.

Company Official: Yes.

Labor Lawyer: Given the language difficulty, how do you arrive at that conclusion?

Company Official: Some of our people are bilingual.

Labor Lawyer: And they spy for you?

Company Lawyer: Objection.

Labor Lawyer: I'll change the question. They report to you?

Company Official: Yes.

This gives an idea of the difference of view between union and company officials, and hints at the gap in understanding between management and labor. The company hired immigrants because they worked for low wages, and were difficult to organize into unions, both because of the language problem, and because they were happy to have escaped even lower wages in Italy and fearful of getting in trouble in America. The opinions and actions of Americans regarding this fictional affair clearly would be bitterly divided, as in the actual Sacco and Vanzetti case of the 1920s. Opinion inevitably would suffer from many forms of bias, mutilation of evidence, cultural misunderstanding, rival views of society, political passion, cries for revenge and punishment, and the like. Many somewhat comparable earlier affairs have suffered similar errors and distortions, without leaving so comprehensive a record as the Worcester Massacre surely would have left, and as the Sacco and Vanzetti case did in fact leave. And the Sacco and Vanzetti case is not yet "settled" to everyone's satisfaction.

2. A CASE OF PECULIAR INTERPRETATION

The investigator must be on guard against authentic documents that use undoubted facts, but interpret them in unacceptable ways. For example, Sen. James Eastland of Mississippi some years ago made a speech in the Senate in which he cited "evidence" and statistics (often so convincing to the uncritical) to give the impression that judges of the Supreme Court under Earl Warren were procommunist.[4] Eastland based his charge on voting behavior in 1953–62, which he asserted showed that Warren voted "pro" communist in 62 of 65 decisions, that Justice Black "supported" the position of the Communist Party in all (102) of his decisions, and that Justice Douglas "reached a conclusion favorable to" the Communist Party in 97 of 100 cases. Eastland's speech offered no real basis for such assertions. Also,

---

[4] *Cong. Rec.*, 87 Cong., 2 Sess., May 2, 1962.

it ignored the complicated questions of jurisprudence involved in the cases before the court, reducing everything to a simplistic and unreal division into "for" and "against" communism. The latter was not the issue in the cases, and Eastland ignored the great constitutional issues that were involved. Unfortunately, the Eastland speech was widely reprinted by critics of the Warren Court.

3. A CASE OF BOWDLERIZATION

Evidence is suppressed or otherwise distorted for many reasons. It is not just panic-stricken or malicious liars who cause trouble for historians. Bowdlerization is a modern form of deliberate distortion of reality designed to protect morals or furbish images according to selected namby-pamby patterns. It is seldom helpful to the historian, always is irritating upon detection, and occasionally can result in serious misunderstanding.

Ex-Gov. Leland Stanford of California commissioned a painting of the "wedding of the rails," the joining of the sections of the transcontinental railway near Ogden, Utah, in 1869. The painter worked from a photograph of the event, but he eliminated two things that it showed—liquor bottles, and ladies of questionable virtue—and added prominent citizens who were not in fact present at the ceremony. The absence of the latter is scarcely interesting, since the ceremony itself was of small consequence, but to show the West without strong drink and strumpets is to distort social history rather sizably.[5]

4. ERROR DUE TO FAILURE OF DEFINITION

The subject of "national character" has produced a large literature, heavily studded with errors, distortions, and

---

[5] Cf. Thomas A. Bailey, "The Mythmakers of American History," *Journal of American History*, LV (June 1968), pp. 5–21.

prejudice. More rigorous questions need to be asked of the evidence. What characteristics, in what combination, demonstrate a national character different from that of other national groups? How to prove the existence of these characteristics in individuals? From their utterances? From their actions? Are these superficial or fundamental indications of the characteristics in question? Are a few statements or actions by an individual sufficient to demonstrate that the characteristic is present in force? In how much force? What is it likely to lead the individual to do? How many individuals must be "proven" to possess the presumed proper mix of characteristics in order to permit a confident assertion that the majority of the population possesses this mix of characteristics? Are there significant ethnic or social variations? To add to these problems there has been added recently the striking proposition that most persons in the larger nations possess similar personality patterns, and that unusual, or "distinctly national" patterns occur only in small minorities. This psychoanalytical approach gives "national" a new meaning in the context, and suggests that "character" has been erroneously defined in the literature on national character.

5. CROSS-CULTURAL ERROR

Error due to cultural differences is common, and often difficult to detect. It may be simple to find error in the reporting of a poorly educated person testifying on something in his own environment, but it is more difficult to discern the misunderstandings in an effort to report on an alien culture. Historians long have been aware of this problem of cultural difference, talking of combatting it with "historical mindedness." This sometimes meant what anthropologists later called cultural empathy. Such cultural or historical empathy comes only with effort. Voltaire, a man of genius, did not make the effort, and so misunderstood the culture of medieval Europe, which he decided was shameful and of no importance to modern times.

How enormous and socially crippling over the centuries were the errors made by Europeans about the black slaves they carried from Africa to America, and about the Indians they found in the New World. It was not simply a matter of clashing interest and European will to dominate. Europeans, being technologically superior in some critical areas, assumed that all aspects of their culture must be "superior" —morally, esthetically, psychologically—to those of black Africans or red Indians. The result was the creation of ideas of innate Indian and black inferiority, which can be eradicated only rather slowly by revisionist studies by historians and others.

Cultural empathy or historical mindedness must be cultivated both as a technical necessity and as an obligation of interpretation. It is necessary for understanding many aspects of a culture, and many of the motivations and actions of individuals. Neither the examination of individual pieces of evidence nor the synthesis of bodies of evidence can be pursued with confidence without this quality of sympathy founded upon study. This does not mean that the researcher abandons his own values in his own world, or that he never applies them to the historical scene he is studying. It does mean that he must first try to think and believe like his subjects, discover how they performed in their own eyes, inform the reader from that point of view; then he may, with identification of his purpose, make a comparison, even a judgment, involving other value systems, including his own.

One frequent error stemming from lack of historical mindedness is when it is assumed that men in the past had knowledge that we possess. That makes it easy to condemn decisions with hindsight. The historian must recreate for himself the terrifying doubts facing military and political leaders. They nearly always have information permitting several interpretations of a situation. The great intelligence services of our own times have done little to reduce this problem. We therefore should be careful, for example, how we describe what Abraham Lincoln *knew* about Southern intentions between his election and inauguration as president.

It is well to close this section by asserting that with a bit of reflection the student can smother the notion that nothing is knowable. It is reasonable to believe that there are degrees of probability regarding the errors in the record and our perception of them. We may be confident that Napoleon lived and did numerous things that we know something about (consider the contrary supposition with regard to Bonaparte, Lincoln, and Julius Caesar), and we have a fair idea of the effects of the American Civil War on the economy of the Confederate states.

D. Checklist for internal criticism

Beginning researchers often get lost in the verbiage of discussions of internal criticism. This minimum (far from exhaustive) list of questions or steps to use in connection with a piece of evidence provides an easy first entry into the critical examination of statements. The amount of evidence being checked may be a sentence, a paragraph, or more. The investigator must decide on the proper unit. Not all these suggestions will apply to all pieces of evidence; others that are not on the checklist often will be needed.

1. Is the real meaning of the statement different from its literal meaning? Are words used in senses not employed today? Is the statement meant to be ironic (i.e., mean other than it says)?

2. How well could the author *observe* the thing he reports? Were his senses equal to the observation? Was his physical location suitable to sight, hearing, touch? Did he have the proper social ability to observe: did he under-

stand the language, have other expertise required (e.g., law, military); was he being intimidated by the secret police?

3. Conditions of *reporting*:

a. Regarding the author's *ability* to report, was he biased? Did he have proper time for reporting? Proper place for reporting? Adequate recording instruments?

b. When did he report in relation to his observation? Soon? Much later?

c. What was the author's *intention* in reporting? For *whom* did he report? Would that audience be likely to require or suggest distortion to the author?

d. Are there additional clues to intended veracity? Was he indifferent on the subject reported, thus probably not intending distortion? Did he make statements damaging to himself, thus probably not seeking to distort? Did he give incidental or casual information, almost certainly not intended to mislead?

4. Are there inner contraditions in the document?

5. Do any statements seem inherently improbable; e.g., contrary to human nature, or in conflict with what we know?

6. Remember that some types of information are easier to observe and report on than others.

7. Are your own biases or preconceptions distorting your view of the document or the exact statement in it?

8. Consult reference works as required to resolve doubts.

9. Does the statement leave you sufficiently confident of your knowledge of that detail so that no corroboration is required?

E. Corroboration, contradiction, and measurement

When we come to the problems of corroboration and contradiction, we have passed beyond the simple internal criticism of the individual document or the specific statement therein. We now are comparing evidence. It is proper to think of this either as a more complex type of analysis than that involved in the single document, or as a low level of synthesis. A major part of historical method relates to efforts to find corroborative evidence and weigh its quality, or to resolve problems arising from contradictory evidence, by corrobation for one explanation or another.

Difficult as this process can be, it occasions less doubt than the problem of the single source, where we have neither corroboration nor contradiction. In such a case we are truly in complete doubt, unless (as is seldom the case) the single source is almost unarguably credible and sufficiently weighty. It should be pointed out that, on the other hand, much of recent history presents us with the opposite problem of almost too much potentially or partially corroborative material.

How much corroboration is required to make us feel comfortable in our interpretation? The answer is that it depends on (1) the problem (i.e., on what is being investigated—an entire culture, the location of a ford over a stream, a man's motives), and (2) what evidence is available (a three-line diary, 6,000 pages of legislation, no eyewitness reports, or the observations of 3,000 witnesses). It is foolish and simplistic to fix a number of corroborators, even of stated quality; e.g., two or more reliable and independent witnesses. We are not in a court of law. Reliability and independence are highly desirable in evidence, but two witnesses may give us no more of either than one witness. It depends both on the types of witnesses and on the types of problems.

We have commented in Chapter IV (C) on the qualities in authors or witnesses that create a supposition of reliability. They relate to ability and willingness to observe and report accurately. The reliability of the corroborative witness is an important element in determining the amount of corroboration required.

Some historical problems are more difficult to handle than others. Sufficient corroboration for a description of Lincoln's assassination is a very different thing from sufficient corroboration of the assertion that class antagonism in France so seriously weakened national morale that it was a critical element in her quick military defeat in World War II. In general, we may say that the corroboration of relatively small events ought to be easier than corroboration of large complex events; that accounts of physical actions are generally easier to feel confident of than descriptions of states of mind; that it is easier to corroborate testimony on commonplace matters than on things people care enough about to lie and to torture their observations; that some matters scarcely can be reliably corroborated, because almost everyone either avoids testimony or feels no obligation to tell the truth (e.g., crime, espionage, illicit sexual activity, treason).

The quantity of corroboration available, as opposed to the quality of an individual piece of corroboration, may seem critical in handling some problems. Corroboration by sampling given portions and types of population groups often seems appropriate for public opinion questions.[6]

Indirect or negative corroboration is better than none, but sometimes not much better. The absence of contradiction in other sources is especially chancy. There are circumstances when we may feel fairly sure that it would have appeared in other sources (e.g., large newspapers in countries with a free press in modern times), but many others when we cannot be sure. Similarly, it is difficult to feel secure with such "corroboration" as the reputation of the author, internal consistency of the document, or lack of anachronism, conformity with the formulations of physical science, or by the lack of bias or the possession of expert knowledge by the witness in place of a multiplication of witnesses. All these have value, but must be used with caution.

Analysis of the problem of corroboration may be furthered by thinking of it in terms of methods of "measure-

---

[6] Cf. Chapter IV (D) on oral testimony.

ment" (or weighting). We tend to think of this in terms of *physical* measurement—i.e., comparison with a fixed physical standard, as the inch, or kilogram, or dollar (which is at least more or less fixed at any given time, and a bit less subject to varying interpretation than the standards of "virtue" or "truth"). This is, indeed, one type of measurement available at times to historians: quantitative method, which we have dealt with.[7]

Another of value is definition or delimitation. One virtue of definition and delimitation of ideas is that it often improves estimate, if not quite measurement, of the value even of qualitative evidence. Merely because definition in this sense does not deal in ergs or decibels does not mean that it does not improve accuracy. The frequency with which we encounter waters muddied by the sloppy definition of concepts justifies calling definition a measurement. Even virtue can be defined against some standard or set of presuppositions or propositions; yet how often the writer merely tosses in the judgment without that definition. The definition of terms and concepts is one of the essential and operating members of the body of scholarly method.

---

[7] Chapter III (C).

VIII

ANALYSIS AND SYNTHESIS

Analysis and synthesis involve such mental processes as comparison, combination, and selection. Although some mental activity of this sort *may occur whenever sufficient evidence is available to require it,* much of it occurs in the later stages of research and writing. By now tentative hypotheses will have helped shape the collection of data, being modified or abandoned at need. Now the hypotheses receive their final test against the evidence collected and against the views of other scholars. Final efforts are made to detect bias in evidence and researcher; also, to sift out irrelevant data. Now all the material needs to be considered together, in a final effort of analysis, interpretation, generalization, and synthesis. Now the researcher engages in the always perilous process of inference. These broad and somewhat overlapping terms encompass the most difficult part of the historical inquiry.

A. Analysis and synthesis

We must not—to repeat in different words—suppose that all consideration of evidence prior to the *final* synthesis is "analysis," untouched by synthesis. We did, indeed, choose to speak of external and internal criticism in terms of analysis. But some of that, and especially in internal criticism, was quite complex, and did in fact involve synthesis. Analysis and synthesis thus proceed together, often overlapping or merging; it is, however, generally true that emphasis will shift from analysis in the early and middle stages to synthesis in the final stages of work.

Analysis is a systematic attempt to learn about a subject or problem by looking at its elements, breaking it into components. The first set of components arrived at is likely to be much altered in the course of investigation. The part may be one or a few pieces of evidence bearing on one aspect of the total subject under study. To these bits and components are brought to bear the resources of the mind, the research files, concepts and techniques of special disciplines, and such added research as may be necessary.

A research project of an author of this guide provides an example. The original question was "What was the relation of transport costs to periodic high prices and shortages of maize in colonial Mexico City?" The evidence quickly generated questions and tentative, low level hypotheses. Why the reliance on pack mules rather than cartage, especially in areas with dense population and favorable terrain, when there were complaints of high transport costs? When large maize growers and distributors (including owners of mule trains) withheld maize to force up prices, why not bring it in from beyond the area of the cornering operation? The answer often given, then and later, was that other surpluses were so far away that transport costs put retail prices at Mexico City above popular purchasing power. The accounts included no analysis, and apparently were based on too little evidence to make analysis possible.

What was needed was analysis of the relative prices of pack mule transport and cartage. Cost factors in each case had to be assembled. That meant, first, charges made for freight at the time. It also meant determination of freight-age profits by calculation of costs, which entailed assemblage of data on a number of factors. What was the cost of animals in transport (some horses and oxen, but mostly mules)? Sale prices of mules were gathered. But what of muletrain operators who bred their own stock? It was decided to assume that their animals cost them 25 percent less, but the evidence was poor and the assumption was a soft spot in the analysis. It was then necessary to have a figure for the average useful worklife of a mule. Not very satisfactory data suggested three to six years. Another soft spot. What about feed, during a freight trip and between trips? During trips it could not just be left to casual foraging. Data were assembled on the costs of cut forage. How much average downtime should be allowed for mules sick, lame, with pack sores?

Costs for personnel? Mule drivers (about one per ten animals), supervisors, guards (sometimes jointly paid for by several mule trains), and their food, wages, and pilferage. Costs of equipment: pack frames, cushion cloths, covers, ropes and rawhides. Fees for corrals; road, bridge, and ford tolls; bribes to officials and potential thieves (e.g., tavern keepers, often in league with plunderers). The data were far less than ideal, and left more soft spots in the analysis, but at least all calculations were founded on some relevant data, and the problems of analysis were clearly stated. Those were gains.

There was more. Rain and river damage. Spillage. Pilfering by outsiders (e.g., whores, corral and tavern workers, and assorted hangers-on at camp sites on the trail). When all this was done, and the results at least tentatively regarded as usable, attention was turned to carrying capacities. A mule load was more or less standard at about 200 pounds, divided into two halves, slung on each side of the

mule. Some cargo, of course, was difficult or impossible
to divide and in those cases either was lashed to more than
one mule or had to go by porter, or by cart or wagon.

In the ordinary mule train ten mules might carry a ton
or a bit more. Carts and wagons used at the time carried any-
where from about 1,000 to 4,000 pounds. A new calculation
of animal, personnel, equipment, and other costs showed
that with large enough vehicles savings could be made in
the number of mules and personnel used, although that depended on terrain. All this required much comparison of
bits of evidence, and synthesis into cost estimates.

Such cost estimates were possible only after breaking the
problem down into its components, a process that required
constant questioning by the investigator of the data on
transport and of much of the surrounding social environment. Recourse was had to specialized works on animal
breeding and transport, and to the work of specialists in
transportation economics. In addition, there was frequent
analysis of the record-keeping system of the colonial age.
How accurate were the reports? What percentage of the
record had survived? Was the extant record representative
of the original record?

Now it was time for an examination of route topography,
vegetation, and climate. As with the analyses discussed
above, the total problem was too large; so it was pared to
a few routes in the central Mexican highlands. Here the
population was relatively dense, living in rather level mountain valleys and basins, generally at 5,000 to 8,000 feet above
sea level. Some of the valleys were quite large (about 60 ×
30 miles for the Valley of Mexico, for example). Mountain
passes between valleys sometimes were quite low and short.
The first step was to find contemporary evidence of routes
followed. This generally was simple. In the valleys it made
little difference where the exact track lay, and in many cases
it went between stated towns or villages. There seldom was
a choice between mountain passes. Mileages were derived
from maps and from surveys by automobile, using the

odometer. Elevations and gradients also came from maps, but had to be extensively supplemented by field observation. Dry river beds (common during much of the year in Central Mexico) had to be inspected to determine the difficulty of carrying simple wagon roads up and down the banks. Vegetation patterns (hopefully not too much changed from colonial time, but only research could suggest answers to that) indicated whether and how much cutting or route deviation was required for carts and wagons. Usually that occasioned little problem. Slopes in the valleys seldom posed a major problem. Most soils in the dry season would sustain wagon traffic without difficulty. That left the mountain passes. As a first calculation, it was found that on most routes they constituted less than 10 percent of the mileage. Then came the difficult problem of inspecting the passes, finding historical data on their use by wheeled vehicles, making estimates of costs of passage under colonial conditions, and calculating the cost of improvements of the mountain stretches of selected routes. This required much labor by the investigator and much consultation with modern road builders. Costs of road building in the colonial era had to be assembled.

All of these separate but interlocked analyses resulted in a preliminary conclusion that little additional road and bridge building was required for broad expansion of wagon and cart freightage. But that left unsolved the question of why Mexicans in the colonial era did not use as much cartage as Europeans, who even had cart routes over the Alps. It was only partly a matter of the freight items and the magnitude of traffic. A whole new line of research was required to arrive at the probable answer that there were not in Mexico dynamic elements much interested in the problem. Government had neither sufficient data nor generally the will to promote cartage, partly because it connived, directly and indirectly, with monopolistic private elements. The great hacienda owners preferred a monopolistic system since it gave them profits from high prices, and they were satisfied with the return using mule trains. Merchants transporting imported luxury goods ordinarily did not need to lower prices to make sales. So it appeared that part of the answer lay in the sociopolitical organization of the Spanish empire, including the system of property division. But that generalization depended on the earlier analysis of relative transport costs.

So, questions guided the search for data, which, upon analysis, proved incomplete and contradictory. Renewed collection and more analysis established some points as probably proved or agreed upon, others were still doubtful in part, and some were entirely unproved. Moving from the more to the less probable, relationships were established. Much historical analysis proceeds in this way.

B. The working hypothesis

The hypothesis is a natural and useful device. Natural in this context means that the researcher cannot avoid thinking of hypotheses. According to an older methodology, premature hypothesis might prejudice interpretation, so should be avoided. But no one with imagination can deal with even a single piece of interesting evidence without having tentative hypotheses flicker through the mind. As we collect more evidence we think we see analogies, and something similar to an hypothesis exists whether we will it or not. And the hypotheses may arrive by interrogation of the evidence: Were these savage beatings and mutilations of runaway slaves a response to law or to fear and greed in the minds of the owners?

A working hypothesis probably will include a preliminary supposition regarding causation, which was discussed in Chapter I. Assignment of a tentative cause or causes is a guess at an explanation. These, obviously, are processes requiring imagination; but it is imagination arising out of evidence, for a useful wording hypothesis can begin only with some facts. A hypothesis should be: (1) founded on all the available facts and contradict none; (2) plausible, and not contradict the laws of nature; (3) capable of disproof or verification (historians scarcely can grapple with miracles); and (4) as simple as possible.[1]

If the researcher did not fairly early develop hypotheses or questions to apply to his material, it would be difficult to know what to collect. In practice, what happens if no preliminary hypotheses or questions are adopted is that the researcher makes selections either helter-skelter and with little discrimination, or he uses poorly defined or even unacknowledged criteria. It is much better to adopt tentative hypotheses and let them shape the search for a time, being alert to modify or abandon them when necessary. Such tentative hypotheses having been adopted from the beginning, the researcher necessarily frequently tests them against the evidence he collects.

The problem is to not let hypotheses become straitjackets; they must be abandoned at need. This is what we mean by "working" hypothesis. It helps our labors. It is tentative, but it must be clear that even the most tentative of hypotheses is apt to guide research, serve as a standard of relevance, to affect our selection of material, or our degree of attention to evidence. The only defense against such dangers is the consciousness that they exist. Finally, it is clear that in the adoption of working hypotheses the researcher must be conscious of the dangers of bias, ethnocentrism, and oversimplification, as in all his research activity.

As an illustration let us proceed a short distance into the use of working hypotheses in connection with the subject "The Spanish Conquest of the Aztecs." Probably we will tell ourselves that we want to be able to describe the process in terms of the following five areas of interest: (1) why was it undertaken? (2) how well did it succeed? (3) why was it accomplished so quickly and easily? (4) what were the results for the Spaniards and for the Aztecs? (5) what did

---

[1] After Wilson Gee, *Social Science Research Methods* (New York: Appleton-Century-Crofts, 1950), p. 197, citing D. Luther Evans and Walter S. Gamertsfelder, *Logic, Theoretical and Applied* (1937), pp. 315–16.

the conquest mean to the rest of mankind? Each of these is a large and complex subject in itself. Here we will deal, for illustrative purposes, only with (3), why was the conquest so easy? We assume that it is beyond argument that the conquest of millions of Amerinds by a few hundred Spaniards in two or three years may be considered easy.

Examination of the testimony indicates that the following factors were explicitly asserted by contemporary Spaniards as contributing to the rapid victory: superior weapons, good leadership, Spanish alliance with Amerind groups, Amerind superstitious fear of Europeans, Amerind military ineptitude of various sorts. There is considerable evidence in Spanish and Amerind sources to make it seem that the probability is very great that these factors had something to do with the matter. We also quickly discover that the contemporaries of the conquerors, and later historians also, do not entirely agree on the *why* of these factors, and that some of the historians suggest weaknesses in the Amerind social structure as also contributory. So our initial hypothesis is that a combination of factors was responsible for the rapid and easy conquest of the Aztecs by the Spaniards.

The researcher at this point discovers that he is not satisfied. More research is required, and different sorts of consideration of both old and new evidence seem to be indicated as a means of trying to identify better the importance of the ingredients in this historical process. The activities sketched above involved location and criticism or analysis of pieces of evidence, and much combination or synthesis of evidence. The synthesis was not, however, final synthesis in this investigation. We will return to synthesis in this research task later in this chapter.

C. Bias and subjectivity

Common usage erroneously makes "bias" and "subjectivity" synonymous. We are subjective in the sense that we are aware of and seek to understand that which has meaning in terms of our personal values. Many values are shared with others, so that groups have common interests and similar responses to certain stimuli, but each individual develops his own reality world. This is the psychological matrix from which his purposeful behavior stems. "As he thinketh in his heart, so is he." Thus runs the biblical proverb, and modern scholarship adds, "He is, in large measure, as he feels."[2] Subjectivity is, therefore, an inescapable human quality. It cannot be willed or wished away.[3]

Bias may mean a judgment reached without examination or without consideration of the evidence in full. It may also mean so strong a commitment to a belief, position, or cause that it precludes consideration, or even awareness, of contrary evidence and opposing views. Few scholars would claim to be free of all bias, and probably none would be justified in such a claim. We cannot eradicate all bias, but we can minimize it. "The safeguard against bias in the writing of history, as in the natural sciences, is not to indulge in useless resolutions to be free of bias but rather to explore one's preconceptions, to make them explicit, to consider their alternatives. . . ."[4]

Students who wonder (and many of them do) if they may properly express opinions in their research papers, or who fear to do so lest they be charged with subjectivity, are worrying about the wrong things. The proper question is not, "Is this an opinion?" but "What are the bases for this opinion?" And the proper follow-up questions are: what evidence was sought? what evidence was found? what was selected for use? what was actually used and for what purpose?

---

[2] For a brief discussion of this by a social psychologist see Handley Cantril, "*Sentio, ergo sum:* 'Motivation' Reconsidered," *The Journal of Psychology,* 65 (1967), pp. 91–107.

[3] See I (C) on the values of historians.

[4] Cohen, *The Meaning of Human History* (1946 ed.), p. 80. Note that Professor Cohen included natural sciences as well as history.

It is proper to demand that an historian be impartial in seeking and using all the evidence, not just evidence that accords with preconceptions or supports a personal thesis. Historians must try to identify and correct for their own biases, as well as for biases in the evidence. They must accept the subjectivity of their perceptions and be prepared to recognize that what is valid for one may often appear invalid to another. It is not proper to demand that an historian be an unperson with no standards, judgments, or opinions. There is every reason for historians to be humble about their performance, but no reason for them to be humble about the scholarly craft they practice.

Bias may take the form of uncontrollable attachment to a church or religious ideas, or to a political party or political views or a social class, or a distaste for certain occupations or for men with beards. It also can be a much larger and pervasive thing, as the cultural patterns of the ancient Maya, so different from those of their European conquerors as to make communication on many subjects nearly impossible. Or how much communication could exist between Polynesians and early New England missionaries on the "duty" of work, the "sin" of nakedness, or the beauties of sexual abstinence? We have mentioned earlier the problems of error due to ethnocentrism.

Bias or prejudice may be thought of as exaggerated points of view. The point of view, the experience, the beliefs, the attitudes of the historian must affect his interpretation of history. What is important is that he should be aware of this, and be willing to discuss opposing points of view.

An excellent example of how changing experience and point of view affected the work of an historian concerns the role of Hernán Cortés in the conquest of Mexico. A Spanish historian wrote in 1935 in praise of the chronicle of Bernal Díaz, one of Cortés's soldiers, who criticized the great captain as having received credit for the achievements of his men. Immediately after this, the historian fought in the bloody Spanish Civil War of 1936–39. This gave him a different understanding of the problems of military leadership, and he wrote a new discussion in which he defended Cortés against what he now called the jealousy, greed, and ambition of Bernal Díaz. He also developed a new explanation of some of Cortés's more devious actions, as being dictated by the need of manipulating his solidiers into accepting intelligent direction by pretending that ideas and decisions came from the ranks.[5] Although we might call this a change in point of view rather than in biases, the similarity is apparent. The fact is that huge amounts of military history have been written by men with no military experience and sometimes with little appreciation of military problems. All this without reference to the fact that some modern scholars so dislike military institutions that they are unable to analyze them with approximate impartiality.

It is difficult to guess whether bias or self-delusion is the more prominent in the following example. The Haymarket Affair of 1886 in Chicago involved an isolated act of terrorism by a lone anarchist. Some conservatives in the United States insisted on viewing it as part of a wave of radicalism threatening to destroy American institutions. The opposite self-delusion or political bias was that of the left, as when the French revolutionary periodical *Le Révolté*, declared of the Haymarket Affair:[6]

> Blood flows in the United States. Tired of leading a life which is not even a mere existence, the worker makes a final effort to struggle against the beast of prey which is devouring him. And this beast of prey . . . turns it slaves [soldiers and police] loose upon the worker. . . . It is open war.

---

[5] Ramón Iglesia, "Two Articles on the Same Topic: Bernal Díaz del Castillo and Popularism in Spanish Historiography and Bernal Díaz del Castillo's Criticisms of the *History of the Conquest of Mexico* by Francisco López de Gómara," *Hispanic American Historical Review*, XX (1940), pp. 517–50.

[6] Quoted in Henry David, *The History of the Haymarket Affair* (2d ed., New York, 1963).

This document is good evidence for one thing only: leftist hope of revolution.

Bias in the form of adherence to Marxist doctrine led to a dubious system of interpretation of evidence in Herbert Aptheker's *American Negro Slave Revolts* (New York, 1943). Aptheker uncovered numerous slave disturbances in the antebellum South, but most historians think he exaggerated their significance. He erroneously concluded that black militance and overt examples of revolt were common, critics contend, in order to advance a Marxian interpretation of slavery in the United States. He wanted to find a high level of slave resistance, so he did, regardless of the evidence.[7]

In assigning error or falsification to bias, probability often is all we can achieve. But this may be a considerable gain. For years a famous quotation was attributed to Woodrow Wilson by virtually every major historian dealing with his presidency or with American intervention in World War I:

> Once lead this people into war, and they'll forget there was ever such a thing as tolerance. To fight you must be brutal and ruthless, and the spirit of ruthless brutality will enter into the very fiber of our national life, infecting Congress, the courts, the policeman on the beat, the man in the street.

More recently it has been argued that Wilson either never made the statement or did so in a different form. The quotation originally was cited in J. L. Heaton, *Cobb of the World* (New York, 1924), as coming directly from editor Frank Cobb, who had it from the lips of Wilson. Now it has been shown that Heaton had it only at third hand, from Maxwell Anderson and Laurence Stallings, as purportedly repeated to them by Cobb at the time of the incident, then given by them

---

[7] Later and much better studies of black slavery in the entire Western Hemisphere have proved that black slaves very seldom could revolt because the system of repression was too strong. That had been true, also, of white slaves in the ancient Mediterranean.

to Heaton many years later. It is pointed out that Stallings and Anderson were such fanatical pacifists, with considerable literary ability, that this argues—with some other evidence—for a verdict of possible fabrication. Their motive assertedly was to endow Wilson with prophetic powers regarding the effects of warfare. The issue is by no means settled to the satisfaction of historians, but some doubt has settled upon the quotation.[8]

Can history be objective when the historian selects both the facts that he will include and the causes that he will assign to events? Does this condemn history to the mere whim and prejudice of historians? That is the view of some of the new left revisionist historians in the United States. They assert that the work of all historians is inescapably subjective, and that the pertinent question is what cause they will favor. A positive aspect of this has been bold reinterpretation of old and possibly ossified views; a negative side of it has been insufficient interest in accuracy and proof in terms of probability, and some glorification of irrationality and intuition at the expense of reason.

In any event, even in the case of the historian who believes in the possibility of maximizing objectivity, and in the necessity of identifying and sometimes minimizing subjectivity, the danger is real that there will be lapses. The honest historian guards against this as best he can. He remembers that he is involved in the process that he is describing and tries to rise above his own biases and limited point of view. If he suggests an hypothesis, he attempts to subject it to rigorous testing, weighing both the supporting and the conflicting evidence. He tries to give a well-rounded account that will include all the *significant* and *relevant* evidence. These last are difficult principles that we deal with later in this chapter. To give way completely to despair of

---

[8] Cf. Jerold S. Auerback, "Woodrow Wilson's 'Prediction' to Frank Cobb: Words Historians Should Doubt Ever Got Spoken," *Journal of American History*, LIV (December 1967), pp. 608–17.

any control over subjectivity in historical studies surely
compels adoption of such attitudes as that public servants
cannot rise above their personal biases, and that we sanc-
tion their refusal to try to do so. To the ordinary person of
common sense, both propositions are rather childish.

D. Relevance and selection[9]

The impossibility in a large research task of using all
evidence remotely touching the subject indicates the need
for selection. Obviously, what is desired is selection of
relevant data. The function of the test of relevance, therefore, is to help in the selection of data. Nothing is more
important in historical investigation, and few things are as
difficult. Sometimes, for one thing, it is not at all clear
whether a piece of evidence is relevant. Also, one's notion
of relevance often shifts during a research task, making
some evidence already selected either totally or partially
irrelevant, and making some evidence that has been dis-
carded now clearly relevant.

One approach is to cast aside "insignificant" evidence—
that is, evidence too picayune or too tangential to be very
helpful. In discussing the development of the blast furnace
we might well decide that the connection with man's original conquest of fire was irrelevant. Often it helps to ask
whether the need in a specific case is to establish facts or
to interpret them or to find causes. If we are simply counting barrels of flour, our needs are different from the case
where we wish to know why congressmen voted taxes on
flour elevators, or in the case where we are interested in

---

[9] The positioning of a discussion of relevance in this part of the
guide must not be taken to mean that the process of determining
relevance occurs only during the later stages of research and composition. Decisions regarding relevance are made from the beginning
of research. Cf. Chapter VIII (A), on hypotheses in the determination
of relevance.

the role American grain played in sustaining the Allies in World War I. It may help to look at parts or aspects of the question under study, and decide what is needed for understanding of each aspect; then, finally, one may know what is relevant to study of the entire subject.

The test of relevance is most easily applied to studies devoted to narrowly defined topics. Suppose the problem is child labor in English factories during the early 19th century. Many facts are clearly relevant: legislation, statistical data, evidence of conditions, etc. But other data may be of questionable relevance: working conditions for adults, general economic conditions, educational institutions. Some of these may help to illuminate the chosen topic, others may not. In any case, there is a danger that the historian will digress more and more from his main concern to the bafflement of his readers.

How can the historian keep on the main path? One useful device is to think of his topic as a proposition, or a hypothesis, to be proved or refuted. The proposition might be: English factories during the early 19th century seriously jeopardized the health and welfare of children. Then the test for inclusion would be whether the data either supported or refuted this proposition. In the light of *all* the relevant evidence, the researcher then selects for inclusion those facts that are important and are representative of the total body of the evidence—that is, they set forth the pros and cons in true proportion.

For longer historical works, the problem of relevance is more complex. Yet analogous methods will be helpful. Certain general hypotheses, or a series of hypotheses, may be set up and tested. Or when analysis proceeds by asking and answering questions, there should be serious restrictions on the temptation to diversion into unrewarding irrelevancies.

There is a broader question of relevance that we have referred to in several places: the changing views of historians as to the importance of various aspects of human activity. Medieval chronicles are replete with miraculous occurrences and prodigious feats of arms, but give little data on life among the lower and middle classes. The monkish scholars placed highest value on divine intervention and knightly valor. In contrast to this, 19th-century British and American historians tended to ignore miracles, minimize battles, and emphasize constitutional and legal growth. They placed their highest value on what they liked to call "ordered liberty." In the 20th century, historians have placed increasing stress on economic and social developments and have related political development to these factors.

At least, in each period of historical writing, certain generally-held standards of values provided the historian with a guide as to what was considered important. The process, moreover, to some extent has been an evolutionary one. The earlier selection of events sometimes seems to us not so much erroneous as fragmentary. As men have raised their sights and enlarged their aspirations, their view of the past has widened. For this reason, astute historians will not select data solely on today's values but upon those they believe will come into increasing recognition tomorrow. For example, if in the future scientists are going to play an increasingly important role in human affairs, today's historian will be wise to increase the attention given to the scientific advances of the past and in so doing help to improve the field of historical inquiry.

E. Final synthesis[10]

The final synthesis, and its expression, are the terminal processes of the historical endeavor. The operative word

---

[10] We have dealt elsewhere with such matters important to the final synthesis as causation, motivation, contingency, values, ideas, relevance, laws, hypotheses.

here is "final." Other syntheses, as we have observed, will be made in the course of the research task.

1. IMPORTANT PRELIMINARY OBSERVATIONS

There are three preliminary observations to make about synthesis in general before moving to final synthesis in particular.

a. Digestion of evidence

Adequate synthesis of evidence at any level will not be attained without proper *digestion* of the evidence. This means sufficient reflection on and manipulation of the evidence to permit its meaningful synthesis. This requires poring over the evidence, reading and re-reading it, making preliminary generalizations and combinations and recombinations. If this seems obvious, let it be clearly understood that our many years of experience in teaching historical methods shows that all too often beginning researchers do not familiarize themselves sufficiently with what they have collected, either for purposes of internal criticism or analysis or for synthesis at all levels. These beginning researchers have evidence on notes, in files, but they do not *possess* it mentally. They cannot see interconnections and contradictions simply because they do not know well enough what they have. They think pieces and small groupings of evidence will reveal larger meanings. Not so. The evidence, or facts, do not speak for themselves. The collector must become thinker and puzzle out meanings for himself. Much digestion may be done during the processes of collecting, evaluating, analyzing pieces and groups of evidence; even so, some final digestion will be necessary. If little digestion has occurred during the process of collection and preliminary analysis, toward the end a great deal of digestion will be necessary. It is impossible to overemphasize the importance of this process of digestion, as a necessary preliminary (or accompanying step) to synthesis. We could mention modern nations whose historical output is distinguished by zeal in collection and publication, and by distaste for the hard work of digesting evidence, with really lamentable results.

b. Using other syntheses

Synthesis requires the use of the work (including the syntheses) of other scholars. This is true of all but the smallest research tasks.[11] The investigator will, of course, have been doing much of this since the beginning of his inquiry; now, however, we are speaking specifically of the conclusions (explicit, or implicit in the structure of synthesis) of other scholars. Thus, successful synthesis involves the capacity to judge the quality of work of other scholars. This is, to be sure, a requirement of analysis in external and internal criticism, as well as at all levels of synthesis; at all these stages the investigator will be making use of the work of other scholars. Now, finally, you will be, in a manner of speaking, synthesizing your research with that of others. It is essential to learn to use the work of others well, in order not only to avoid repeating what has been done adequately by others, but to incorporate into your own research and interpretation everything worthwhile that has been done before you. This is not an easy task. Nor is it so obvious a requirement to the beginning as to the experienced researcher. The beginning researcher too often thinks that all his work must be with "sources"—i.e., evidence. Maximum use must be made of what others have done with evidence.[12] One of the many great talents of the 18th century

---

[11] There are few subjects so new that no literature touching them exists.

[12] Cf. Langlois and Seignbos, *Introduction to the Study of History*, pp. 229–31: that "the operations of history are so numerous" that no man can do it alone; history, with its need for millions of facts, should have a proper division of labor, but has never enforced sufficiently rigorous and accepted standards so that such division exists, thus it is difficult to be sure of the quality of scholarly works; but the latter must be used, although "with the same critical pre-

historian Edward Gibbon was his skill in blending the scholarship of others into his own work with evidence.

c. Synthesis as generalization

Some historians affect to be leery of generalization. All historians practice generalization, willy-nilly. It changes nothing to call generalizations explanations. The problem, of course, is finding sufficient evidence for the specific generalization. This means not certainty, as we have emphasized, but sufficient evidence for the assertion of degrees of probability. Few generalizations about large-scale human affairs should speak of certainty. Generalizations usually require qualification: nearly always, usually, almost, in the majority of cases, most likely, perhaps. The term "always" must be used with precision; if there could be exceptions, so far as the researcher knows, the word cannot be used. If all the causation of an event cannot surely be assigned to one source or influence, multiple causation must be admitted as a possibility. Finally, improper use of analogy is a special form of generalization from insufficient evidence. It may not properly be asserted that the creation, development, and disappearance of human cultures involves a natural process akin to the birth, growth, and death of biological organisms, or the fixed procession of the seasons on earth.

The above points having been made, we now discuss final synthesis under four headings: interpretation, emphasis, arrangement, and inference. These processes are interacting and overlapping, but to promote communication they must be considered separately. The first two require little attention. For one thing, they are in fact included under other labels (e.g., generalization, relevance, arrangement), and have been or will be discussed there. But the terms are so often used as to require a word of explanation, and there are some minor points to make.

---

cautions" that are given to contemporary evidence. See Chapter V (C), on preliminary analysis in note taking.

2. INTERPRETATION

Some scholars consider it useful to insist that all of final synthesis is interpretation. And there is value in the claim that most of interpretation is either (1) the finding of causal relations that permit explanations of human events, or (2) assertions of value judgments by the researcher or author. To say that these are the same thing is a counsel of despair; we must assume that there are some things that most (possibly all?) complex human cultures will interpret the same; e.g., some causal relation between loss of nine tenths of the population by plague and a decline in economic production. To be sure, cause of the plague may be assigned to virus, an angry God, emanations from comets, or noxious airs. In any event, interpretation often is in fact synonymous with the usage of explanation, or causation, or generalization.[13]

3. EMPHASIS

Interpretation, generalization, arrangement all result in emphasis; the process cannot work in reverse. There are, however, two things to say about emphasis in the final synthesis: (1) Remember that the *amount* of the account devoted to the subject may give emphasis, as may the *intensity* or skill devoted to a part of the treatment, and even the very order in which matters are discussed. (2) The historian should at least try to define his intended emphases, and struggle to see that they are in fact executed as he wished. The last injunction relates as much to composition as to the mental operations of synthesis.

4. ARRANGEMENT: CHRONOLOGIC, GEOGRAPHIC, TOPICAL

Arrangement, or the grouping of evidence, is interpretation, although it also is necessary in the more narrow sense

---

[13] Cf. Chapter IV (B), on a similar terminological morass involving classifications of evidence as sources, secondary, etc.

of communication.[14] Almost any arrangement except the bare chronologic involves some sort of interpretation or judgment and results in emphases.

The commonest ways of arranging historical evidence during research and in the final synthesis are chronological or topical. Geographical (usually meaning by the territories of political units) is fairly common. In a large synthesis it is common to combine two or all three of these schemes. Even when a primary chronological or topical organization is elected, the major sections probably will be arranged internally in the other manner (i.e., a chronological section may be developed topically and vice versa). Most historical studies might be described as being the chronologic arrangement of topics, or the topical development of periods of time. The easy advice is to suit the arrangement to the evidence and to the principles of interpretation adopted. What is most suitable is not, alas, always clear. Sometimes, indeed, two or more types of arrangement might be equally meaningful.

It is at least clear that all historical arrangements are to some extent *time oriented.* Even if the major divisions are political jurisdictions, and the next level of arrangement is by topics, within each of these the treatment or arrangement will be chronological. The major problem usually is whether the primary divisions should be chronological or something else. In any event, it should be remembered that a merely chronologic organization does not order elements by their importance and a purely topical tends to blur the flow of events in time—that is, to maim the historical content.

It should be noted that following chronological treatment within a geographical, topical, or chronological order, is not the same thing as determining the time period in the first instance. This last, the process of *periodization,* can scarcely be done purely on the basis of time; e.g., a history

---

[14] See Chapter IX (A), the outline; also Chapter VIII (C), on bias and subjectivity, which may affect arrangement.

of the 19th century makes no sense as a group of years from 1800 to 1900, since human affairs do not begin, end, or undergo significant changes in such arbitrary 100-year periods. The regnal dates of monarchs, or the years of presidential administrations, make some sense from certain limited points of view. These must, however, be carefully specified. Much of the life of a nation begins long before the reign or administration commences, is little changed during it, and endures long after it. The value of such "periods" as "The Age of the Enlightenment" or "The Progressive Era" is that they permit emphasis on certain aspects of life during the period stated. The danger is that the impression may be given that all was either enlightenment or progressivism in such periods.

In connection with periodization, the modern tendency is to determine what important developments occurred, in selected realms (e.g., Europe since the fall of Rome, France in the first decades of the industrial revolution, Hispanic America in the colonial period, or the suffrage in England from the Great Revolution to the present), and declare the periodical divisions to fit the results of such inquiry. Thus James Shotwell put it tersely that, since facts can be arranged in various ways, "arrangement is argument."[15]

5. INFERENCE

Inference is the process of reasoning from facts that are not entirely connected. It is used to fill gaps in the record or to supply connections between bits or classes of evidence. To call it "informed invention" is possibly overly pessimistic. At any rate, it should be done tentatively, provisionally, even modestly. Although this type of reasoning or interpretation is as chancy as the assignment of causes, in most investigations it must be used. Remember, that all

---

[15] *The History of History* (New York: Columbia University Press, 1939), p. 198.

inferences are probabilistic. An inference may even be thought of as an hypothesis; that is, a suggestion as to relationships between facts.

The process is to some extent intuitive, undemonstrable, partially free of fact; but it should cling to whatever facts are available. It is not mechanical, but a creative process. It is not, however, inventive in the sense that fiction is contrived. The historian may not move the first voyage of Columbus to 1516 to suit his whim. He must "create" attitudes toward facts by the processes of selection and combination, and by his ascription of motivation and causation. The possible errors to be avoided are numerous, and only a few are mentioned here. It is erroneous to suppose that the ideas, life-styles, etc., of an upper class, or a specialized group (e.g., intellectuals) represent a total society, and therefore to infer connections between "elitist" facts and others that probably have at least some of their grounding in the common folk of the society. It also is dangerous to base inferences involving large groups of people upon what is known of an individual.

Common sense suggests that the more inference is involved in a synthesis, the greater the likelihood of error. The greater the inference, the further removed the interpretation is from the evidence. Common sense also suggests the probability that the larger the synthesis the smaller its relation to reasonably demonstrable fact or what we must call probability. Such metahistorians as Toynbee necessarily deal largely in inferences. This does not mean that the largest possible synthesis should not be attempted. It does suggest that modesty might be appropriate in the presentation of grand syntheses.

6. CHECKLIST FOR SYNTHESIS

At this point, some beginning scholars might do best to proceed with the suggestion made above that synthesis is combination, comparison, arrangement of evidence, with connectives provided by inference, and explanations provided by assignment of cause. Other beginning researchers will benefit from further attention to the elements of synthesis, and the approximate order in which they occur. This will assist understanding of a process that is intrinsically difficult both to use and to explain.

We can list at least 15 elements considered in this guide that are important in the process of synthesis. There is no single, always best, answer to the questions of in what order or in what intensity these elements are to be used. In addition, we cannot expect always to be conscious of their use. Practitioners of the craft do not proceed on such a basis. Their synthesis or correlations often are instantaneous (after a lot of preparation); and may be intuitive in the sense that correlation sometimes leaps to the mind apparently without an effort to create it. But researchers do need *sometimes* to be conscious of the elements of synthesis. In any event, in order to discuss synthesis at all, we must specify the elements of the process.

The 15 elements in synthesis are here numbered and grouped into five categories.[16] The roman capitals in parentheses indicate the chapters of this guide in which the primary discussion of each element occurs.

Category one. We may think of the elements in this category as being essentially preliminary to synthesis: (1) literal and real meaning (VII); (2–3) observation and reporting of the detail (VII); (4) bias and subjectivity (VIII).

Category two. We will call this initial synthesis: (5) corroboration, contradiction, and measurement (VII); (6) plausibility, probability, and certainty (III); (7) working hypothesis (VIII).

Category three. We will label this secondary synthesis: (8) causation (I); (9) motivation (I); (10) individuals and

---

[16] There is some overlap—unavoidable and useful—with the nine operations in the "Checklist for internal criticism" in Chapter VII (D).

institutions (I); (11) contingency (I); (12 facts as values, ideas, objects (IV).

Category four. Final synthesis: (13) inference (VIII), which supplies the ultimate speculative connectives.

Category five. Which is really the implementation of synthesis: (14) relevance (VIII), often used earlier in the process also, but now operating at the highest or final level of synthesis; and (15) arrangement (VIII).

7. AN EXAMPLE OF SYNTHESIS

Illustrating the process of synthesis, we continue discussion of "why was the conquest of the Aztecs so easy?", which we began above in dealing with working hypothesis. We will not grapple with all the 15 elements of synthesis listed above (some of which are not even synthetic), but merely try to help the beginning researcher understand the complex process of synthesizing evidence.

We left the conquest of the Aztecs with the tentative hypothesis that a combination of factors was responsible for the easy Spanish victory. We were not certain, however, that we had identified all the factors; even less that we knew the values of the elements in the mix, or how the mix operated; nor were we sure that the factors operated the same in all combat and other decision-making actions involving Aztecs and Spaniards and the Amerind allies of the latter. And we were wondering whether the Spanish conquests of other Amerind groups were replicas of the Aztec conquest; and whether other cases would illuminate the Aztec case. Further, we were aware that explanation of the Aztec conquest is chiefly interesting as it helps explain the larger question of the Spanish conquest of the Amerinds generally.

So the next step is to look at Spanish conquest of Incas and Mayas. These turn out to have been accomplished rapidly by small bands of Spaniards, and much as in the Aztec case. We become convinced that the Amerinds simply could not resist the Spaniards. We put to one side the special difficulties in the Maya area, and decide that the most advanced cultures and largest concentrations of population succumbed quickly to small forces because of certain identifiable factors.

The next step is examination of relations between Spaniards and the lower Amerind cultures. At once we are in trouble. The Spaniards found it difficult in many cases to conquer Amerinds of simple culture.

Great doubts remain in some cases, involving both higher and lower cultures; about the observation and reporting of details of negotiations, agreements, battles. But so many cases have been investigated, and so much corroborative evidence has been found, that at least the gross physical events seem clear—we believe that we know *what* happened with a high degree of probability, who fought when and where and with what casualties and with what physical results.

We now state that the highest Amerind cultures succumbed more easily than many of the lower. This raises questions: (1) why did not *all* of the lower resist with about equal success? and (2) why did *many* of the lower resist more successfully than the higher? As for the former, we find that sometimes the location (e.g., on islands) of the Amerinds made it difficult for them to resist, because they had few remote redoubts into which to retreat and from which to sally forth to the attack. We find, also, that some Amerind groups were less accustomed to warfare than others.

The next question might be: Of those who resisted rather successfully, did some do better than others? The answer is yes. Some groups put up serious resistance for centuries —e.g., in Costa Rica, Chile, Argentina, northern Mexico. Why? Terrain? Leadership? Strength and persistence of Spanish effort? We inquire: Did the Spaniards try as hard against the lower culture groups? How do we measure this? By the number of Spaniards? The number of Spaniards in proportion to Amerinds? By weapons (e.g., number of firearms)? By persistent effort over the years? By the intensity of Spanish effort? And how do we measure? A possible approach to intensity can be made by coupling it with statistics on the size and direction of Spanish efforts and with indications of the nature of Spanish interest in their efforts.

The size of Spanish efforts usually can be tabulated. The nature of Spanish interest is clear: it was economic (understanding that a desire for status and authority depended upon the acquisition of wealth). Wealth meant either precious metals or access to large numbers of Amerinds who were accustomed to working regularly under direction. We find some correspondence between the size of Spanish efforts and the presence of one or both of these factors; and we speculate that the intensity of Spanish effort varied in proportion to the presence of these two possible rewards.

We are further encouraged by the observation that the patterns of early Spanish settlement tended to coincide with the presence of precious metals or of the Amerind concentrations mentioned. We accept this as a working hypothesis, but soon must temper it with the observation that Spaniards also settled in places without these characteristics, so that the generalization is: early Spaniards *often* settled in areas offering precious metals or concentrations of Amerinds accustomed to working regularly under direction.

Does there seem to have been some relationship between the schedule of Spanish military operations, their size, their intensity, and their uninterrupted duration, on the one hand; and on the other the presence of either precious minerals or concentrations of Amerinds accustomed to working regularly under direction? The answer is that there is considerable correspondence, but some at least partial exceptions.

We have not yet grappled with the possibility that variations in Amerind culture affected the ability of the indigenous population to resist conquest. (We may have begun by now to consider the possibility of limiting research to specified aspects of a problem frequently sprouting new ramifications.)[17] Important cultural differences between Amerind groups clearly existed. It is sometimes difficult, however, to demonstrate that they were pertinent to the question of easy conquest. Some cultural characteristics we consider were not relevant to this issue, some we cannot know about, and some apparently had some relevance (considerable inference is involved here). Aside from the high population concentrations and regular patterns of labor under direction, there were in higher and quickly conquered cultures rigid class systems with little social mobility, high differentiation of labor, elaborate political structures, religious legends involving white gods, systems of tribute between dominant and inferior states, military mobilization systems and armies of considerable size with hierarchic organization, and governmental jurisdiction over wide territories. We find some high cultures paying tribute to others, even warring with them. The Spaniards allied themselves with some groups against others. We hypothesize that the lack of political unity among Amerind groups, and the lack of a sense of "Amerind nationalism or culture unity" were major factors in conquest everywhere. But where the largest political jurisdictions existed (Inca, Aztec) conquest was most rapid because the defeat of the "national" armies left much of the population ready to accept the result without much further resistance. Indeed, the loss of an important leader of the military hordes of the higher cultures tended to lead to panic.

Things were otherwise with lower culture groups. Defeat of a group in battle often resulted in tribal retreat, continuing the struggle as guerrillas. Further, the fate of one small tribal group might have no influence on decisions of another. There was no winning a war at one fell swoop. There was no war, but unending skirmishing.

---

[17] This problem of confining the subject is introduced to warn the beginning researcher of a problem surely to be encountered. See Chapter II (B).

We will not pursue the problem of interpretation of this difficult subject of the character of the Spanish conquest of the Amerinds, to say nothing of the even more important question of the results of that conquest for the Spaniards, the Amerinds, and the rest of humanity.[18] Let us consider, instead, two possible ways, with variations, of arranging materials on the subject.

The large mass of evidence might be arranged into three categories: (1) activities before battle, including negotiations, treachery, acquisition by Spaniards of Amerind allies against other Amerinds, and the benefit Spaniards received from Amerind fears of Spanish animals (horses, war dogs) or weapons (especially firearms) or supposed supernatural origins; (2) the evidence of the battlefields; and (3) post-battle activity, which sometimes included astounding surrenders by huge populations. This arrangement permits a form of comparison of critical elements that might be illuminating. A variation of the arrangement would be to use the three divisions, but group the cases being analyzed into lower and higher cultures.

Another potentially useful arrangement would be in terms of two classes of Spanish advantages over the Amerinds: (1) physical, and (2) psychological or social. Or the latter might be divided into two classes. The entire arrangement could be under these headings, or there could be subheadings under the prebattle, battle, and post-battle arrangement suggested in the preceding paragraph.

Physical advantages included such things as acquisition of Amerind allies (psychological and social factors also were involved here), horses, iron or steel swords and lances,

---

18 It likely, of course, that the historian would have developed interest in other important matters also; e.g., whether the differing ease of conquest with reference to culture groups related to crown impatience with the actions of *conquistadores*, cruelty to Amerinds by Spaniards, ease of chistianization, introducton of new labor systems among the Amerinds by the conquerors, introduction of African slaves, or the incidence of race mixture involving Spanish men and Amerind women.

firearms, war dogs, sometimes ships. The psychological and social advantages of the Spaniards may be said possibly to have had their basis in human nature, and they clearly related to the Amerind cultural condition. Panic in the Amerind ranks sometimes resulted from relatively minor events. It seems that if the Amerinds had possessed the fierce individualism of the Europeans, they might have resisted better, both in battle and thereafter. Thus, among the higher cultures, great populations and territories fell into Spanish hands after a few battles. Fighting the lesser groups was different because all territorial jurisdictions were small; no event in a tribal area much affected another area; no grand conquest was possible because no grand culture existed, with a rigidly compartmentalized social structure and an authoritarian and hierarchic governing system.

We thus have the beginnings of a multiple-causation explanation of the ease with which a few Spaniards conquered millions of Amerinds. We have considered several possibilities for the arrangement of materials, both for final synthesis and interpretation and for communication or exposition. The latter is considered in the next chapter.

COMMUNICATION: WRITING AND REWRITING

Communication of what was decided is probable fact and most plausible interpretation is the end of the researchers' endeavor. If they can communicate with clarity, strength, and grace they will have achieved all that can be hoped for from craftsmanship and style. The materials of the next two chapters will aid in the development of that craftsmanship necessary to clarity in communication, and hopefully they may lead beyond that to strength and grace in expression.

A. Outlines—Adjusting organization

An outline helps the organization of materials and thoughts, a subject we discussed above.[1] Such attention to arrangement for sense and communication, to be sure, can

---

[1] Chapter VIII (E) 4.

be done without a written outline. Some writers prefer to rely on unaided memory to remember decisions made on a complicated organization, believing that outlines interfere with spontaneity of thought and unduly freeze a composition. A compromise is to have small outlines of sections of the subject, and even to destroy them after a draft manuscript is prepared. Formal outlines, however, seem to serve most beginning researchers best.

Outlining involves: (1) a decision as to the primary categorization of materials; (2) subdivision of those categories; (3) the use of sketch or telegraphic style rather than sentences. Lesser injunctions are that (4) no level in an outline have only one unit (e.g., with an "A," there must be at least a "B," with a "1," at least a "2," etc.); (5) some consideration of correspondence between the number of outline entries and the length of the sections of the manuscript that will be based on them, although this sometimes is not appropriate; and (6) the repetition of materials must be the minimum consistent with good sense. This last apparently simple rule is easier to state than to achieve.

The primary organization of the study usually is chronological or topical; a geographical organization is rarer for historical or social science studies; other types of primary organization (e.g., biographical) are rarer yet. Even when a primary chronological or topical categorization is elected, the major sections probably will be arranged internally in the other manner (i.e., a chronological section may be developed topically and vice versa). Of course, no paper will follow strictly chronological order. Most historical studies might be described as being the chronological arrangement of topics or the topical development of periods of time.

The most important advice about outlines is to remember that they are merely working devices, and that the worker always should be willing to change them. He needs to be on guard against resistance to such change that is apparently based on substantive grounds, but masks rejection of tedious labor and the risk of getting materials confused. Care will minimize the last, and care is the spinal column of the scholarly life.

The following is part of a possible outline of the subject "United States Intervention in the Dominican Republic in 1965," chopped down from an initial effort to deal with all United States interventions in Latin American since World War II:

I. Background of United States
   A. Concern about world communism
   B. Economic and strategic interests in Dominican Republic
   C. Relations with Latin America
II. Situation in Dominican Republic
   A. Major political elements
      1. Armed forces
      2. Political parties
      3. Economic interests
      4. Church
      5. Public opinion and the media
         a. Literacy and levels of education
         b. Press and censorship
         c. Responses of populace to news
            (1) General apathy
            (2) Role of minorities
   B. Socio-economic situation
III. Situation in Washington
   A. Information
   B. Interpretation of information
   C. Interest groups and points of view
IV. Decision to intervene
   A. Reasons and timetable
   B. The intervention
V. Reactions to the intervention
VI. Withdrawal of American forces

This organization pretty well covers the subject and provides for a generally chronological arrangement, with ample provision for analysis of major topics. It might serve as a beginning outline for a book or as the final outline for a paper of 20 to 30 pages.

Some researchers find it valuable to use not only the rather short outline of the main features of organization, but also more detailed "writing outlines," even to guide the composition down to the paragraph level. Such writing outlines can be made just before composition of the first draft, and whenever desired thereafter.

Although the mechanics of the outline device are of some consequence, remember that the purpose of the exercise is the effective organization of materials, both for improvement of the researcher's understanding, and in consideration of the needs of communicating findings.

If a student has properly considered the organization of a study, possibly using the outline device, many of the audience's (instructor's) queries will have been anticipated—partly by perceiving deficiencies in the student's own knowledge and thinking.

B. The importance of writing

Effective writing is a necessity for successful communication, as beginning researchers are told insistently by guides and instructors. The student must accept the seriousness of this injunction, and he must expect to be criticized for defects of sentence and paragraph construction, grammar, spelling, punctuation, word selection, and allied matters.

A number of subjects treated in this guide relate to the final act of writing or communication: for example, the need for thorough digestion of evidence; the problem of organization, aided by general and detailed outlines and the form and types of footnotes. Here we add some suggestions that are valuable for their own sakes, and that will emphasize for the student the need for care in composition. As a practical matter, there is not time in the beginning course in historical method to devote much attention to problems of exposition. If the student's first research paper is returned with severe criticism of the writing, and continued research is a goal, the student must settle down to the study of usage obviously neglected in earlier years. There are excellent guides to the subject.[2]

The student must be clear that good writing is necessary to maximum performance of the historical task. As Pericles put it long ago, "A man who has the knowledge but lacks the power clearly to express it is no better off than if he never had any ideas." The student must be aware also that it is a common mistake of the beginning researcher to allow too little time for writing and rewriting. Many fine professional writers of historical prose have testified to the many times they have rewritten passages of their works. Ask yourself: Have I said exactly what I intended? Is it possible that what I have set down might confuse or seem ambiguous to others? Remember that the first draft is a device for putting initial flesh on an outline or scheme of organization; subsequent rewriting may almost completely replace the initial wordage.

C. Drafts—especially the first draft

Writing is hard work, and the excuses authors find for postponing it are legendary. Force yourself to begin, regardless of mood; there should be no waiting for "inspiration." A poor beginning can be changed later. If the outline properly reflects the material you have collected and your decisions as to its arrangement, the direction of writing should be fairly clear. Of course, work on the first draft often discloses defects in the tentative organization of the paper as set down in the outline. It is common to find that

---

2 Bergen and Cornelia Evans, *A Dictionary of Contemporary American Usage* (New York: Random House, 1957); H. W. Fowler, *A Dictionary of Modern English Usage* (2d ed., rev. by Sir Ernest Gowers; Oxford: Clarendon Press, 1965); Kate L. Turabian, *A Manual for Writers of Term Papers, Theses, and Dissertations* (3d ed., rev.; Chicago: University of Chicago Press, 1967); E. B. White and William Strunk, *The Elements of Style* (New York, 1959). These are compact and sensible guides.

the material will not sustain a separate section that had been planned, and it will in the draft have to be combined with something else. Working with a typewriter is better than handwriting, especially because errors are more evident in typescript; but many writers prefer to do first drafts in longhand. It is not necessary to defer writing until all the research is finished. You may prepare drafts of sections as soon as the evidence seems adequate for a coherent account. Researchers differ, of course, as to how much they require before preparing a first draft.

A good paper or book almost always goes through two or more drafts, at least of parts of the manuscript. At the first try, thorny matters of evidence and emphasis will not always be well arranged, to say nothing of well expressed. The second or later drafts will result in tightened language. Standard proofreader's marks for changes may be used where that is appropriate.[3] First drafts inevitably are wordy, hence the saying, "I could have made it shorter if I'd had more time." Almost always it is possible to delete verbiage to advantage. Certain words—for example, "very" —habitually creep unneeded into sentences. Also, it will be found that phrases used in early drafts can be replaced with shorter phrases, or even with single words by some reconstruction of sentences.

Figure 4. A corrected first draft

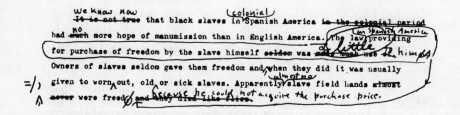

---

[3] See Appendix A for proofreader's marks.

In revising drafts, scissors and paste sometimes will save time, but beware of scrambling the sense and especially of mixing up the citations. In all drafts attention should be paid to having sufficient evidence, examples when they are required for clarification, clearly reasoned interpretations, no excess data or language, no irrelevancies, and an organization that is clear, that carries the argument logically from beginning to end, and that provides strong and clear linkages between the parts of the investigation.

Writing should be directed to an audience, often simply intelligent, educated people. The audience for these papers is the scholar, which means that the exposition probably will be suitable also for the audiences of many public and private report-writing agencies. Clarity—in organization and statement—is the first aim. Whatever the audience, put yourself in the place of the reader as a means of making sure that you state exactly what you have in mind, and leave no room for ambiguity or misinterpretation.

There are several workable methods for putting citations into the first draft. They can be put in brackets in the text; in the margin; at the bottom; on filler sheets of a different color inserted between sheets of the text. Also, it is possible to use short footnote references in the first draft, if it is clear that they will lead to the proper research notes when completed footnotes must be made later. Some scholars use a code (letters or numbers) in the manscript and on research notes to refer to materials that will be used later for footnotes at the designated places in the draft. Some scholars turn on edge in the files the research notes to be used for footnotes later; some separate them entirely from the general files. Occasionally, it is possible to clip research notes to the proper pages of the draft for later composition of footnotes at designated points; but in a large research task this seldom is feasible, except when working with small sections at a time.

This last offers one method of reducing the difficulties. If the investigation is well enough arranged, and is of the proper character for such procedure, you may be able to write a draft of a small section of the subject, with indications of places for footnotes; then immediately do the section over, improving style and organization as required, and making the footnotes from the small research note file being used for the section. Some writers do not put citations in the first draft; others put only some of the major items; others feel comfortable only when fully documenting as they go along. The only requirements are that the final draft be adequately documented, and that the method used for that purpose be the result of thought and planning, and as efficient and accurate as can be contrived.

How long should the paper be? In our experience most good papers resulting from one semester of work and following our procedures and requirements are between 25 and 30 pages, including footnotes and bibliography. Most longer papers would benefit from tightening of the exposition and especially from strengthening of the supporting evidentiary base.

A few other suggestions may be made. Avoid crowding pages, so as to leave room for insertions and other changes. Sometimes gaps may be left (properly labeled) for material that clearly is required. When inserting extra pages, be careful not to get the citations scrambled. The draft need not be pretty, so long as it can be puzzled out from deletions, insertions, and other changes. Avoid excessive quotations. Yes, give your own "opinions" (i.e., views founded on stated evidence). Do not hesitate long over style and polish at this stage.

D. Aids to effective writing

Effective writing certainly should be precise and clear, and if possible also vigorous and interesting. Some rules and precepts generally are accepted in this area, but there is much disagreement on usage and style, and even more on how to teach them. There is agreement, however, that above all practice and thought, writing and rewriting, are needed to develop clarity, facility, and grace. Logic and consistency in argument also are qualities that are indispensable for effective writing.

1. *Sentences and paragraphs.* At the least, a sentence should make sense and have a subject and predicate. Phrases masquerading as full sentences obviously must be altered. Aside from that rule, the most important requirement is that a sentence be clear beyond doubt. Few sentences are as badly formed as the following: "The sheep strayed while the shepherd ate his dinner and nibbled the sparse grass." And this sentence is easy to reconstruct as "While the shepherd ate his dinner the sheep strayed and nibbled the sparse grass." More common than such cripples are sentences that simply have too many or unsuitable words. We no longer admire 18th-century sentences that spread their dependent clauses over a dozen lines. The following is a moderately horrible example of a sentence that should be broken into several: "The pack-mule driver in 19th-century Arizona, often a Mexican or a Mexican-American and part Indian, possibly knowing little English, in many cases entered into agreements with store-keepers—usually Anglo-Americans, to purchase supplies in return for haulage business, with the result that a species of monopoly raised transport prices for persons not a part of the arrangement, and that led ranch-owners to set up their own mule-trains and mulewagons." The example is at least clear, but indulgence in such interminable sentences inevitably leads to trouble.

It usually helps to have close together nouns and the adjectives describing them, verbs and modifying adverbs, and qualifying phrases and the things they relate to. Varying the length or the construction style of sentences often will lend both force and charm to the composition. Finally, it often is thought useful to open a paper or a chapter with a statement (sentence or paragraph) of intent, which may also set the tone of the work. It is important to compose (and recompose) these with the greatest care. The same may be true of concluding sentences or paragraphs.

The successful paragraph is a joy to writer and reader. Generally, it consists of one subject or closely linked subjects, with the linkage made explicit. Often, it should begin with a topic sentence, stating, or at least intimating, the matter to be discussed. It requires ingenuity to provide variety in such opening sentences, to avoid a stiff and mechanical effect. It is helpful if the opening sentence also serves as a bridge from the preceding paragraph, but that sometimes is difficult to arrange satisfactorily. The argument or elaboration after the opening sentence should be relevant to the subject or linked subjects of the paragraph. Abrupt changes of subject within paragraphs should be avoided; they probably indicate that the material should be in a different paragraph. Nothing is more common in student compositions than sentences that have little or no connection with the matter immediately at issue. Delete or transfer such material.

Also, the order of discussion in the paragraph is important; that is, the meaning of each sentence should flow from that of the preceding sentence. Finally, the paragraph often should conclude with a sentence summarizing or concluding an element the next paragraph can echo. Thus, a large part of successful paragraph construction consists in *transitions*—between paragraphs, and between sentences within paragraphs. This calls for care in the use of transitional or connective words or phrases; e.g., still, yet, of course, nevertheless, but, moreover, even, all too often. But more than anything else, the paragraph must be *coherent*. If it is not, the reader will not rearrange it for you. He may forgive a poor sentence, but a poor paragraph is too much. It is for this reason that careful authors lavish care on paragraphs.

There is no law on the length of paragraphs. Those of only two or three lines are more common in journalism than in scholarly work, but some of that length are allowable in the latter. Single-sentence paragraphs should be used sparingly, but they occasionally are useful.

Most of the above should be regarded as guidelines. Paragraphs are not made precisely to formula. Sometimes, for example, a coherent subject is split into more than one paragraph in order to give the reader smaller units to grapple with.

2. *Word selection.* An interest in language and writing often begins with a fascination with words. That fascination has fastened itself on a person when a dull pebble in the heap of words suddenly blazes like a ruby in a new or newly-perceived context. We see this happen with children, with newly-literate adults in underdeveloped countries, and with students taking up seriously for the first time the tasks of researcher and writer.

Without a touch of that fascination it is difficult to become an accomplished writer, because much of that art consists of word selection. That selection is firstly to attain precision and secondarily to compel attention. Precision needs no defense, but the importance of capturing attention needs emphasis, as in the old prescription for giving orders to a mule: "First, hit him between the ears with a two-by-four; then, having caught his attention . . . ." Readers, alas, have learned from experience that full alertness while reading often is wasted energy. A writer, therefore, is well-advised to find graceful equivalents of the two-by-four.

a) Emphasize nouns and verbs in writing. This means both selecting them with care, and making them bear the burden of the sentence. Adjectives and adverbs, thus, should be used sparingly. It is obvious that much gooey writing is due to overuse of adjectives. Excessive adverbs also are common, with "much" and "very" often used without adding to content or to euphony. An example of excess verbiage is: "Industrious and conscientious Charles V labored long and hard and without success to contain within minimum limits the spread of what he considered the pernicious and disgusting Protestant heresy." Much the same is said briefly and with more impact in "Charles V spent his life trying, with sparse success, to defeat Protestantism."

b) It follows from this that all "overwriting" should be avoided. Although that most often results from a surplus of phrases making the same point, or from excessive adjectives or adverbs, there can also be too lush a supply of nouns or verbs. As a variety of overwriting, sensationalism also should be avoided; that is, exciting—even brutal— effects for their own sake. Pretentiousness also is a form of excess, and one to which scholars are not strangers.

c) Empty, tired, or pallid words should be eschewed. Try to make the important words in the sentence serve a semantic rather than simply an esthetic purpose. Words that are rather empty of meaning because they have been overworked can be filled with meaning by use in a new context. Even words that have not been overworked can be given fresh or different vigor by new use. "Sanitary," for example, is a word with sufficient content in discussions of drainage, but it can be given a new and strong content by use in the sentence "Smith's conversion to sound tax principles had a sanitary effect on the financial policies of his party." Writers may invent such new uses of words, but in case of doubt reference should be made to a good dictionary.[4] For synonyms a thesaurus is useful.

d) There is, of course, no rule more important than accuracy. It does not do to have physicists "feeling" that particles act in certain ways; they "think" about particles. "Not all that large" is a linguistic abortion that does not really mean "small." "Chaos" is not the merely messy social disturbance that some journalists imagine, but something much grander. "Anarchy" is not merely "violence," as

---

[4] Use *Webster's New International Dictionary* (2nd ed., unabridged). The condensation, *Webster's New Collegiate Dictionary*, is much cheaper but excellent, and includes in the back abbreviations, rules of punctuation, capitalization, compound words, hyphenization, and allied matters.

some people suppose. An "ironic" occurrence is not merely somewhat comic, as seems to be the supposition in some quarters. "Always" and "never" should seldom be used; they are too drastic for most of human history.

e) A successful war on jargon and "trendy" expressions will do something for sense and grace, thus appealing to the interest of the reader and to his understanding. Jargon has been called "language which is more technical than the ideas it serves to express," fake technical language, and technical terms used out of the context in which they are technical. Jargon was present in writing before modern times, for example, in theological tracts; and there is nothing wrong with technical terms in specialties. But jargon now flows into general use from many specialties, including advertising, the universities, and the great government bureaucracies. Such specialized language often conveys insufficient or incorrect meaning to the general reader; even more often will it be irritating; and in any event usually it is unnecessary. It is irritating when the stock market suffers a "technical decline," and when "methodological models" are thought classier than "research methods."

Jargon merges into the trendy vocabulary of the moment, fashionable terms. "Seminal" is one that scholars have adopted with enthusiasm to stand for "extraordinarily fruitful," or simply for "important." Unfortunately, we now have seminal studies of subjects that do not matter. "Empathy" threatens to become a synonym for almost any form of sympathy or understanding. Many persons currently seem afflicted with the idea that "motive" is something different and less elegant than "motivation." "Crucial" is now the outcome of football games, which rather dilutes a strong word. "Classical" now is anything that has a history of a few years, as the "classical Packard touring car of 1926."

f) Clearly, faddish language sometimes slops over the border into slang. We have no need for "truthwise" or even for "meaningwise." "Like the Civil War was some buzz," we can easily do without. The locution "at this point in time," so depressingly aired at the Watergate hearings, offers nothing to students of the language. The obscenities that a few professors recently thought necessary in order to achieve rapport with their students, and more than a few novelists think necessary to keep up their royalties, happily appear unlikely to become common in historical literature. All subjects now can be discussed, and that is salutary, but it creates no requirement for a scatalogical vocabulary.

g) Use care in the use of linkage words (and phrases). "But" shows an opposition; e.g., "Paul loved Mary but she would not talk to him," is better than "Paul loved Mary and she would not talk to him." It will not do to say "Napoleon was a great general; however, he was a tyrant." The connective "however" requires the existence of a link between the statements. Better usage would be: "Napoleon was a great general; he also was a tyrant." Or, it is proper to state: "Napoleon was a great general; however, that did not mean that his military judgment was infallible."

"Although" is another problem link: for example, "Although Charles V was moral and hardworking, he failed to achieve his aims as king of Spain or as emperor of the Holy Roman Empire." The "although" is used improperly because it implies that morality and industry should have ensured success in the cutthroat domestic and international politics of 16th century Europe, whereas (another connective) the policies and strengths of other states also were important, as were Charles's intelligence, the information and advice available to him, the economic and military forces he had available, and a number of other factors. Care also is needed in using the following: moreover, nevertheless, whether, and since.

h) Beware of misuse of the definite and indefinite articles, as in: "An emperor of China once had kidnapped the beautiful princess of Central Asia." That is a large area of indefinite boundaries and often contained a number of kingdoms. Better would be "a beautiful princess," or "the beautiful princess of a Central Asian kingdom," or, if appropriate, "the beautiful princess of the Kingdom of Central Asia."

i) Many combinations in English of verbs with prepositions are exact for given purposes only: shake up and shake down, call up and down. You play with a baby and to an audience. You run on in conversation and also run on the playing field, but with a difference. You dance to the tune of the dictator or dance in tune with it, and a court may some day decide which. It is one thing when you agree to the boss's suggestion and another when you agree with it.

3. *Grammar and usage.* Grammar, usage, punctuation, and spelling are important to writer and reader. A few common rules and problems are listed here. The reference books recommended above deal with many others. (1) Be careful of verb tenses. This is a matter both of avoiding confusion and ambiguity, and of arriving at a pleasing style. Beware of mixing tenses unduly in a paragraph; sometimes it is not proper. (2) Use the active (subject of the sentence performs the act) voice rather than the passive (subject is acted upon). The active voice usually is shorter, clearer, and stylistically more pleasing. It is better to state: "The herald blew the trumpet at dawn, arousing the army for battle," than, "The trumpet was blown at dawn by the herald in order to arouse the army for battle." (3) Search for errors and ambiguities in the agreement of pronoun and antecedent and of subject and verb. An example: The lieutenant told the sergeant to get the men moving as soon as they ate, and the sergeant relayed the order to the corporal, and he shouted, "Everyone hit the road in twenty minutes!" So, which of the three men shouted? Probably the best guess is the corporal, but the writer should not make the reader guess.

(4) Avoid misplaced modifiers; be certain that it is clear what word is being modified. (5) Watch for proper usage of I and me, and who and whom. (6) The usual rule is to spell out numbers of one or two digits, or any at the be-

ginning of a sentence. (7) Beware of such compound nouns as "peer contestant types," in this case doubly abhorrent because it is jargon. (8) It is good practice to overdo guidance of the reader, rather than the opposite. Beginning researchers tend to overestimate the knowledge of readers. (9) Write in the third person, although now a frank "I" often is preferred in some contexts (for example, discussion of bibliography, method, interpretation) to such awkward phrases as "the present writer." (10) Sexist expressions should be avoided, as a matter of justice and to meet current publishing standards. (11) It is pretentious to try to inflate the importance of findings by adopting the language of other disciplines; e.g., voting habits can be described adequately without recourse to the locution "inversely proportional to." (12) Be careful in the use of figurative meanings, as sarcasm, irony, deliberate exaggeration (hyperbole). The problem is that readers may take the expressions literally. (13) Euphemisms, deliberate retreat from fact by using obscuring terms, now are considered feeble and unnecessary: for example, "passed away" for "died" or "fallen in battle" for "killed in battle." (14) It is worth repeating that excessive repetition is bad usage, split verbs should be kept to a minimum, and excessive modifiers are a plague. (15) Abbreviations seldom are used in the text of an historical paper; they are more acceptable in footnotes, bibliographies, and appendixes.[5]

Diligently look for mistakes in spelling and punctuation. It is amazing how easily they can be overlooked. When in doubt, consult a dictionary or manual of usage. You cannot throw this burden onto the instructor, just as the professional researcher cannot expect it all to borne by an editor. Great care and patience are nearly as important in achieving proper spelling and punctuation as are knowledge and access to reference works. Sloppy practice in these realms not only may affect meaning, but it tends to reduce general

---

[5] See Appendix B for some common abbreviations.

confidence in a writer's sense of responsibility and dedication to precision. "Pray" when "prey" is intended, or "council" when "counsel" is meant create a sad impression.

Reading a sentence aloud is a useful way of determining whether the punctuation contributes to the intended sense. Among the commoner rules to bear in mind are: (1) if you are not firm on the use of the semicolon (and many people are not), you had better construct two declarative sentences separated by a period; (2) use a comma to separate the coordinate clauses of a compound sentence when a coordinating conjunction (e.g., but, for) is used, but if there is no conjunction, use a semicolon; (3) put a comma after a subordinate clause that precedes an independent clause in a sentence; (4) if you are not firm on the use of hyphens, see a usage manual.

4. *Progression of ideas.* The progression of ideas to be followed by the writer usually is set by the organization worked out by him in the process of collecting and analyzing evidence; that is, the organization has dictated a certain progression of ideas before any drafts have been composed, except, possibly, of isolated aspects of the subject. With full-scale drafting, the organization may be altered drastically, but more likely the changes will be in detail rather than vertebral. In any event, ultimately the writer has an order of themes or ideas or sub-subjects that he wants to flesh-out with full sentences, paragraphs, and illustrative material; and he will expect the whole succession or progression of ideas to have a cumulative impact upon the reader. That cumulative impact will be made up of weight of evidence, cogency of reasoning, and linkages between all the parts that will make up the whole body of work. Alternative flows may be possible at certain points, but the main line of argument must progress. This is a matter of good judgment, close observation, and art.

When the proper flow of argument has been determined by research, analysis, and synthesis, the chief peril to the progression of ideas is digression. We have spoken of digression in connection with the paragraph. Digression that interferes with the progression of ideas in the total paper obviously may be more damaging than when it mars a paragraph. Unfortunately, digression is one of the besetting sins of the writer, so beguiling that even people who really know better will defend the practice, if not in theory, at least in specific instances. The multivolume philosophy of history of Arnold Toynbee, often damned by historians as a hash of vast generalizations put together out of scanty evidence, sometimes is praised by the same critics for the erudition and fascinating detail of its illustrative material. Since that constitutes some three quarters of the work, its quality and quantity are serious matters in judgment of the total. Too much of the illustrative material deviates, much or little, from the main line of argument, thus is plain digression. In addition, great stretches of pertinent illustrative material seriously interfere with the main line of argument simply because of their length, so length itself at times amounts to digression. The question of course, is how to know when illustrative material appropriate to the argument approaches excessive length. Only taste—of writer and reader —can decide.

It is obvious that many digressions are irrelevances, and the human mind cannot easily follow an exposition that allows too many irrelevances. So, stick to the subject. Do not wander, or if you do, consider whether you lose more than you gain with the reader. It is the reader and his understanding and appreciation you care about. Do not be that bore, the narcissistic writer, who wallows in admiration of his words regardless of their effects on others. Cultivate instead a satisfaction with effects you think you are likely to achieve with readers.

5. *Errors of reasoning.* There are compositional faults that amount to errors of reasoning or logic or to the obscuring of fact. Some might also have been discussed in our section on grammar and usage. Many of these occur during the data collection and analysis processes and are perpetuated

in the exposition later; some others are introduced during the process of final composition. Whatever the origin, they must be watched for during the writing of drafts and revisions. A few of the more common are listed. (1) The *non sequitur*, as in "President John Kennedy had great difficulty getting congressional approval of his domestic legislation, and he was assassinated." Clearly, the last part of the sentence does not follow in reason from the first. (2) Tautology —hidden or needless repetition. Poor Pres. Calvin Cooledge is picked on frequently for having supposedly intoned: "When people are out of work, unemployment results." That is a delicious howler. Only a trifle less tautological was the common declaration of Spaniards in colonial America that came close to an assertion that Indians worked little because they choose not to work, being invincibly lazy. It was an explanation that did not explain—and in addition was untrue.

(3) Anachronisms deal with events or ideas as though they occurred at times other than those times when they did occur. You thus have events occurring before other events that in fact preceded them in time, or ideas or attitudes supposedly current before they in fact existed. The historian must be careful in dealing with human slavery in the past so that in his proper condemnation of the institution he does not impute to its ancient practitioners our contemporary attitudes. When that imputation is made, it becomes difficult to understand what those ancient slaveholders thought they were doing, or why they did it, or what were the surrounding sociopolitical conditions that made their attitudes workable. A somewhat less obvious example is: "President John Kennedy, in not ousting Castro, opened the door to his later interventions in Africa." The statement implies that Kennedy should have guessed that Castro might later intervene in Africa, something that only a veritable crystal ball would have made possible. Even if the statement is taken only to mean that Kennedy's failure to oust Castro made him responsible for any later Castro actions, it implies anachro-

nistic ability to guess Castro's trouble-making propensities and capabilities with aid from the Soviet Union that scarcely could be predicted.

(4) It is squalid practice to depend on factors not pertinent to the argument; for example, by flaunting one's expertise or reputation in an effort to muffle criticism by the unanointed. Blatant efforts of that sort occur. Less obvious varieties of the same malpractice are seen in excess quotation in obscure languages, jungles of footnotes, convoluted syntax and pretentious vocabulary, and efforts to bury dissent under multivolume sets of redundancies.

A form of this is the *ad hominem* argument, which shifts attention from the question to its critics so drastically as to obscure the central argument. The history of legislative bodies offers rich examples of flight from argument to character befoulment, the dirtied opponent being supposedly incapable of clean argument. Historians sometimes do much the same by battening on a critic's faults rather than replying to his complaint of their own.

(5) Misleading use of analogy. It is common to state or imply that when things agree in one or some respects, possibly they agree in even more. That notion certainly has led to discoveries of value in science, and suspicion has been converted to certainty. In historical analyses, however, that is not to be hoped for, although analogy may usefully stimulate the imagination of the researchers. Historians do use analogies (and metaphors as a form of analogy) in profusion, either because they cannot prove their contentions with evidence, or because they love the imagery, or to make a point of probability or plausibility rather than of proof, or because they do not understand what they are doing.

The heart of the matter is that no analogy is "perfect," because that would be not an analogy but an identity. What analogies all too often do is create illusions of proof. Some analogies are "better" than others in that the distance from identity is less, so the degree of illusion is less. Of course, in practical affairs analogy is used constantly; for example, to combat "appeasement" of an aggressive foe, said to resemble fatally an earlier one supinely unopposed; or against stronger rules against libel by the media on the grounds that censorship by the Inquisition started in a small way. Military intelligence and journalism are only two of the fields that labor under the illusion that analogy aids prediction. Reliable historical statistical series may aid prediction— for example, of population growth—but analogy will not, except by stimulating thought.

We alluded in Chapter III to the perils of analogies between meteorological and human social phenomena. The "winter of our discontent" is excellent poetry, but civilizations know no seasonal changes. Possibly it does no harm to depict a "culture withering in the freezing wind of tyranny"; except that some readers may develop the erroneous notion that there must be an exact correspondence between the degree of popular participation in government and the florescence of literature and art.

(6) False dichotomy (two-part division). This currently fashionable "either-or" opposition is easily abused, and often is more misleading than it need be. If the two elements of the supposed dichotomy in fact overlap, it is no dichotomy. It is no answer to say they overlap in no "essential" way, or that the dichotomy "essentially" exists. Such essentiality requires much proof when the supposed dichotomy involves complicated historical questions.

A dichotomy often asserted or implied in Brazilian economic history is that it has known only "boom or bust." Even when that is reduced to the claim or imputation that the two conditions have strongly and unusually affected the Brazilian economy, some of the dubious and pernicious effects of the dichotomy remain. Whether or not it has been "unusually" subject to states of boom or bust is not established, for that would require a huge comparative effort. Even to define the proper units (countries, colonies), and establish the time periods, would be a formidable problem. Furthermore, no one defines either boom or bust, so we cannot define the chronological limits of either. In addition, the booms that are mentioned involved parts of the economy only, and the thesis ignores the other parts, or simply asserts (or even only implies) that the booming sector had a governing effect on the nonbooming. In fact, some of the nonbooming sectors pursued their way without much influence from the booming, unless it can be claimed that they would have boomed if not damped by the booming sector.

Possibly worst of all is the fact that the judgment is stated or implied to rest heavily on a fatal Brazilian passion for speculation as opposed to productive investment. This passion for speculation permeates interpretation of the supposed dichotomy like a genetic disorder to which Brazilians presumably have been more subject than Roman senators, European supporters of the Mississippi Bubble, or American investors in the stock market in the 1920s.

(7) Cancellation of partial "small" differences. This arises from the practice of declaring that small shades of difference can be ignored. Thus, all grays become white or black, all communists are equally red, socialists of dozens of stripes may be lumped, racism and sexism come in no varieties worthy of distinction. This sort of "lumping" has some use and much abuse.

(8) Supplying answers to metaphysical questions. Beware of claiming to *know* why things happened, and especially large complicated events. You can find out much of the apparent *why* of things, but not all the motives involved or all the intricate chains of events and interests and passions. The impossibility of this search is suggested, for example, by disagreements as to the why of World War I or the American Civil War, and as to whether they were "inevitable." Historians cannot find *proof* for answers to metaphysical questions, in the end because they cannot know everything; neither can scientists. When you come— as most of us do—to *speculation* about *why*, or about in-

evitability, be frank about the speculative part of the answer.

E. Quotations and translations

Each of these aspects of communication has a body of rules and sound practice.

1. *Quotations.* The first two rules are: (a) keep quotations to a minimum, and (b) do not throw the burden of interpretation on the reader. A good beginning will have been made if most research notes consist—as we advised— of summary and paraphrase rather than long quotations. Keep quotations to a minimum, chiefly because you usually can make *your* point most exactly in your own words. As for using quotations to give "flavor" to the paper, remember that condiments in cooking should enhance, not overpower. It is bad practice to drown the reader with quotation, so that he almost has to write your study for himself by puzzling out what the quotations mean.

(c) Do not appropriate anything without giving credit— by using quotation marks and indicating the source. There are three ways of putting quotations into the text. (1) As an integral part of the sentence: Moctezuma complained to Cortés, "You destroy our gods without explaining your own," according to Bernal Díaz. (2) Following a colon at the end of the sentence: Moctezuma said to Cortés: "You destroy our gods without explaining your own." (3) Several lines of quotation may be put as a separate paragraph, *without* quote marks, but distinguished from the text proper by indentation, by smaller type, or by both: Moctezuma said

> You destroy our gods without explaining your own, and expect us to be grateful. And when we attempt to expostulate, you brand us on the face as slaves. How can we make a decision as men under these conditions?

(d) Use single quotation marks for a quotation within a quotation, as in "The historian Oviedo states that Moctezuma complained, 'You destroy our gods without explaining your own.' " (e) Changes you make in quoted material (e.g., spelling, punctuation) must be indicated in brackets or in a footnote. Also, when you supply words in a quotation, to improve the sense, they must be put in brackets: "When 'red beard' [Pedro de Alvarado] arrived at the place, he found 20,000 Indians drawn up for battle." (f) *Sic* (thus) is inserted in brackets in a quotation to indicate that something (e.g., bad sense or bad spelling) is thus in the original, when the reader might suppose the quotation to be inexact, as in "Perfect responsability [sic] I made the mark of my administration." (g) Follow the punctuation and spelling of the original or explain that changes—usually for "modernization"—have been made. (h) Omissions from quotations are shown by three dots; a fourth is added if at the end of a sentence. (i) Put the final quote marks outside of the punctuation mark. (j) Put the footnote reference number outside the quote marks at the end. (k) Authors about to publish should look up the legal position on quotation of copyrighted material. For nonpublished exercises there is no problem. Current law does, however, put limits on the photoduplication of copyrighted material.

2. *Translations.* (a) The most important rule is to get the exact sense in English; that is, you need not duplicate in English the construction of the foreign language; instead, paraphrase. That means for one thing, that idioms need not be translated literally. In translating from English to another language, for example, you might not dare translate literally "Has America lost its edge in innovation?" That meaning of "edge" does not exist in some cultures. You would either explain what the idiom means, or find an equivalent—if any—idiom in the foreign language. And what would you do with: "Stevenson ran again for president, and 'Third strike and out!' "—if the target language had no knowledge of baseball?

(b) If you are not a true bilingual, always remember that you probably are making mistakes; at least that will induce care. (c) The best guides are fine dictionaries and, above all, friendly experts, often at universities. (d) Most foreign language material used in studies meant to be read by others should be translated. This is primarily to aid communication, but it also is a courtesy. (e) There frequently is no need to translate the titles of books. (f) Sometimes a word or phrase needs to be put down in both languages, when there might be dispute as to the translation: for example, "masculine aggressiveness (machismo)," which is a tough one to translate, and depends partly on context. (g) Foreign words inserted into English sentences usually are italicized: The owner of an *hacienda* was the lord of a little empire and the *patrón* of his people. In this case, hacienda might be considered anglicized, thus left without italics; *patrón* more probably would be italicized.

F. Style

Much of what has been said in this chapter about writing relates to style in one sense of that word; that is, it deals with what is necessary and appropriate to good English style. The word style also is used to denote an individual style, as the style of the 18th century historian Edward Gibbon. This latter type of style, an individualistic mode of expression, *in addition to* acceptable English style, cannot be taught. Teachers can help you learn to write—that is, decent English style; the other type of style comes, if it comes at all, only with much labor, and is developed by the writer himself. When he has done that, the style can be recognized and described. Whether a recognizable individual style will be admired depends, however, on the standards and prejudices of the judges, and almost certainly those will be heavily influenced by the fashion of the times. Gibbon's style, admired in his day, is not accepted as a model today; and it is doubtful that Ernest Hemingway's style would have found much favor in Gibbon's time. But you need not try to please posterity, or even everyone today.

You are not writing for comic books, cheap newspapers, porno magazines, shoddy adventure stories, tawdry romances, technical journals, or institutional reports. Your audience is potentially rather large, but it is far from including all readers.

The beginning researcher and writer, following the suggestions of this guide, and of appropriate reference works, may certainly hope to attain clarity of expression; in addition, with much practice, and possibly the help of God, he may aspire to achieve some day that style which Edmund Wilson defined as a combination of "lucidity, force, and grace."

X

COMMUNICATION: FOOTNOTES AND
BIBLIOGRAPHY

Footnotes and bibliographies are important to scholarly activity. There is no need to make a fetish of them, however, and pedantic overuse, to say nothing of downright padding, irritates and disgusts the reader. On the other hand, it is silly to sneer at footnotes and bibliography. They are not confined to scholarly production. Many national and international public bodies (the U.S. Department of Agriculture, the World Bank), and many private institutions, including large business firms, issue reports and studies that have notes and lists of references. Even strategic surveys and estimates by military intelligence agencies use specialized kinds of citations and bibliographies.

A. The form and use of footnotes

In most studies, without citation of evidence (in text or notes), the assertions of the author cannot be checked.

The requirement of reference notes in scholarly work therefore tends to discourage slipshod or dishonest work. The apparatus is lacking in some interpretations of history that have a use in promoting general understanding and discussion, but those works can add little to our store of knowledge. It is only a partial exception when a short study tells us in the text that enumerated new—and usually small—bodies of evidence form the basis of the study; for example, a letter or a diary. Another specialized partial exception is a restricted analysis of quantitative data.

i) There are three common types of footnotes, and they may be combined. One type cites the source of the statement or quotation that occurs in the text. This citation of source is required because there is a quotation, or because a statement of the writer is controversial, or because the origin of the evidence is not obvious, or simply because new evidence is being used. Although there sometimes is disagreement as to which statements require citation of evidence, that is not a major problem. It certainly is agreed that well-accepted facts need no citation, and there are more of those than beginning researchers realize. Finally, the use of one note for an entire paragraph of text is acceptable when the evidence will support all the paragraph's statements. But a multiple-citation footnote for an entire paragraph whose elements cannot clearly be matched with statements in the text is an abomination.

ii) The second type of note is a cross-reference to another part of the paper (e.g., [23]See p. 221 for discussion of this point). The third type of note explains or elaborates the text. This may be done when the material is not critical to the point being made in the text or would unnecessarily interrupt the argument. Examples are: originals of translated passages or discussions of the translation, explanations of foreign or obsolete measures or weights, notes on variant spellings, examination of chronological questions, and presentation of tangential material of many other types. Beware of abuse of this third type of note, which in some works seems to overwhelm the main text.

Footnote styles are numerous, although some of them agree in many respects. Many scholars in social and humanistic studies use either Turabian's *Manual*,[1] or the system of the Modern Language Association. There also are systems for citation of specialized materials in law, religion, poetry, and ancient Greek and Latin classics. Writers subject to the fiat and whim of professors, graduate schools, and editors must, of course, accept their footnote rules. Writers seeking publication do well to request the style sheets of the journals and presses they are interested in, and adjust their manuscripts accordingly.[2] On the position of notes in a manuscript see the section on "Drafts" in Chapter IX.

The detail of footnoting is not difficult, but it requires meticulous attention to rules and to all possible ways of reducing both verbiage and the possibility of confusion from any cause. The following items cover most of what is needed for footnoting.

1. *Different types of materials.* (a) Italicized (underlined in typescript) are titles of books and of series of books, newspapers, and journals and magazines. (b) Articles in journals and magazines are in quotes and not italicized. (c) When citing newspapers give name and date, but not pages, but do indicate (in text or note) whether the item referred to is an editorial, news dispatch, cartoon, or signed column. (d) Volume numbers of magazines and journals are put in capital romans, without "vol." (*Magazine of History*, XV, No. 1, Oct. 1922, pp. 66–69). (e) Manuscript materials take neither italics nor quotation marks. Examples: Manuscript account book of Sergio Goicoechea, August 12, 1792, *Archivo Nacional de Guatemala*, leg. 461, exped. 33; James Delp, New York City, April 18, 1854, letter to Mallory Carpenter, New York Public Library, Delp Collection, File 88.

---

[1] See Chapter IX (B) above. See Appendix B for abbreviations commonly used in notes.

[2] The most radical changes may be in footnotes, but others may be in date forms, capitalization (e.g., for Spanish publishers), or spelling (for British publications).

Oral interviews are treated much the same: Clark Powell, editor of *Manifold,* personal interview with the President of Nigeria at Lagos, November 5, 1978. But an unpublished typescript dissertation is treated thus: Henry Smith, "History of Rye in Dakota," unpublished Ph.D. dissertation, University of Kansas, 1948, p. 33.

2. *Authors.* The author's name is put first, and in regular (not inverted) word order, as John Henry Smith, *History of York* (New York, 1966), p. 12. Be careful to state if there is an editor or compiler instead of an author. The following is an acceptable way of dealing with anonymous or pseudonymous authors: Mary Bopeep [pseud. for Beula González], *Carrie's Kittens* (Boston, 1902), p. 76. A work with a number of authors may be cited: [24]Mark Poole *et al., History of Manumission in Virginia* (3 vols., Boston, 1976), III, 178.

3. *Publication data.* (a) A common style, which we recommend, is to put publication data in parentheses in footnotes, but not in listings in bibliographies. In notes the parentheses often help separate the publication data from comments by the author or other textual material, as in the immediately preceding example. (b) When little-known towns appear in notes, their location sometimes is pinpointed: Geneva [N.Y.] *Crier,* January 12, 1876. (c) If there is more than one volume in the work cited, a volume must be specified (as in the item by Poole under "authors," above). Also, the number of volumes in the multiple-volume work may be given on the first citation, but not thereafter. (f) Put the name of the publisher at the first citation if it serves a purpose. Most modern commercial publishers in countries with a reasonably free press may be omitted.[3]

---

[3] It is easy to locate such publishers if they are wanted. The citation should include publishers if they are apt to be strongly biased (e.g., communist publishers, some church publishers). The publishers of older works sometimes are included as part of the means of identification. For underdeveloped countries, even though the press may be relatively free, the name of the press often is an aid to finding materials and sometimes helps in judging the quality.

4. *Some other important practices.* (a) Use superior numbers in the text to indicate the notes. There can be no deviation from this. Note numbers put in parentheses on the same line as the text are confusing. On the other hand, note numbers sometimes are not raised from their position preceding the note itself. (b) The order of citation is author (or ed. or comp.), title, edition (if other than first), number of volumes (if more than one), place of publication, publisher (if approprate), date (or dates) of publication. Sometimes editors or compilers are put after the title; the usage is not fixed. (c) Be careful with collections of documents not to cite the entire collection if (as is usually the case) a specific document needs to be cited, as in: [12]Parker Johnson to the Rev. Matthias Carter, Pittsfield, Mass., May 19, 1763, in *Collection of Doctrinal Disputes*, III, 67–68. The form of the note indicates that it has been cited before. The point of the present illustration is to assert that frequently you cannot simply state: [12]*Collection of Doctrinal Disputes*, III, 67–68, unless the identification of the document does not matter.

(d) *Op. cit.* (the work cited) and *ibid.* (the same) are used frequently. The use of *op. cit.* is limited to cases in which you have no more than one work by an author; otherwise, a short title system must be used. *Ibid.* refers to all of the preceding citation that you choose to use. If you have more than one work by Boyd, the citations may go:

[5]Henri P. Jacquard, *The Mountain People of Haiti* (New Orleans, 1927), 6. | |

[6]Boyd, *History of Atlanta*, 92.

[7]*Ibid.*, 105

[8]Boyd, *In the Deep South*, 15. (You cannot use *ibid.* here.)

[9]*Ibid.* (That is, even the page number is the same.)

[10]Jacquard, *op. cit.*, 43.

N.B.: Many style systems are strongly insistent that publishers always be supplied at first mention in a footnote or in bibliography listings; others consider that it is enough to have the publishers in the bibliography; still others agree with us that not all publishers are needed; some want no publishers.

5. *Other rules.* (a) Do not use "p." before the number of a page unless confusion might result (*History of France*, II, 66; but *Paris in 1916*, p. 122). (b) We prefer not to repeat in the footnote material that is in the text (e.g., if you name the author and title in text, give only the other bibliographic data in the footnote). (c) Abbreviate bibliographic data as much as possible without creating communication problems. Some style systems insist that in notes the names of months be spelled out; we do not. (d) Any material you supply in notes (e.g., in a quotation) is put in brackets, as in the main text. (e) The first letter in a footnote is capitalized, just as in a sentence: [17]*Op. cit.*, 98. (f) Evidence (primary material) quoted from a study (secondary material) is cited thus:

> On municipal meat contracts the ordinance stated that "no person shall be at the same time involved in the contracts for more than one of the three slaughterhouses."[34]
>
> [34]*Actas del cabildo de Buenos Ayres*, 21 de mayo de 1746, as quoted in Luis Calderón, *Historia municipal de Buenos Aires* (3 vols., Buenos Aires, 1928–33), II, p. 64.

Rather than in such niggling—but necessary—rules, critical methodology resides in the guideline: *It will not always do to give a bare citation of source.* At least in some important cases there must be comment on, even discussion of, the character and value of the data cited (either in the text or the footnote or in both). The citation Henry Adams, *History of the United States*, II, pp. 33, 67–69, means nothing by itself except that Adams was willing to make some statements (and was a talented, diligent, and responsible scholar). What sometimes is needed is some indication of what he based his statements on; e.g., Adams, II, p. 33, citing a letter of Jefferson to Gallatin recounting his own observation of the affair at the wharf, and in 67–69, citing a convincing number of other accounts by 12 different witnesses, most of them members of Congress.

Such analysis may be most complex when a number of sources—hence a number of citations—is involved. Thus, we use the *multiple citation footnote* as a training device in the bringing together of substantial bodies of analyzed evidence in support of findings, weighing the evidence, estimating probabilities, describing the boundaries of doubt, enunciating the question, "What do I *know*, for sure, and how?" In short, this is a struggle with uncertainty, contradiction, and corroboration. Clearly, not all aspects of a research task require or permit such elaborate analysis. A few cases suffice for training purposes. Since a complicated multiple citation footnote can be confusing, the technique of putting together the citations and arguments is of some consequence.

Figure 5.   Illustrative multiple citation footnotes

Number 1. This contrasts the evidence for differing interpretations, thereby implicitly criticizing previous work and supporting the present author's viewpoint.

27   John Chasuble, "Intellectual Origins of Swinners," GHST, XVIII, No. 3 (April, 1947), pp. 58-97, insists that the sect permitted essential freedom of expression, but supports his view only with a few examples of open heterodoxy in a period of 157 years; Pi y Margall, Justificación, 101, suggests that since "everyone" supported control of publication and expression, it was not oppressive, and dismisses imprisonment for heresy as having political rather than intellectual or religious aims, but he cites no evidence for this view; F. T. View, The Swinner Controversy (New York, 1951), 16, 76, 144-56, argues that censorship was unimportant, on the basis of some 1,000 copies of works on the Index that he found in library lists for the relevant period. Cf. W. Blackton, "How to Count," Lancer, X, No. 1 (November, 1959), 90-103, demolishes the View thesis, pointing out that the 1,000 copies of condemned books represented only one percent of the volumes View himself found listed, and probably represented no more than one-tenth of one percent of all the books in the country, even at a modest estimation of the contents of the known libraries of the country at the time.

N.B.: Some of these sample footnotes were invented to illustrate points, others were taken from historical works. Each element in a long note is, of course, illustrative of the rules and guidelines listed above.

234

Figure 5 (continued)

Number 2. Having cited the essential evidence on this issue, this note suggests that an assumption made by well-known scholars may be unwarranted. In this, as in the previous example, the author expresses opinions that are not important enough to include in the body of his text.

18 George Paisley, "Graustark Grain Trade," History
Magazine, XV, No. 3 (March, 1913), 22-56, assigns the policy
almost exclusively to the royal family's interest in the
condition of its estates, founding his view on extensive
examination of the personal correspondence of the royal
family, and on the printed record of the debates in the
parliament. Only Maffick, Diplomatic History, II, 77-78,.
disputes this thesis, on the basis of three letters by
Duke Elmer, and without commenting on Paisley's massive
collection of evidence.

Number 3. Here is detailed the nature of the evidence that underlies the accepted position, but citation of a dissenting opinion demonstrates that the author has not uncritically adopted the argument presented in the text.

27 Numura Cable No. 277, May 8, 1941 (Foreign Office
Archives). Statements in Hull, Memoirs, II, 996, and Langer
and Gleason, Undeclared War, 470, to the effect that Nomura
sent Hull's four principles to Tokyo in April, together with
the "Draft Understanding," represent what would normally
have been a logical assumption in the circumstances.

Number 4. The assumption of other scholars is noted here in support of the opinion in the text, which, as this note makes clear, nevertheless remains merely an assumption.

18 Some leading scholars believe that this was the main
purpose of Lincoln's question. See Benjamin P. Thomas,
Abraham Lincoln (New York, 1952), 189; Baringer, Lincoln's
Rise to Power, 24.

Number 5. In addition to citing the basic document, the author adds to the opinion of contemporaries the evidence he has himself uncovered, evidence that supports their opinion of events and justifies his using that opinion in his text.

Figure 5 (continued)

112 Ravidavia's manifesto of 1821, Ravignani, "El Congreso
Nacional, in "Levene (ed.), <u>Historia de la nación argentina</u>,
VII, Part I, 28. See also Ignacio Núñez to Woodbine Parrish,
July 15, 1824, Alberdi, "Derecho público provincial
argentina," <u>Obras selectas</u>, XI, 101-102; Ravignani, <u>Historia
constitucional</u>, II, 179-183, 186-191. In advocating free
trade between the provinces, Ravadavia undoubtedly had in
mind conditions on the Paraná River. Entre Ríos detained
ships engaged in the trade between Buenos Aires, Santa Fé,
and Paraguay, and taxed them heavily. Agreement between
Buenos Aires and Santa Fé, August 22, 1821, Ravignani,
<u>Asambleas constituyentes</u>, VI, Part II, 150.

Number 6. This is a minimal footnote. It gives an original source for the narrative presented in the text and adds
an important interpretation which challenges a part of that
source.

43 For Botha's speech and an account of this stormy meeting,
see Lloyd George, <u>Memoirs</u>, I, 359-63. Paul Birdsall,
<u>Versailles Twenty Years After</u> (New York, 1941), comments on
Wilson's position, arguing that the President won a considerable victory.

Numbers 7 and 8. These two notes summarize the con-
trasting views of scholars on controversial issues discussed
in the text, a technique that informs the reader of the author's ability to weigh the evidence as well as naming the
authorities on the questions.

1 For good examples of the "conventional" treatment of the
ideas of the Avenir movement, see Alec R. Vidler, <u>Prophecy
and Papacy</u> (London, 1954), 163-83; Charles Boutard,
<u>Lammennais, sa vie et ses doctrines</u> (3 vols., Paris, 1905-13),
II, 137-69; and, more briefly, Adrain Dansette, <u>Histoire
religieuse de la France contemporaine</u> (2 vols., Paris,1948-
51), I, 300-302. A far more perceptive treatment may be
found in André Trannoy, <u>Le Romanticisme politique de
Montalembert avant 1843</u> (Paris, 1942), 170-94.

14 William B. Hesseltine, <u>Ulysses S. Grant, Politician</u>
(New York, 1935), 77-79; Stanton to W. P. Fessenden, Oct. 25,
1866, Huntington Library. Including Stanton as a popular
figure may surprise some, but see a contemporary attestation
to Stanton's general prominence in <u>Miscellaneous Writings of
the Late Honorable Joseph P. Bradley</u>, ed. Charles Bradley
(Newark, N. J., 1901). Such evidence is strikingly
different from recent commentaries on Stanton in Otto
Eisenschiml, <u>Why Was Lincoln Murdered?</u> (Boston, 1937), and
Theodore Roscoe, <u>The Web of Conspiracy</u> (Englewood Cliffs,
N. J., 1959), which should be measured against James G.
Randall's plea for a realistic appraisal of Stanton, in
"Civil War Restudied," <u>Journal of Southern History</u>, VI
(Nov. 1940), 455-56.

Figure 5 (concluded)

Number 9. This is a footnote that contains material some scholars would prefer to put in the text. The decision depends both on the purpose of the study, and on the judgment of the author as to the relative importance of the data.

35 Consulting numerous files of southern newspapers for 1858, I found that Douglas' Chicago speech had a much greater effect upon editorial opinion than did the Freeport doctrine. Denunciation of the latter was confined almost entirely to newspapers already bitterly inimical toward him like the Washington Union, North Carolina Standard, Charleston Mercury, Mobile Register, and Jackson Mississippian. A few journals which had either condoned or only mildly reproved Douglas' anti-Lecompton stand actually defended the Freeport doctrine. Among them were the Louisville Democrat, Richmond Enquirer, and Augusta Constitutionalist. A surprising number of southern newspapers, furthermore, took little or no notice of the doctrine in the weeks after its denunciation, and some, like the Memphis Appeal and Montgomery Confederation, even became more friendly toward Douglas after the debates began. Thus southern press opinion concerning Douglas in 1858 was both varied and variable, but one conclusion appears to be sound: The Freeport doctrine produced no significant change.

B. The formal, annotated bibliography

The list of materials at the end of the paper, after the bibliographic essay, must include everything cited in the paper. In addition, the following materials often are listed: materials that made a contribution to the paper but were not cited, or materials probably of some importance to the subject but which were not used (either because not available or because time did not allow), or materials consulted but found of no use (especially if readers would be likely to suppose they might be useful, a not uncommon circumstance). Usually, do not list trivial and irrelevant items.

Listing styles vary somewhat; if the information is clear, the style is satisfactory. The style in the Turabian *Manual* is acceptable. An entry is much like the first mention of an item in a footnote, except that the last name of the author is given first. The following rules are useful:

1. Arrange items alphabetically by authors (by title if there is no author or editor or compiler).

2. Listings begin at the left margin, and continuation lines also go to the margin.

In the case of multiple-volume items, *do* give total volumes, but not the volumes and pages used (footnotes will show that, where necessary) in most cases.

4. With newspapers, lump the dates of issues used, when feasible; e.g., (a) 1939–42; (b) Aug. 1927–Sept. 1928; (c) scattered issues in 1950–57, 1959, 1960, and all of July 1961–Sept. 1962; (e) March 3–14, 1860, April 1861, scattered issues in 1862.

5. With magazines (e.g., *Saturday Evening Post, The Atlantic Monthly*), as opposed to scholarly journals (e.g., *American Historical Review*), you may sometimes want to list the dates of issues used (e.g., *Review of Reviews*, May 1910–April, 1912), if your chief purpose was to survey public opinion insofar as indicated in the press, rather than to list the names of authors and articles. Your footnotes, however, may often show the names of articles and authors (or editorials or cartoons) from such magazines.

6. Listings may be grouped or categorized. Nearly always materials should be divided between materials contemporary with the period of the study, and more recent studies of the period (sometimes labeled primary and secondary materials). Often the contemporary materials should be subdivided into manuscript and printed materials, government documents, newspapers, diaries, etc. Either the contemporary materials or the studies may require divisions into topical, geographic, or chronologic subsections.

7. Whether bibliographic aids are included depends on the subject or individual preference. Generally, they need not be listed.

8. The extent of annotation varies according to the topic, the item under review, and, in the case of manuscripts prepared for publication, the printing budget. For the beginning researcher, it is wise to over- rather than under-annotate, because the process is valuable in developing a critical attitude. If an item is so nearly valueless as scarcely

to merit annotation, the fact may be stated in a sentence, with a clause indicating why that is the case. The following suggestions usually will be helpful:

(*a*) Indent the first line of the annotation considerably, but carry continuation lines to the left margin.

(*b*) Few items require more than two or three lines of annotation.

(*c*) Annotate: (i) the most useful items; (ii) well-known works (if only to say they were useless); (iii) those you list but do not cite in the paper.

(*d*) Observe the ways in which the annotations in the formal bibliography differ from those on the working bibliography cards; e.g., abbreviations, language, data of interest to the researcher but not to the audience.

(*e*) Do not abbreviate, but be as succinct as possible.

(*f*) In the case of multivolume works, usually it is not necessary to identify the volumes used (footnotes will show that where necessary). Just indicate what the set contains that is important to your subject, and your judgment of the value of that data.

(*g*) The content of the annotation depends to a large extent on the subject under investigation; therefore the annotation comments on the portions of the item relevant to that subject. It is not a book review for the general reader so coverage, style, and "interest" are irrelevant.

(*h*) Strive for meaningfulness in annotation; e.g., a common weakness is to say that an item is "good" or "definitive" or "indispensable," without adding a phrase or two to indicate why. The examples in Figure 6 illustrate some of the suggestions made above.

Figure 6.   Bibliography entries, with annotations

Example 1. This annotation describes, but does not comment on, the content of a multivolume work.

Chalkley, Lyman. Chronicles of the Scottish-Irish Settlement in Virginia. Extracted from the Original Court Records of Augusta County, 1745-1800. 3 vols. Rosslyn, Va., 1912.
Abstracts of will books, muster rolls, deed books, fee books, vestry books; lists of bonds given; reprints of letters. Contains information on Lewis' surveying operations west of the Valley of Virginia, and his land-holding in the same area.

N.B.: These entries generally follow the University of Chicago style and the Turabian *Manual* based on it. We do, however, omit publishers. On this question see footnote 3 to this chapter.

Examples 2 and 3. These annotations explain both the usefulness and the bias of two modern studies.

Justice, Arthur Z. The Patriot Party and the Industrialization Program. Zion City, 1935.
Useful for the party point of view, by a partisan.

Menéndez y Pelayo, Marcelino. Historia de los ortodoxos españoles. 2d ed. 7 vols. Madrid, 1911-32.
A great deal of comment on the Economic Societies, by an advocate of Roman Catholic orthodoxy, who considered the Societies instruments of materialistic philosophy. Undocumented, biased, repetitious, sometimes absurd, it has had great influence.

Example 4. Here, a brief explanation is necessary to describe what an unedifying title does not.

"The Preston Register," Virginia Magazine of History and Biography, II, No. 4 (April, 1895), pp. 399-404.
A contemporary document listing the people killed, wounded, or captured by Indians in Augusta County from autumn, 1754, to May, 1758.

Figure 6 (continued)

Examples 5 through 9. These annotations briefly record those characteristics of items that are important to the author's study.

Arcila Farías, Eduardo. <u>Comercio entre Venezuela y México en los siglos XVI y XVII.</u> Mexico, 1950.

    A valuable and challenging scholarly work, emphasizing the great problems Spain faced in contriving an economic policy for the entire empire, and demanding a re-evaluation of interprovincial trade, especially that centering on New Spain.

Basterra, Ramón de. <u>Una empresa del siglo XVIII: los navíos de la Ilustración.</u> Real Compañia Guipuzcoana de Caracas y su influencia en los destinos de América. Caracas, 1925.

    A mass of assertion without demonstration.

Bunkley, James N. <u>History of the Province of Catawba.</u> 4 vols. Boston, 1920-24.

    A much-quoted and much-condemned economic interpretation of history. It is difficult to determine the basis for most of his sweeping generalizations.

Calvo, Carlos. <u>Anales históricos de la revolución de la América latina, acompañados de los documentos en apoyo.....</u> 5 vols. Paris, 1864-67.

    The Introduction (I, pp. V-CXXXVII) has many statistics (not always well certified) on colonial economic life, especially overseas trade, mining, and government revenues.

Cappa, Ricardo. <u>Estudios críticos acerca de la dominación española en America.</u> 26 vols. Madrid, 1889-97.

    Father Cappa's work is pro-Spanish, and literary rather than scientific, but contains some interesting information and views on the colonial economy, largely that of Peru, and emphasizing the 16th century.

Figure 6 (concluded)

Example 10. An extensive, general, important or "standard" work is assessed and its general line of interpretation outlined in this long annotation.

```
Carrera Pujal, Jaime. Historia de la economía española. 5
vols. Barcelona, 1943-47.
     Covering 1500-1808, emphasizing economic literature
rather than economic life, it is an excellent account of
Spanish views of the country's economic woes, but less satis-
factory as a description of the economy itself. Carrera is
critical of scholars (e.g., Colmeiro) who oversimplify
economic history, but he does believe that the weakness of
manufacturing was the critical element in Spain's economic
thought and action from the 17th century to the 18th, and
notes that the revisionists of the latter were not invariably
sound in their proposals. Fairly extensive use was made of
the publications of Spanish Economic Societies. The study
is primarily based, however, upon writings on economic sub-
jects, rather than on government, business, or other types
of records.
```

C. The bibliographic essay

In the finished work, the bibliographic essay precedes the annotated list of materials consulted. Because it summarizes the nature and adequacy of those materials, however, it is composed after the writer masters these problems by completing the annotated bibliography. The bibliographic essay is valuable to the user of a scholarly work in giving a succinct estimate of the adequacy of the evidence available for study of the subject, and the quality of previous studies touching the matter. Such discussion may, of course, be put in the preface, or scattered throughout the text and footnotes. It is, however, especially valuable when associated with the bibliographic list.

Preparation of the bibliographic essay has great value in the training of the researcher: it forces him to discuss the adequacy of the evidence as a whole, and it compels consideration of the entire body of relevant scholarly studies. Beginning researchers often will not do these things if permitted simply to comment individually on studies and bits of contemporary evidence.

Although there is no standard form or length for the bibliographic essay, in most cases it should:

1. Be short—usually not more than two pages.

2. Deal in a general way with the source problem (i.e., contemporary materials) on the one hand, and with studies of the subject on the other hand. These often should occupy clearly distinct sections of the essay; two large paragraphs should be sufficient. The discussion should emphasize special difficulties, schools of thought, or prejudices affecting workers in the field.

3. Deal with broad *classes* of sources (e.g., manuscripts, public opinion materials, government documents) and studies (e.g., biographies), rather than repeat the annotations to individual items in the bibliographic list that follows the essay.

4. Enlighten the reader as to the researcher's grasp both of the subject and of the research problems involved in dealing with the subject.

5. Give the reader immediate understanding of the adequacy of the materials consulted, and the precise merits or deficiencies thereof for the study of the subject.

6. Be keyed to the subject studied. Remember, you are engaged in a scholarly investigation of a specific subject, not writing book reviews for the heterogeneous audience of the *New York Times*.

7. Do not give full bibliographic data (e.g., author's first name, number of volumes, date of publication), since they are in the list that follows the essay.

The material on bibliographic essays in Figure 7 is meant only as a suggestion; it should not be followed slavishly.

Figure 7. Bibliographic essays
A. *An example, from a study of "The Policy of President Winkler on Graustarkian Watches." This invented bibliographic essay is very informative, but other subjects and bodies of material would require a different analysis. Since the possibilities are numerous, no other complete essays are offered; instead, some extracts from bibliographic essays are supplied.*

Figure 7 (continued)

The official policies and statements of the two governments are well covered in the U.S. Department of State's blue book, *The Graustarkian Tariff Controversy,* and the Graustark Foreign Ministry's *American Economic Imperialism.* While the considerations that entered into American policy remain obscured in the classified files of the State Department, an excellent survey of the elements involved is the article in *Foreign Affairs,* "American Choices in the Current Tariff War," by "N," believed to be a high official in the State Department. The *Congressional Record* reflects the opinions of various interests on the issue, which was widely discussed in the United States. Since the Graustark legislature possesses little authority, and engages in no debate, the few proclamations issuing from that body are merely reflections of the views of the executive power. These proclamations were printed in the officially-controlled newspaper *Verity.* The attitudes of other governments toward this controversy are well summed up in the report of the United Nations Committee on Current Trade Barriers.

President Winkler's rather tortuous course through the dangers of the crisis may be followed in newspaper reports of his public speeches and press conference statements. Of some relevance, also, is the statement of the Democratic National Committee on the occasion of the first meeting of the platform committee at the last national convention, since it gives exactly the justification of Winkler's twistings and turnings that he himself usually gave.

Public opinion in the United States was badly divided on the matter, partly because of the technical intricacies of the tariff, partly because of Winkler's habit of obscuring the issues. The *New York Times* and the *Washington Post* maintained a reasonably dispassionate editorial tone, and occasionally called both pros and cons to task. A good example of rabid opposition to Winkler's policy was the *Chicago Tribune.* A passionate supporter of the president's views was the *St. Louis Post Dispatch.* On the whole, Democratic papers supported the president, and Republican papers opposed his policy on the issue. Generally speaking, editorial opinion was more divided on the moral issues involved than on the strictly economic matters in question.

A peculiar difficulty confronting the student of this affair resulted from the burning of the U.S. Embassy in Graustark, a conflagration that consumed almost all the records of the

244

Figure 7 (continued)
affair kept there. According to a State Department spokesman, some of this data was reconstructed from memory by a three-man team of embassy staff members. The reconstruction is classified and not available to scholars.

Many studies, scholarly and otherwise, have dealt with the question; a large proportion is spoiled by obvious prejudice. These prejudices are sometimes patriotic, sometimes related to political party affiliation, and sometimes related to the ancillary religious controversy between the United States and Graustark. The best analysis of the economic issues is Green, *Graustarkian Economic Aims,* although it is marred by his excessive dependence on the letter of statements in *Verity* and by his neglect of historical materials demonstrative of an undeviating Graustarkian policy in this field over many years. Best on the political-moral implications of the United States surrender to the Graustarkian Tri-State Formula is Smithers, *Appeasement Again,* which is admirably objective.

B. *Some extracts from bibliographic essays.*
(1) From a graduate paper on "The Censorship Struggle in Guatemala, 1800–1821":

This paper was written largely from the eight or nine primary sources noted previously. The historians, as Marure, Montúfar y Coronado, and Montúfar y Rivera Maestre, give little information directly pertinent to the subject. The general literary studies, as Henriques Ureña or Quesada, treat these matters very loosely. A fair amount of scholarly work has been done on small aspects of the censorship and publication subjects; much of it has been published in the *Anales de la Sociedad de Geografía e Historia de Guatemala.*

(2) Two extracts from R. Shafer, Economic Societies in the Spanish World:

Society publications available for the period to 1821 totaled some 10,000 pages (more than 6,000 for Spanish Societies; more than 3,000 for American). Manuscript material in the Archivo General of Guatemala provided necessary additional evidence on the Society of that place. A considerable amount of evidence on the Societies was gleaned from non-Society publications of the late 18th and early 19th centuries. For Spain these were largely the writings of literary figures and government officials, as Jovellanos, Sempere y Guarinos, and Fernández de Navarrete. For America more information was

Figure 7 (concluded)
derived from periodicals, as the *Gazeta de Guatemala,* the *Mercurio Peruano,* and the *Telégrafo Mercantil.*

Previous studies of the Economic Societies are of restricted value. There has been no study of any magnitude of all the Societies—Spanish and American or of all the American Societies. Studies of individual Societies tend to be based on too little evidence, are usually badly organized, and spend much interest on origins, motives, and general attitudes, and relatively little on chronology, statistics, and physical accomplishments, to say nothing of a precise and orderly analysis of ideas and objectives.

(3) *Extract from a paper on piracy:*

The quantitative data available on piracy in the Mediterranean in the 16th century are spotty, but what exists, together with mercantile complaint and lament, and government measures for control, suggest the extent to which it affected marine insurance rates.

And finally

If you have come this far, you have begun a journey that can last a lifetime, and from now on you can teach yourself. There is great satisfaction in collecting, interpreting, organizing, and presenting information. And great service, too. Nor is the need for such service likely to diminish in our complex world.

PROOFREADING

As lines come from the compositor's machine they are arranged in a tray called a "galley," which holds enough lines to make about 2.6 pages in a book. A printing of each galley is a "galley proof," and it goes to the author with marks and queries by printer and editor in the body of the proof or the margins. The author should answer all queries raised by editor and printer, crossing out (not erasing) those that are not satisfactory, and adding his own marks or instructions as desired. Corrections should be made in the margins, opposite the line containing the errors. Use right margin for right half of a line, and left margin for left half of line. If several corrections are needed for one line, the marks are made in the order the errors occur. If there could be doubt as to where the correction is to be made, draw a line from the mark in the margin to the word to be corrected. Matter written in the margin as an explanation or a direction for the printer should be encircled, or it may be set in type.

Figure 8 lists commonly used proofreader marks. Figure 9 shows a proof sheet with proofreader marks in use.

Figure 8. Commonly used proofreaders' marks

Mark	Meaning	Mark	Meaning
∧	Insert marginal addition	wf	Wrong font
ℨ	Delete	x	Broken letter; bad type
ℨ	Delete and close up	tr	Transpose (Mark letters ∪ in text)
⊃⊂	Close up		or
#	Insert space	⌐⌐	Transpose (Mark in margin and also mark words in text)
⊂/#	Close up and insert space	=	Straighten line
∨∧	Space evenly	‖	Align type
ꭚ	Reverse; turn upside down	⊥	Push down space
¶	Paragraph	⌐	Lower
no ¶	Run in same paragraph	⌐	Raise
	or	]	Move to right
run in	No paragraph	[	Move to left
sp	Spell out	□	Indent 1 em
?	Query to author	□□	Indent 2 ems
⊙	Insert period	bf	Set in bold-faced type
⌄	Insert comma		or
:	Insert colon	∼∼∼	Set in bold-faced type (Indicated by wavy line under word or letter)
;	Insert semicolon	rom	Set in roman type
=/	Insert hyphen	ital	Set in italic type
∨	Insert apostrophe		or
∨∨	Insert quotation marks	___	Set in italic type (Indicated by one line under word or letter)
?/	Insert interrogation mark	lc	Set in lower case (Used in margin; draw slant through letter in text)
!/	Insert exclamation mark	caps	Set in capitals
[/]	Insert brackets		or
(/)	Insert parentheses	===	Set in capitals (Indicated by three lines under word or letter)
em	Insert em dash	sc	Set in small capitals
en	Insert en dash		or
		==	Set in small capitals (Indicated by two lines under word or letter)
2/	Insert superior figure or letter	c+sc	Set in caps and small caps
3	Insert inferior figure or letter	stet	Let it stand; restore words crossed out
			or
⌒	Use ligature (Mark ff, æ, etc.)	······	Retain words under which dots appear (Write "stet" in margin)

Figure 9. Marked proof sheet

TYPES OF CONSUMERS' GOODS

Consumers' goods may be classified in not the following three main groups, based on the buying habits of the purchasers: convenience goods, shopping goods, specialty goods.

Convenience Goods

Definition and Examples.—Convenience goods are consumers goods which the consumer usually desires to purchase with a minimum of effort at the most convenient and accessible store. Purchases are of small unit value, are frequent, and are made soon after the idea of purchase enters the buyer's mind.

In a great majority of cases, little fashion element is involved. Groceries, meats, and drug items are important examples. Soap, chewing gum, tobacco, small hardware items, razor blades, ice cream, and gasoline also are in this category. Since such goods are usually purchased in small quantities day after day, they are sold in stores located close to consumers, such as neighborhood or smalltown stores, or are delivered to the consumers doorstep, as with milk, ice, and newspapers.

Many studies make it clear that people actually do treat these goods as convenience items. One study of the buying habits of people living in small towns, for example, reveals that they buy locally 98.6 per cent of their gasoline, 98 per cent of their food, and 95 per cent of their toilet goods. These are primarily convenience goods. In contrast, items such as pianos, high-priced automobiles, furniture for the home, and expensive clothes are usually bought in the larger cities" (*The Main Street Plan* New York: Outdoor Advertising, Inc., 9000]). It was also shown that, while farmers traveled an average of 4.9 miles for gasoline, oil, and groceries, they went 10.1 miles for their furniture and 10.6 miles for their automobiles. In a 1944 study of buying habits, it was discovered that the families of Greater Milwaukee went less than 3 blocks for 46 per cent of their groceries, while an additional 29.2 per cent were purchased within three to six blocks from home.

Marketing Convenience Goods. Since customers wish to purchase convenience goods with a minimum of effort, a manufacturer marketing such goods will place them in as many stores as possible, that is, he will attempt to gain maximum exposure to sale. Similarly, the retailer will locate his store as near as possible to the consumer. Otherwise, either consumers will accept products substitute or sales will be entirely lost.

The fact that convenience goods are placed in as many stores as possible and that the stores are located close to the consumer produces an

COMMONLY USED ABBREVIATIONS

These abbreviations often are used by historical and other scholars. The abbreviations are a mixture of Latin and English, and the latter are tending to drive out the former. There usually is no point in using the Latin when the English term is equally clear and about as short. Editors and publishers do not agree as to which Latin abbreviations should be italicized, which is a nuisance.

ante: before; the English is preferred
c., ca.: *circa,* meaning "at or near the date"; ca. is preferred because c. also is used for "copyright"
cap.: capital letter
cf.: meaning "consult" or "compare"
ch., chaps.: chapter(s)
ed.: used for "editor" (pl. "eds.") or "edition"
e.g.: meaning "for example"
et al.: meaning "and others," used for authors
et seq.: meaning "and the following"

f., ff.: "the following page" or "pages"; preferred to *et seq.*

fl.: meaning "flourished," about the mid-date of a person's life

ibid.: meaning "the same reference;" may be used to represent as much of the title given *immediately above* as is needed

id., idem: meaning "the same person"; sometimes used to avoid using an author's name, but not always clear—better to repeat name

i.e.: meaning "that is"

infra: meaning "below"; the English is preferred

ital.: italics

l., ll.: line(s)

l.c.: lowercase letter

loc. cit.: meaning "the place cited;" use sparingly, often ambiguous

MS, MSS: manuscript(s)

n.: note or footnote

N.B.: meaning "please note" or "note well"

n.d.: meaning "no date," when publication date cannot be supplied

n.p.: meaning "no place," when place of publication unknown

op. cit.: meaning "the work cited" previously

p.; pp.: page; pages

passim: meaning "here and there" in a publication; *et passim* is "and here and there"

post: after; the English is preferred

rev.: revised, revision

q.v.: meaning "which see"

sec.: section

sic: meaning "thus," to indicate that an apparent error was in the original

supra: above; the English is preferred

tr., trans.: translator, translation, translated by

vide: meaning "see"; the English is preferred

viz.: meaning "namely"

v., vol.: volume

ADDITIONAL READING ON HISTORICAL METHOD

The following items give additional information on the subjects covered in this guide, and provide further bibliographic leads into the literature. See Chapter V (B) for references on bibliographic aids.

1. Meaning and scope of human history

Raymond Aron, *Introduction to the Philosophy of History: An Essay on the Limits of Historical Objectivity* (trans. from the French; Boston, 1961). Isaiah Berlin, *Historical Inevitability* (New York, 1955). Grace Cairns, *Philosophies of History. Meeting of East and West in Cycle—Pattern Theories of History* (New York, 1962). Edward H. Carr, *What Is History?* (New York, 1962). Ernest Cassirer, *The Logic of the Humanities* (trans. from the German; New Haven and London, 1960). Morris R. Cohen, *The Meaning of Human History* (La Salle, Ill., 1947). R. G. Collingwood, *The Idea of History* (Oxford, 1946). David Hackett Fischer, *Historians' Fallacies: Toward a Logic of Historical Thought*

(New York, 1970). Leon J. Goldstein, *Historical Knowing* (Austin, Texas, 1976). Pieter Geyl, *Debates with Historians* (The Hague, 1954), and *Use and Abuse of History* (New Haven, 1955). J. H. Hexter, *The History Primer* (New York, 1971). Sidney Hook, *The Hero in History* (2nd ed., New York, 1955), and Hook (ed.), *Philosophy and History* (New York, 1963). H. Stuart Hughes, *History as Art and as Science* (New York, 1964). Erich Kahler, *The Meaning of History* (New York, 1964). Karl Löwith, *Meaning in History* (Chicago, 1949). Bruce Mazlish, *The Riddle of History. The Great Speculators from Vico to Freud* (New York, 1966). Hans Meyerhoff (ed.), *The Philosophy of History in Our Time* (Garden City, N. Y., 1959). Murray G. Murphey, *Our Knowledge of the Historical Past* (Indianapolis and New York, 1973). Emery Neff, *The Poetry of History* (New York, 1947). Don Karl Rowney and James Q. Graham, Jr. (eds.), *Quantitative History. Selected Readings in the Quantitative Analysis of Historical Data* (Homewood, Ill., 1969). A. L. Rowse, *The Use of History* (rev. ed., New York, 1963). Social Science Research Council, *Generalization in the Writing of History: A Report of the Committee on Historical Analysis of the SSRC* (Chicago, 1963), and *Theory and Practice in Historical Study. A Report of the Committee on Historiography* (New York, 1946). Pardon G. Tillinghast, *The Specious Past: Historians and Others* (Reading, Mass.: Addison-Wesley, 1972). Morton White, *The Foundations of Historical Knowledge* (New York, 1965).

2. History of historical writing

Matthew A. Fitzsimons *et al., The Development of Historiography* (Harrisburg, 1954), covers nearly all human groups that have had a written history, and is an excellent starting point for references. Coverage is largely Occidental in Harry E. Barnes, *A History of Historical Writing* (2nd rev. ed., New York, 1963): and James W. Thompson, with B. Holm, *A History of Historical Writing* (2 vols., New York, 1942). Noah E. Fehl *et al., History and Society* (Hong Kong,

1964), deals with Chinese, Israelite, ancient Greek, and modern Western historiography.

3. The older auxiliary disciplines

Two general treatments are Tom B. Jones, *Paths to the Ancient Past* (New York, 1967), and John M. Vincent, *Historical Research* (New York, 1911; reprinted 1929). For archeology see Ivor Noël Hume, *Historical Archaeology* (New York, 1969); *Larousse Encyclopedia of Archaeology* (New York, 1972). On chronology see J. C. McDonald, *Chronologies and Calendars* (London, 1927); Willis I. Milham, *Time and Time-Keepers* (New York, 1947); Stephen Toulmin and June Goodfield, *The Discovery of Time* (New York, 1965). On genealogy: Gilbert Doane, *Searching for Your Ancestors. The How and Why of Genealogy* (3rd ed., Minneapolis, 1960); Nal D. Greenwood, *The Researcher's Guide to American Genealogy* (Baltimore, 1973); Noel C. Stevenson, *Search and Research. The Researcher's Handbook; A Guide to Official Records and Library Sources for Investigators, Historians, Genealogists, Lawyers and Librarians* (rev. ed., Salt Lake City, 1964). On numismatics see Elvira Eliza Clain-Stefanelli, *Numismatics—An Ancient Science. A Survey of Its History* (Washington: The Museum of History and Technology, 1965); Stanley E. Lane-Poole (ed.), *Coins and Medals: Their Place in History and Art* (3rd ed., London, 1894). For diplomatics and paleography see André Blum, *On the Origin of Paper* (Lydenberg, New York, 1934); Sven Dahl, *History of the Book* (tr. from Danish, New York, 1958); Hubert Hall (ed), *A Formula Book of English Official Historical Documents* (2 vols., Cambridge, 1908–9); William Mason, *A History of the Art of Writing* (New York, 1920); E. M. Thompson, *Handbook of Greek and Latin Paleography* (New York, 1893); B. L. Ullman, *Ancient Writing* (New York, 1932). On modern linguistics see Joseph H. Greenberg, *Anthropological Linguistics: An Introduction* (New York, 1968); Mario Pei, *Invitation to Linguistics: A Basic Introduction to the Science of Language* (New York,

(1965); Josephs Vendryes, *Languages: A Linguistic Introduction to History* (London, 1925; tr. from French of 1921).

4. Social and behavioral sciences and history

William O. Aydelotte, Allan G. Bogue, Robert W. Fogel (eds.), *The Dimensions of Quantitative Research in History.* (Princeton, 1972). Bernard Berelson and Gary A. Steiner, *Human Behavior: An Inventory of Scientific Findings* (New York, 1964). Robert Berkhofer, Jr., *A Behavioral Approach to Historical Analysis* (New York, 1969). Cahnman and Alvin Boskoff, *Sociology and History: Theory and Research* (Glencoe, Ill., 1964). Thomas C. Cochran, *The Inner Revolution: Essays on the Social Sciences in History* (Toronto, 1962). Charles M. Dollar and Richard J. Jensen, *Historian's Guide to Statistics: Quantitative Analysis and Historical Research* (New York: Holt, 1971). Folke Dovring, *History as a Social Science: An Essay on the Nature and Purpose of Historical Studies* (The Hague, 1960). Maurice Duverger, *An Introduction to the Social Sciences* (New York, 1964), including a section on the methods and problems of sampling opinion by interviews and questionnaires. Roderick Floud, *An Introduction to Quantitative Methods for Historians* (Princeton, 1973). Wilson Gee, *Social Science Research Methods* (New York, 1950). Bert F. Hoselitz, *A Reader's Guide to the Social Sciences* (Glencoe, Ill., 1959). Robert Hyman *et al.*, *Interviewing in Social Research* (Chicago, 1954). *International Encyclopedia of the Social Sciences* (17 vols.; New York, 1968). Mirra Komarovsky (ed.), *Common Frontiers of the Social Sciences* (Glencoe, Ill., 1957). Susanne K. Langer, *Mind: An Essay on Human Feeling* (Baltimore, 1967). Val R. Lorwin and Jacob M. Price (eds.), *The Dimensions of the Past: Materials, Problems, and Opportunities for Quantitative Work in History* (essays presented to the American Historical Association's Committee on Quantitative Data; New Haven, 1972). Eugene Meehan, *Explanation in the Social Sciences: A System Paradigm* (Homewood, Ill., 1968). Richard S. Rudner, *Philosophy of*

Social Science (Englewood Cliffs, N. J., 1966). Edward Saveth (ed.), *American History and the Social Sciences* (Glencoe, Ill., 1964). Social Science Research Council, *The Use of Personal Documents in History, Anthropology, and Sociology* (New York, 1945); and *The Social Sciences in Historical Study* (New York, 1954). Pauline Young, *Scientific Social Surveys and Research* (3rd ed., New York, 1956).

INDEX

W–X

This book has been set linotype in 10 and 9 Aster, leaded 3 and 2 points respectively. Chapter numbers and titles are 12 point Aster bold. The size of the type page is 24 by 42 picas.